Montana
AMERICANA
MUSIC

Montana Americana Music

Boot Stomping in Big Sky Country

Aaron Parrett

Foreword by Smith Henderson

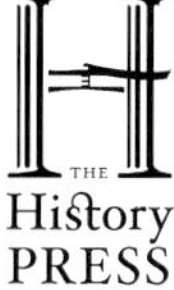

Published by The History Press
Charleston, SC
www.historypress.net

First published 2016

Manufactured in the United States

ISBN 978.1.46713.514.6

Author's note: Chapter 5 appeared in somewhat different form as "'Ditch Dvorak, They Want Turkey in the Straw': A Brief History of Old Time Fiddling in Montana," in the *Old-Time Herald*, 13, no. 7 (Fall 2013).

Library of Congress Control Number: 2016936012

Contents

Foreword

I recently attended a wedding with about forty New Yorkers and one other fella from Montana. The Montanan was an affable, highly intelligent neuroscientist. Naturally, the New Yorkers asked if we'd met, and an astonishingly ignorant young woman asked whether or not we knew each other back in the Big Sky.

I am used to this sort of thing from long experience. When I used to frequent Charlie B's in Missoula, the people I met would be a little astonished that I was actually born and raised in the town in which we were both standing. Even in Montana, a Montanan is something of an exotic.

Anyway, to the young woman at the wedding I admitted that Montanans do, in fact, all know one another, but that seven hundred souls (give or take) in the vastness of the great state means we don't know one another as well as we'd like. She took this at face value, and if I am amused, I'm also not too crazy about it.

An old friend of mine used to wear a T-shirt with the outline of Montana and "Gutshoot Them at the Border" starkly stated across it. I had an identical one that read, "You Can't Drink All Day if You Don't Start in the Morning." I used to wear it when I lived in Texas until I was pulled over for speeding one early morning by the DPS. I believe I narrowly avoided an arrest that night, and the T-shirt was no help.

I've no doubt the gutshot T-shirt would've played better. Which brings me to a correspondence—almost magical—between Texas and Montana. Both peoples possess a combative, contrarian streak that doesn't usually express itself well in politics but nevertheless has its local charms. Texans and Montanans are a little punchy, and you'll never encounter people more proud of where they're from. Of course, being proud of your hometown or state is about as dumb as being proud of the weather. But I am proud of the damn weather in Montana! I love the way all the activity in the sky is cupped in our tremendous valleys, how the clouds move across the rises in massive slow shadows like great beasts on a drive-in screen. I love the sunsets in Missoula and Bozeman and the killer wind in Livingston. I love the mind-altering cold of Butte or Wolf Point.

No doubt, to visit Montana is to develop a crush on the landscape, all the cloudwork and shadowcraft, the vistas and wildlife and the cold and snow and lancing sunshine. There are a good deal more than seven hundred people living in the state, but visitors might be forgiven for thinking there are not many more. To be a Montanan is to be a little invisible, to stand in the shadow of all the beauty. Which is quite the opposite of being Texan, which means to be as big as the land, to cover it in cattle and oil derricks.

A West Virginian writer I know argues that the people out west don't have much of a culture. America is yet a young country, but at least back east you're in immediate possession of some history. The maddening layout of a city like Pittsburgh or Boston reminds you of the age of the place. The polyglot of New York never lets you forget you're in a world-class city. The quaking heatscapes of Atlanta and Houston might be overrun with cars, but you cannot deny their teeming nightlife, their museums and their fantastic food.

But as you go west, the local charms turn more Protestant. More meat and potatoes. More salt of the earth. When you see the young bros gassing up their Ford F-150s and blasting some absolutely inane rock-rap hybrid or the latest Aerosmith ballad reengineered by the Country Music Industrial Complex, it's hard not to feel a cultural lack. The airwaves from the Mississippi to Salt Lake are a numbing mixture of right-wing nutjobbery and whatever "rock" is programmed by the Clear Channel cloud. And there you are in the midst of the Corporate Middle America Zone, the McDonald'ses and Starbuckses and all the rest of the vast sameness of America's midsection.

Maybe that's why the land—the weather!—are so romanticized here in Montana. As though the landscape itself is rearing up against the blandness of once Great Plains. Mind you, the blandness is a cultural outcome. Capitalist culture more or less paved flat a landscape that was chock full of grand fauna, whole ecosystems wasted. So now, if a serviceable river runs through it, well, that's enough. Some place has to be unspoiled (even if that's not the case), and it ain't gonna be Texas.

Anyway, this all toward saying that natural beauty and fewer people per square mile does not necessary mean less cultural output. Mississippi has turned out America's finest writers, and this is in spite of, or perhaps because of, its schools being so notoriously poor.

I can't speak for Kansas or the Dakotas, but Montana is not culturally sparse. The latest proof is in this volume by Aaron Parrett. I met Aaron more than fifteen years ago in Athens, Georgia. I don't know if he remembers, but he was at the legendary 40 Watt Club setting up for a gig. His incredible album, *The Sinners*, had been in constant rotation in my house for over a couple years. It was, like this book, an unfolding revelation. The melodies on that album still move me to rapture, but it was Aaron's lyrics that revealed a deep consonance between myself and the tradition of American music called Americana. The high lonesomeness that characterizes all the artists in this book informed my writing deeply and lastingly. *The Sinners* was a key to discovering it, just like this book is a key to discovering Montana's signal contribution to one of this country's finest musical modes.

Since our first meeting, Aaron has become a printer, a professor and, of course, an author. Thank God. This book will save you *years* of research in finding Montana's musical headwaters. Unfortunately, *Montana Americana* isn't perfect and remains incomplete, in my humble opinion. This book is missing Aaron Parrett, one of Montana's most significant musicians.

So let it be said now: read the book for the treasures of Montana music with which it will acquaint you. But find Aaron's music, and when you're in Montana and get the chance, hasten to see him play.

–SMITH HENDERSON

Acknowledgements

Many thanks to all the folks who were kind enough to talk to me at length about their music and whose names appear in the list of interviews and throughout the text. A special thank-you to Dave Martens and Doug Hawes-Davis for sharing their fantastic collections of vintage Montana Americana and to Artie Crisp for pitching me the idea and encouraging me along the way. Thank you to Seonaid B. Campbell for the last-minute photos of Louis Armentaro. I would like to express my sincere gratitude to Smith Henderson for his kind words about my own music. I am in debt to Brandi Foster Brockbank and Rick Ryan, who were kind enough to read the manuscript and offer advice and feedback. I'm grateful to my wife, Nann Parrett, for her computer savvy and skills in proofreading and for giving me so much time to write. And a special thank-you to Maizy Θ Lorraine Parrett, whose sense of wonder and fascination is an inspiration. A small grant from the English department at the University of Great Falls helped make this project possible.

Introduction

Americana in Montana

Sometime in the mid-1980s, a "new" kind of music began to inundate the bars and nightclubs of nearly every college town in America, standing note to note with the alternative sound popular then as produced by bands like REM and the Smiths. Actually, this new music sounded old, mainly because a lot of it had steel guitar in it or a twanging Telecaster, like an old Merle Haggard or Buck Owens record. It was retro, which was cool because retro was hip, and this stuff hit the ear like someone opening the door of a honky-tonk way out on some dirt road in about 1960. To seasoned listeners in most parts of Montana and the rural rest of the country, however, the music sounded more like a slightly glossier version of what the old folks had been listening to for what seemed like forever. Anyone hip enough to know about Gram Parsons or the Byrds knew that "country rock" had been around at least since the 1960s, even if it was just now becoming popular enough to earn its own category on the Billboard charts.

Critics and fans struggled to find a name for this new take on an old theme, especially those who prefer their musical tastes strictly categorized—and almost every nerd with a library of vinyl in his or her basement seems to be enamored of categories and subcategories. By default, most of it became known as "alternative country," which was vague, but at least it made clear that this stuff existed outside of, and apart from, most of the nauseating crap that Nashville had been fogging the airwaves with since the late 1970s. Edgier critics opted for the double-entendre of "alt-cunt," a mashup of "alternative" and "country" that also contained an oblique reference to the pervasive influence of rock-and-roll, at least its taste for irreverence and sexual suggestion. "Y'allternative" was yet another possibility, a slip of the tongue that rolled out with a nod to the South, where a lot of the original country music had been made—and that was true whether you thought of country music as Hank Williams (Alabama) and Ted Daffan (Texas) or you were savvy enough to know about Bill Monroe (Kentucky) or Jimmie Rodgers (Mississippi).

The most enduring fanzine for the music went by the name *No Depression*, and for a while some critics just referred to the musical genre using the same name. The title referred to an old Carter Family song, "No Depression in Heaven," so it had that, but *No Depression* also happened to be the name of an album by the Missouri band Uncle Tupelo, one of the earliest popularizers of this new style, and so the phrase tended to be too narrowly associated with that band's particular sound.

There were other names, too, but in the end, the one that stuck was pure and simple: "Americana." Americana worked well because it was itself an old word, one that had a long pedigree, even if it had never been expressly applied to music. Rob Bleetstein usually gets credit for adapting the old word to a new usage in 1995, but Capitol Records had a country music series on 78 rpm in the late 1940s bearing the label "Capitol Americana." The term also appears appropriately applied in, of all places, a 1958 science fiction story called "All You Zombies" by Robert Heinlein, wherein "Americana" appears in reference to the contents of a jukebox on which happens to be playing the 1947 Lonzo and Oscar novelty song "I'm My Own Grandpa."*

The root of "Americana" was "America," of course, but the "-na" suffix hinted a little at its sort of built-in collectability: people who collect cigar tins, for example, advertise for tobacciana. Americana certainly seemed to capture what rock critic Greil Marcus had a few decades earlier spoken of as "the old, weird America," as he sought to describe an aesthetic that culminated in the lyrics of Bob Dylan. That America included the peculiar religious residue of the First and Second "Great Awakenings"† and the eerie Appalachian gospel music that helped form the roots of blues and country

* Even odder, the story is a complex tale of time travel, which includes a visit to the year 1986. The passage reads as follows: "[T]he juke box blared out: 'I'm My Own Grandpaw!' The service man had orders to load it with Americana and classics because I couldn't stomach the 'music' of 1970, but I hadn't known that tape was in it. I called out, 'Shut that off! Give the customer his money back.'"

† The First Great Awakening (1730–43) was limited to New England, but the Second Great Awakening (1790–1850) was more relevant to this thesis, as its influence permeated the Midwest and figured significantly in states like Kentucky and Tennessee.

music. Accordingly, Jonathan Edwards's sermons became as relevant to Americana as Civil War narratives and chain gang singing—echoes of all of which resonate through the music of "old, weird America."

Whatever Americana music may be, it is apt to be one important remove from America itself, which may be reassuring to anyone tending toward contempt for red, white and blue jingoism, kneejerk nationalism or just plain old authority operating at the categorical level, especially since mainstream country music so often embraces those values. Americana offers some kind of commentary on all of those inelegant features of the American landscape that—like them or not—make the country what it is. Americana may be a mirror, but it also shines a lamp.

This helps explain why even if the music sounded country, it wasn't—at least not completely. A good deal of it came out of the speaker with the same jangle and snap as country-fried rock-and-roll. After all, the suburban kids were listening to it, and while the suburbs may not be the city, they're still a long way from the country. The way it contained echoes of so many other genres explains a considerable part of its appeal.

Pinning down true allegiances always proves exasperating, but parsing those genres drives most discussions of music in the first place. Doing so also serves the useful purpose of supplying new alleys and back roads for collectors to get lost in, and America loves its hoarders and collectors, many of whom are vinyl-addicted Alices repeatedly diving down thrift shop rabbit holes.

But like Columbus, who thought that he was "discovering" a "new world" that was in reality quite old and already inhabited, many collectors and music aficionados alike are not uncovering new music so much as they are recovering old territory with new purpose. Robert Crumb provides a good example: as a consequence of his success as a cartoonist, he has amassed an inimitable and museum-quality collection of 78 rpm records, opening for new generations of collectors a "new world" that was already quite old. Collectors in general are the long-range reconnaissance patrols preparing the way for critical theorists, and eventually the information gleaned from their expeditions gets passed on to the rest of us shopping at the record bins. Collectors are also pragmatic and succinct, if not downright pithy, which proves helpful to anyone searching out new music, mainly because their idiom of critique usually starts out something like this: "If you like Gram Parsons, you'll love these guys…." Collectors are all about nuance and the seduction of obscurity, and it is only when some marketing genius tries to commercialize taste that we end up searching for the perfect categorical "brand." Meanwhile, the best collections, like Harry Smith's 1952 *Anthology of American Folk Music*, are always idiosyncratic and highly personal. As the French philosopher Jean Baudrillard wrote in an essay in 1968 called "The System of Collecting," "It is invariably oneself that one collects." Americana music developed as a consequence of the American urge to collect its own musical expressions.

In any case, as longtime Nashville music writer Craig Havighurst pointed out, "Americana isn't a genre." To those in the industry, it is better understood as a radio format, like "easy-listening" or "hard rock," both of which encompass a host of genres and subgenres. As radio promoter Pete Knapp defined it on his website, "Americana is an amalgam of American folk music formed by the confluence of the shared and varied traditions that make up the musical ethos of the United States; specifically those sounds that are merged from folk, country, blues, rhythm and blues, rock and roll and other external influences," which is about as comprehensive a denotative definition possible. And while one admires the impulse for inclusiveness, using Knapp's definition, it's hard to imagine an American form of music that would not be Americana.

One of the younger up-and-coming musicians I interviewed for this book had some interesting insights regarding the term that might not immediately occur to older generations of musicians and critics. "I had never thought about the definition of the word, nor about whether my music was Americana," wrote Cameron Boster. "I thought the best first step would be to look for a definition on the Internet, and compare it to my unformed concept of Americana. The definition I found ('Contemporary music that draws from American roots music') didn't seem to be much a definition at all. That was comforting. It allowed me to conclude that although I didn't know what it meant, neither did the experts." Further scrutiny turned up some elements that did make sense to him, and he went on to say, "If you're innovating, and you're drawing your inspiration from American roots, you're an Americana musician. What defines Americana depends on the precursors, the things copied." But Boster also made an inference that many other critics have voiced as well: "You have to wonder, though, whether this definition doesn't really mean all roots music. One day, hip hop (arguably an American innovation) will be seen as a 'root' from which other types of music grow—in fact, we're probably already there. It's more likely that Americana is drawn from the lyric-driven, simpler folk-country-blues 'roots,' and not any others."

What Boster captured and Knapp perhaps missed is that Americana might very well fall under the influence of all those disparate strains of American music, but what emerges at the other end of that confluence is some form of musical expression that is somehow—for lack of a better word—country, whether it is hillbilly or the blues. The 78 collector Christopher King gets at what a person could take as a pretty fair definition of Americana in his description of what exactly he seeks out: "If there's any one continuous thread through everything that I have, it's deeply, deeply, rural and backwoodsy. It's almost like it turns its back on the city."* One of America's finest writers and collectors, Larry McMurtry, advanced a similar view in his 1968 essay "A Look at the Lost Frontier," in which he observed that "hillbilly is a music of estrangement—the estrangement of country people who have moved to the city and not found the city good." Not all of the music surveyed in the present book would fall into that category, but a lot of it would, and almost all of it would trace its roots to that category.

It is also interesting that the word *Americana* made its first appearance in print in 1841, according to the Oxford English Dictionary, as a kind of summary reference for "books, manuscript, or other literary artefacts relating to or made in the continent of America or the United States," a definition that over time came to invoke the entire cultural heritage of the United States and, as such, became an almost metaphysical term invoked to clarify everything from politics to furniture styles. By 1940, in fact, the term had come to refer to anything characteristic of the United States, though especially for those things touched with the patina of Marcus's "old, weird America."

It may be relevant to a musicological investigation of the term to reiterate that while all the artifacts of our country's history are Americana, they are especially so once they have become somehow commodified: repackaged, say, into the sort of cheap kitsch found at a Stuckey's or a Cracker Barrel or practically any national park. A snow globe of Mount Rushmore, for example, has transformed the original sculptural project into a cheap plastic gewgaw that in perfect spite of itself crystallizes the essence of a kind of distinctly American arrogance—that is, our failure to understand how four immense human visages carved into wilderness rock is an affront to decency and good taste, not to mention a transgression of land that is sacred to Indians. Americana is to America as marble is to limestone, although the transformational agency is not heat and pressure but rather irony. As American as the actual Statue of Liberty on Liberty Island may be, it really becomes embodied Americana in all those little copper tchotchkes lurking among the detritus of the junk drawer in nearly every American kitchen. Campbell's soup in the can is just a grocery item, but Andy Warhol

* Quoted in Amanda Petrusich's book *Do Not Sell at Any Price* (New York, 2015).

transformed it into the epitome of Americana. For that matter, the Rolling Stones may be English, but Warhol made them (or at least their lips and tongue logo) Americana.

Americana music is both a reflection of this commercial cannibalizing of American culture as well as a reaction against it, both of which appreciate the inescapable contradictions inherent in that culture, the streak of schizophrenia that has split the American psyche ever since a bunch of slave owners decided to form an independent country ironically dedicated to the proposition that "all men are created equal."

That schizoid essence in many ways defines us and ensures that the phenomenon of Americana is uniquely ours. Longtime musician (in Los Hermanos Brothers) and raconteur Frank Ruffolo of Butte, Montana, acknowledged that the term Americana may be somewhat hazy but pointed out that whatever it is, "it only happens here"—meaning, that is, the good old United States of America. The Blasters may exhibit a certain strain of Americana, but the Clash do not and cannot. "It's not like there's a formula," he admitted. "Something works in the context of a soup pot. There's no recipe, but we all agree on the ingredients." The result of this Yankee bricolage is a recipe that relies as much on impromptu experiment as it does on tried-and-true practice. After all, whether you're working in a bakery or playing bluegrass, a certain amount of the technique derives from habits that just make sense in context. At the same time, what gives both a great bagel and a great bluegrass "break" distinction depends somewhat on improvisation within the context of a well-defined idiom.

And so the term Americana retains all these aspects of irony when applied to the style of music that now bears its name. The music, like the other artifacts, is America taken one remove from itself—country music that isn't exactly the sound pouring from beer joints and roadhouses back in the '50s but is, without question, a reaction to the anemic, corporate country rap polluting Top-40 radio nowadays.

Twenty-first-century Americana does recycle certain attitudes that pay homage to its rockabilly past, often invoking both the angst of punk as well as its old-school sensibility. Americana music seems to revere a halcyon if imaginary past (when country music was pure and good) even as it often repudiates the vacant values espoused by those living in that era. Lyle Lovett's cover of Tammy Wynette's "Stand by Your Man" cuts to the heart of what I mean. Americana music often involves its writers and players standing a little outside and looking back in at the United States and its singularly schizoid culture. Americana both sonically and lyrically can sometimes seem like what linguists call a meta-language—a language used to talk about the way language itself functions. Americana music similarly has a strange ability to furnish its own critical commentary, taking note of its own often vulgar affection for the old honky-tonk sound as a method of reinventing the past, of talking about the process of cultural history itself. The music of Robbie Fulks provides many good examples, but start by giving a listen to his anthem of atheism, "God Isn't Real," which is about as soulful a "gospel" song as you'll ever hear. Like Sturgill Simpson's "Turtles All the Way Down," Fulks's song wraps the philosophical sentiments of Sam Harris and David McAfee inside a warm and reassuring cocoon of classic American country. The result is a masterpiece of irony that says as much about our paradoxical relationship with religion in the United States as it does about the history of country music, clinging to a kind of sardonic humor that presumably the obtuse "good old boy" will miss.

What all this means for the book in your hands is that while Americana in the abstract covers an immense amount of territory, I focus mainly on hillbilly, country, country-blues and old-time folk music, as well as its modern offspring, bluegrass. Especially in Montana, those Americana styles are most prevalent and most often drive the discussion. As one person I spoke with put it, it would be hard to find a style of music coming from Montana that was not Americana, since a good part of the descriptive definition covers music that is more rural than urban, more "country" than "city."

That makes sense because Montana has very few urban centers: Billings is the closest thing to a city by the rest of the country's standards, and it barely surpasses 100,000 people. Missoula is a close second with 70,000, but the rest of the urban centers in Montana are better described as large towns rather than small cites: Kalispell and the surrounding area (60,000), the Helena valley (50,000), Bozeman (40,000) or Butte (30,000). Demographically speaking, one of the most striking facts is that almost half of Montana's paltry population of just over 1 million people happens to be congregated into that handful of urban centers—the rest of its people live decidedly rural lives. And while rock-and-roll is in general a "radio format" distinct from Americana and mostly associated with big-city music scenes, it's worth pointing out that Montana has produced some notable rock-and-roll musicians—Colin Meloy of the Decemberists, Steve Albini of Shellac and Jeff Ament of Pearl Jam, to list three easy examples.

And as one of the last states to come fully into what passes for civilization, Montana also retains ties to a nineteenth-century past that continues to influence its art, its ethos, its aesthetics and its music. As recently as 1927, a writer for *TIME* magazine expressed a sentiment no doubt embraced by much of the rest of the country when he disparaged the Treasure State by saying that "Montana [is] generally considered by the world as musically a lummox." Obviously such an attitude demands disabusing, and I hope that if this brief and superficial survey does nothing else, it will at least adduce evidence of a rich and complex history of Americana music in Montana reaching back much farther than 1927.

Traces of Montana's nineteenth-century origins and history have a way of bleeding into twenty-first-century Americana music in Montana as well. The last major altercation between the U.S. Army and the Indians happened in 1877 in Montana, when Chief Joseph surrendered to General Miles just shy of the Canadian border in the Bear Paw Mountains, thus ending the so-called Plains Indian Wars. In 2016, with seven Indian reservations inhabited by a dozen tribes, Montana remains home to almost seventy thousand Native Americans—about 7 percent of the state's population. As the chapter on Montana fiddling reveals, some of the most authentic roots music in the United States may be discerned in Metís fiddling. For that matter, Indian drum circles and related genres of music are among the most enduring and influential aboriginal musical sources across the country. And some of the most innovative music coming out of or tracing its roots to Montana at the moment happens to be Americana music made by musicians from Montana's Indian reservations.

In short, as a low-population, decidedly rural state that has preserved—for better or worse—much of its persona from the nineteenth century, Montana provides a fascinating archive of Americana musical expression to explore. From the fiddlers Pierre Cruzatte and George Gibson, who were among the first European immigrants to bring the earliest Americana music into Montana, to the impressive achievement of the Lil' Smokies at the Telluride Bluegrass Festival in 2015, Montana Americana music has been integrally connected to the musical development of the country itself.

Although this documentary history is brief and constrained by time and space, it is offered in the earnest hope that others will explore in greater breadth and depth the rich archive of Americana music in Montana.

Chapter 1

"Don't Let My Spurs Get Rusty While I'm Gone"

The Snake River Outlaws and 1950s Country Music in Montana

Long before the University of Montana became known as a hipster magnet, drawing millennials from all over America, Missoula, Montana, made its fortune as a logging and timber mill center in the state. The city began as a mercantile stop on the old Mullan Road between Fort Benton, Montana, and Walla Walla, Washington, but in the era of the Copper Kings (1880–1910), the road from Missoula was an artery to the heart of Montana's mining industry in Butte, as the town's sawmills processed massive quantities of timber harvested from all over the western part of the state. In the 1950s, the city became home to several pulp mills as well, and even into the 1970s, the timber products industry dominated the economy. The state university had been founded there in 1893, but in the 1950s, most of the population remained working class; the night life in Missoula flourished in the clubs and saloons in a three- or four-block section of town down near the railroad tracks, in the vicinity of the Great Northern Train station and terminal. These clubs included the Sunshine Bar, where an old-time country and western band from Weiser, Idaho, created a stir in the rosy years following the war.

The 1950s might very well have been the most blissful period in Montana history. After the agony of the Depression and the lean years of rationing during World War II, Montana, like the rest of the country, enjoyed a booming postwar economy, a host of technological benefits that were part of the unanticipated largesse of the war and a pervasive sense of optimism at having made the world safe for democracy. The euphoria was tempered a little by the chilling realization after Hiroshima and Nagasaki that human beings now had the power to destroy their planet with shocking ease, as well as by the postwar fall of Eastern Europe to communism that would eventually grow into the Cold War, but for the most part, in the 1950s Americans in general and Montanans specifically were riding high.

With the radio-friendly format of the 45 rpm phonograph record and affordable TV sets leading the way, Americans started booking passage on a juggernaut of media obsession that would continue to define American culture for generations to come, culminating in our current obsession with smart phones and iPads and wall-sized flat-screen TVs. For perspective, consider the fact that before the war, fewer than one in ten families in America owned a television set, but by the beginning of the 1960s, only one in ten did *not* have one. (According to Nielsen, the average American home today has 2.86 televisions.) In Montana, television's gradual domination of the domestic household was delayed a little from the rest of the country: Ed Craney founded KXLF in Butte in 1953 as an NBC affiliate. It was not until 1955 that he added ABC as a second affiliate.

In the days before cable networks, the big three—ABC, CBS and NBC—controlled the national market almost exclusively, and all programming was delivered through syndication via local broadcasters, which meant that many local communities did not have a station at all or had only spotty reception from one of the bigger cities. Even in the urban areas like Butte or Great Falls, many homes lacked television until the late '50s.

In spite of the rapid cultural changes, Montana, like much of the rural West and the Deep South, remained in touch with a remote past—at least more so than those parts of the country that were heavily urbanized. Before television arrived to overwhelm the entertainment market, people in Montana devoted a considerable share of the time they budgeted for entertainment to live music, dances, picnics and similar social functions that seem far less commonplace today. From the beginning of recorded history, listening to music has been one of humankind's universal passions, and the archaeological evidence suggests that the same was true before we began keeping historical records. But until Edison invented the cylinder phonograph in 1877, there was only one way to hear music: the live performance. Before the widespread availability of cheap phonographs and 78 rpm disc records (the brainchild of Emile Berliner in 1890), people living rural lives might go weeks without hearing music—unless they owned an instrument and played it themselves. It wasn't until the development of public radio transmissions

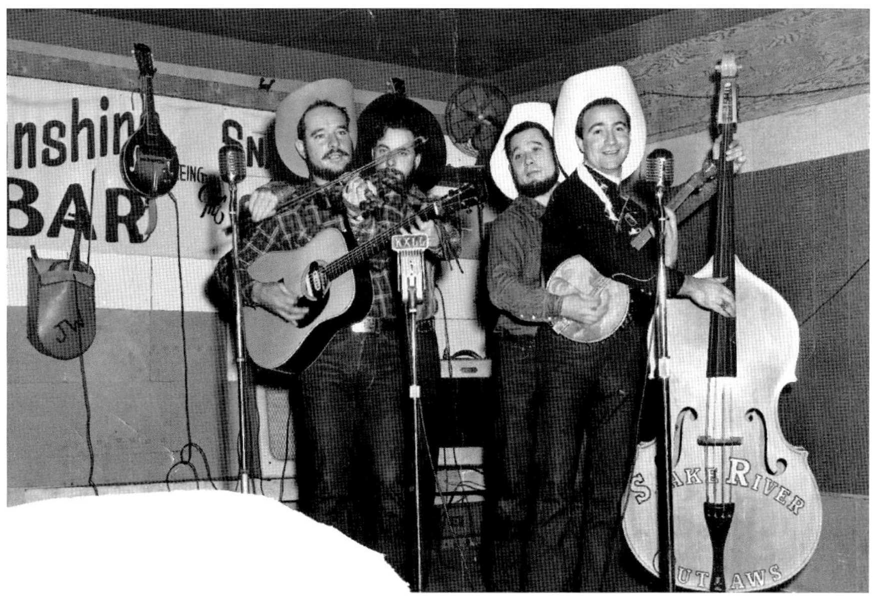

The Snake River Outlaws. *From left to right*: Orval Fochtman, Jimmy Widner, Vern Wilburn and Harold Wilburn. *Courtesy of T. Scot Wilburn.*

in the 1920s and the popularity of radio in the 1930s that listening to music on demand became routine. Nevertheless, in the rural parts of the country, going to a nightclub or "honky-tonk" to listen to live music remained one of the primary choices for entertainment up into the late 1950s.

Enter the Snake River Outlaws into Missoula, Montana, in 1953. Down on the corner of Woody and Alder Streets, in the heart of the "skid row" section of a city whose economy depended mainly on the timber and lumber mills, well-heeled men and women in business suits and evening dresses elbowed their way into Jimmy Rose's Sunshine Bar to listen to the hillbilly music provided by a collection of musicians from across the hills in Idaho. And they didn't mind standing next to winos and workingmen drinking schooners of beer to do it.

Music historian Hal Cannon painted a vivid picture of the scene in liner notes that he wrote for a long-awaited 2008 CD that captured live performances of the band as they were recorded in 1953: "Squeeze inside the bar and it's steamy. The place reeks of cigarettes and alcohol. The place is too small for dancing, with a stage cramped into the corner and faced with a picket fence. By the looks of the band, this is pure cowboy honky-tonk."

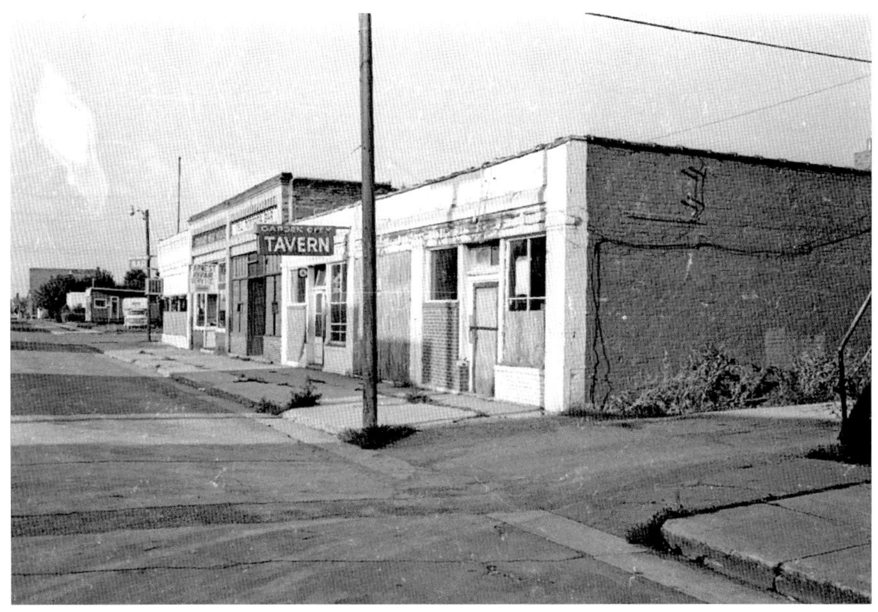

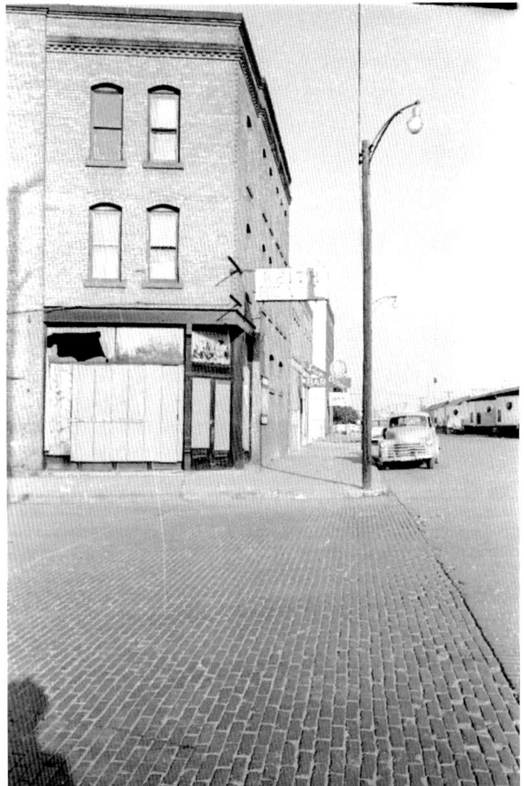

Above: One of Missoula's iconic country music venues in the 1950s, the Garden City Tavern (image circa 1968). *Photo by Stan Healy, courtesy of Archives and Special Collections, Mansfield Library, University of Montana.*

Left: The Silver Dollar bar and the Keith Hotel on Woody Street in Missoula, circa 1968. *Photo by Stan Healy, courtesy of Archives and Special Collections, Mansfield Library, University of Montana.*

Nearly everyone still alive who saw the band perform in Missoula recalls how egalitarian the crowds were, with Missoula's elite rubbing elbows with its drunks and downtrodden, all united in pursuit of some of the best live music in the history of the state.

Just down the street stood the Silver Dollar Bar, and the Outlaws played there on occasion, too. Other honky-tonks in the Missoula area included the Garden City #1, the Garden City #2 and Spider McCallum's Maverick Bar—all places the band would visit over the years.

But the Sunshine Bar was the Outlaws' mainstay, and for most of 1953, they played there six nights a week, from 9:00 p.m. until closing, which in Montana meant 2:00 a.m. That was a brutal work schedule for a musician, but it forced the band to learn a lot of material and play together with the precision of a well-oiled engine. In recalling those years more than half a century later, the band's front man, Orval Fochtman, estimated that he learned well over two hundred songs, mostly from listening to the radio.

In addition to Fochtman, the band consisted of Jimmy Widner, who played fiddle and guitar; Harold Wilburn, who handled the upright bass and sang a few tunes; and Vern Wilburn, who played guitar, tenor banjo and fiddle, singing an occasional number in a beautiful voice reminiscent of Lefty Frizzell. The de facto fifth member, Vern's young wife, Ruby—"the

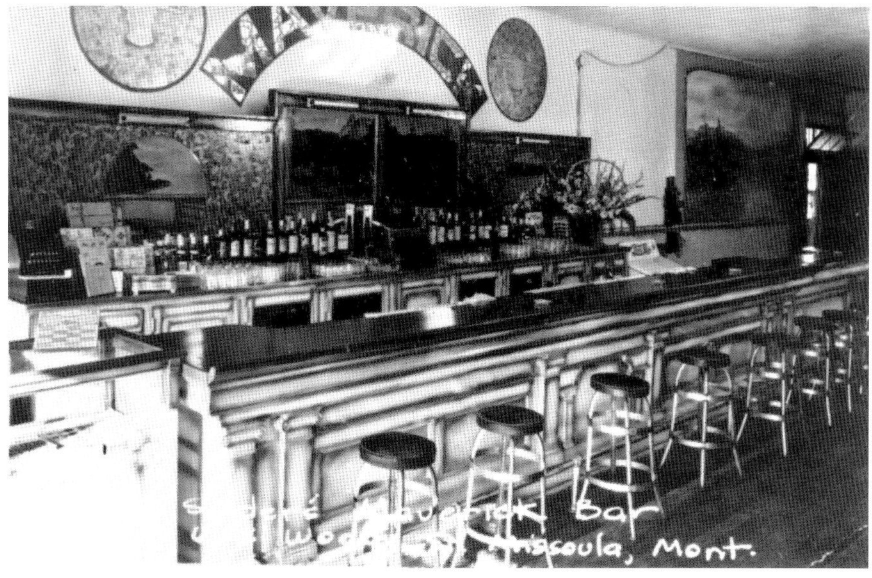

Spider's Maverick Bar interior, late 1940s. *Courtesy of Archives and Special Collections, Mansfield Library, University of Montana.*

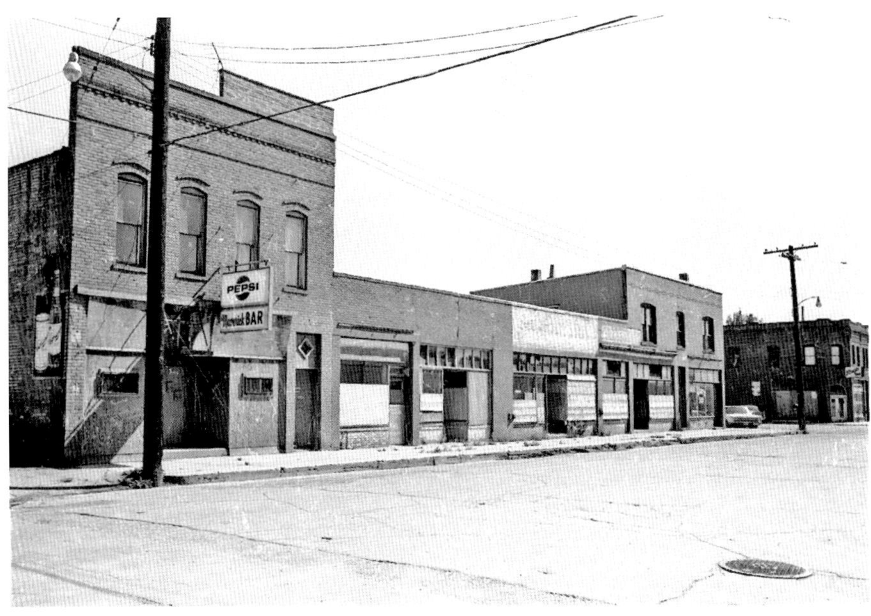

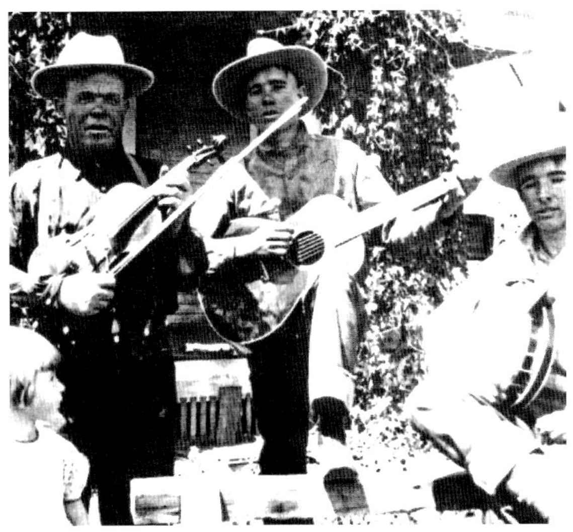

Above: Maverick Bar exterior, Woody Street, circa 1968. *Photo by Stan Healy, courtesy of Archives and Special Collections, Mansfield Library, University of Montana.*

Left: Snake River Outlaws fiddler Jimmy Widner, here playing guitar with an uncle on fiddle and brother on banjo. *Courtesy of T. Scot Wilburn.*

nightingale of Woody Street"—would also step up periodically to sing a ballad in a clear and wistful voice. Her two most popular numbers were "Careless Hands" and "I'd Rather Die Young."

All of the performers hailed from the little town of Weiser, Idaho, about a three-hundred-mile drive away over what is now Highway 12 and then down 95, which landed you in the hot, dusty hills along the Snake River, sixty miles north of Boise. For kids in their late teens and early twenties, a town like Weiser didn't promise much of a future. Jimmy and Orval and Vern had played together for fun a good bit and decided that they might as well put together a real group and hit the road.

Harold Wilburn's son, Scot, related a story he heard from Jimmy Widner about how the Snake River Outlaws started out.* "Jimmy and Orval and Vern had all decided on starting the band, but they needed Harold to play bass. The thing was, Harold was running a lot of moonshine from a still he had set up way down in the bottom of Hell's Canyon, and Jimmy and Vern rode horses all day long to get down there to him." They arrived around sunset, although it was hard to tell down in the bottom of what happens to be North America's deepest river gorge—the encyclopedia lists it at a few feet shy of eight thousand feet deep. Harold was reluctant to go in with the others, but they eventually talked him into riding out with the two of them. "A few days later, they drove down to Boise to go to the big music store there to get Harold an upright bass," Scot said. They walked into the store and started perusing the merchandise. Harold tried out a beautiful blonde upright and played on it for ten or fifteen minutes, but no sales clerk came forth to make the sale. In fact, Harold played for thirty minutes, Jimmy guessed, and in all that time they didn't see anyone working in the store at all. Then Harold paused in his playing and said to Jimmy, "Why don't you hold that front door there open." Jimmy obliged, and Harold walked out with the bass.

"So you see, there was something to the outlaw part of their name," Scot said with a grin. "They were pretty square fellows, but I believe that story because I knew my dad." Wilburn also pointed out that when Vern and Jimmy first started playing together in Weiser, an old hobo who lived in a car down by the railroad tracks used to sit in with them and yodel. He called himself "Wild Bill" Lloyd, the Snake River Outlaw. Lloyd lived hard and died before the band had even fully formed, but the boys immortalized him with their band name.

Once they had roped Harold into the outfit, they headed for Montana, although they spent a few months in Elk River, honing their chops in a rough-and-tumble bordello known as the Up and Up Club in the remote timber town. Elk River lies sixty miles down secondary roads off Highway

* Scot, Harold's son, inherited his father's musical taste and talents. He fronts a top-notch country swing outfit out of Spokane called T. Scot Wilburn and the Shut up and Playboys. Born in Libby, Scot spent his formative years musically in Montana—mostly Missoula, playing in numerous bands.

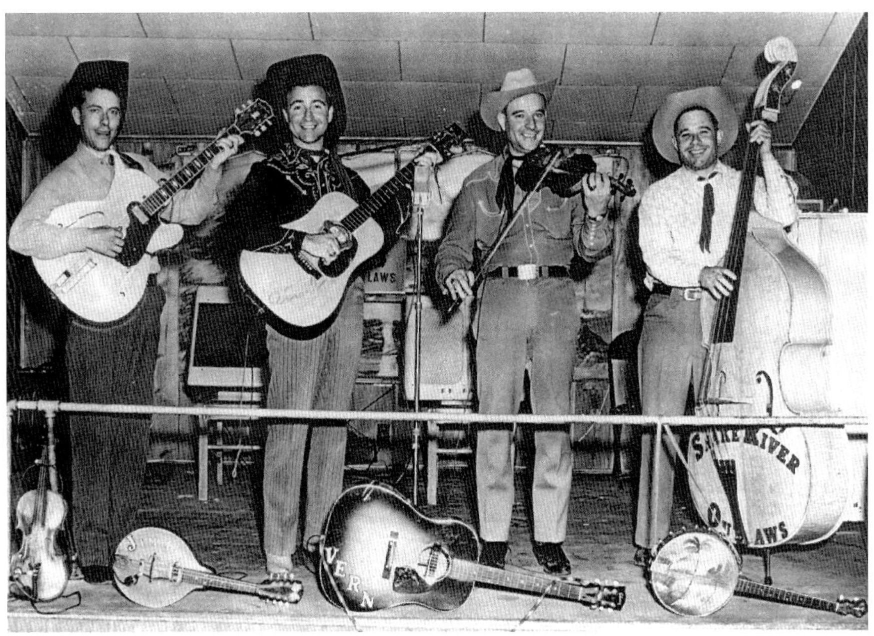

The Snake River Outlaws were one of Montana's finest country bands in the 1950s. In their prime, they played six nights a week at the Sunshine Bar at the corner of Woody and Alder in Missoula, Montana. *Courtesy of T. Scot Wilburn.*

12, the main corridor between Lewiston and Missoula. They slept in tents or cabins near the bar after their shows, and they learned quickly how to keep a rowdy crowd entertained. As Ruby Wilburn recalled in her contribution to the liner notes of *The Snake River Outlaws*, "We went to Elk River, and that was boomtown…Diamond, Potlach, Weyerhauser, all them big timber outfits. No cops, no law, everything was on the go. There was one lady shot her husband and it took about a week for them to get up there and take her to jail." Jimmy Widner's biographer, Tom Brown, described that region of Idaho similarly: "All that country is just plain wild. In fact, the wildness of it along with the distances between pockets of civilization, like Salmon, made the whole area an ideal place for 'refugees from the law' to hang out."

When they decided they'd had enough, they climbed back into the old panel truck they drove in their early days and headed onward to Missoula, where they signed on with Jimmy Rose at the Sunshine Bar, proudly employed as the house band. The Snake River Outlaws held court at the Sunshine on and off for two or three years, punctuating their tenure with occasional tours around the Northwest. At one point, the band moved their operation to Butte, where they played six nights a week at the famous C.O.D. Bar. Owner

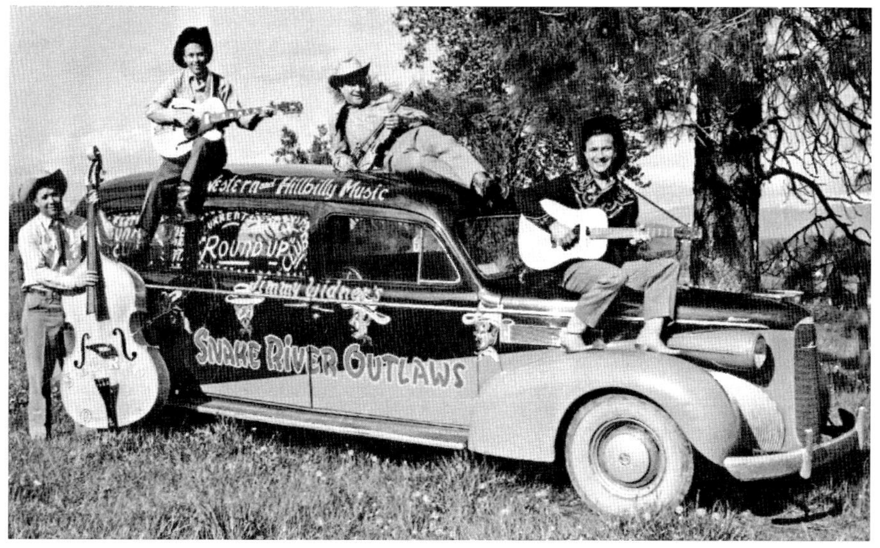

In the days before band busses, the Snake River Outlaws traveled the West in a hand-painted 1939 Cadillac LaSalle. *Courtesy of T. Scot Wilburn.*

Louis Buenni paid the band $600 per week and provided each member an apartment—a lucrative arrangement that, adjusting for inflation, would be worth approximately $6,000 per week in today's dollars.

Thirty-five years after the Snake River Outlaws were in their prime, their performances and on-stage antics at the Sunshine had become legendary and passed around by Montana and Idaho musicians, many of whom probably hadn't even been born in 1953. Most of the stories starred Jimmy Widner, the virtuoso hillbilly fiddler with an insatiable taste for whiskey. Almost every bluegrass or country musician between Salmon, Idaho, and Missoula, Montana, for example, knows the story of one especially wild night at the Sunshine when Jimmy threw back so many shots of whiskey that he vomited right in the middle of a fiddle break, rivulets of the mess making their way down the face of his fine instrument and through the f-holes down into the interior of his fiddle. Unfazed, he sawed with frenzy through the tune, raising shouts and cheers from the crowd. After an exuberant and obligatory "shave and a haircut" tag ending, Jimmy slipped off stage into the men's room, where fans laughed as they watched him rinse out his fiddle under the water spigot. Fifteen minutes later, he was back on stage, sawing out another inspired solo on his still-damp instrument, the sort of escapade more in line with a band like the Sex Pistols in 1976 than a country band in Montana in 1953.

Although the band played every night of the week except Monday, Saturday night was the featured performance. Not only would the bar be especially crowded, but local radio station KXLL, in conjunction with bar owner Jimmy Rose, also hosted *The Sunshine Jamboree*, a radio show broadcast across the entire Pacific Northwest.

The announcer for Jimmy Rose's Sunshine Bar jamboree was a local college student, Bob Balzac, an energetic emcee with a rich radio voice and a fluid delivery. He began each show with a "Yessiree, John! It's another Sunshine Jamboree down here at the corner of Woody and Alder in Missoula, Montana!" Throughout the broadcast, Bob periodically invited listeners throughout the Pacific Northwest to make the drive to Missoula to see the show. Missoulians old enough to remember the little dive bar down on Alder Street recount how the crowd routinely spilled out into the street. "The bar probably only held sixty or seventy people," recalled Harold's son, Scot. "But people would listen in their cars with their radios tuned to KXLL." People danced in the streets and congregated around cars to hear the show coming over the radio, driving the neighborhood if they couldn't find a parking spot. In fact, according to Widner's biographer, Tom Brown, people *had* to dance in the streets—the odd licensure laws at the time apparently forbade dancing in the club itself.

Orval Fochtman was the recognized front man, even if the 1939 Cadillac LaSalle they had acquired as part of their Missoula success had "Jimmy Widner's Snake River Outlaws" painted on the side, probably to capitalize on Jimmy's wild character and reputation. Fochtman had a baritone voice reminiscent of Hank Snow, a '50s western singer who rivaled Hank Williams in popularity. Like Snow, Fochtman happened to be a little more sedate and clean-cut than the original Drifting Cowboy. By all accounts, Orval Fochtman was also blessed with handsome looks that drew attention from every woman in the bar.

The Outlaws only put out two singles in their career, both in the 78 rpm format. Stuart Hamblen's "I Won't Go Huntin' with You Jake (But I'll Go Chasin' Women)" had been a chart topper in 1950 and one of the Outlaws' most requested numbers. For that reason, they chose it as the feature side of the disc they released in 1953 on the Outlaw label (on the B-side, they featured Jimmy Widner playing "The Orange Blossom Special" in his characteristically feverish but succinct arrangement). Bob Balzac liked to remind radio listeners that it was "available in Missoula at Vega Record Company or right here on stage, where the boys'll be glad to autograph the label for you. And both sides are good, you can

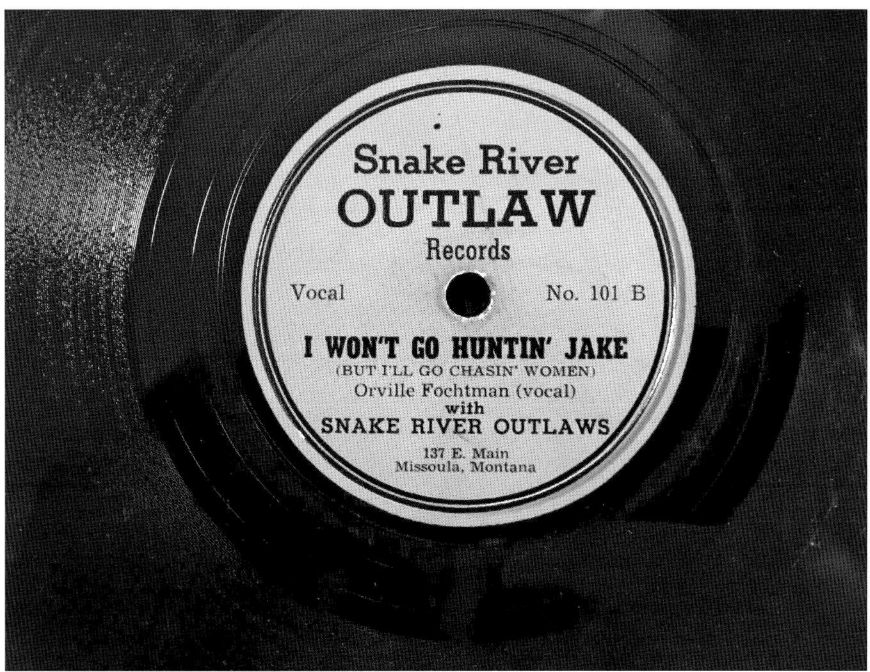

The Snake River Outlaws claim to have released two 78 records on the Snake River Outlaw label (recorded at the Vega Record Company in Missoula circa 1952). Probably only five hundred copies were pressed, and very few survive. *Courtesy of Doug Hawes-Davis.*

be sure of that!" Fochtman claimed that a second disc was also recorded at the Vega Music Company in downtown Missoula around the same time that featured two of the Outlaws' original numbers: "My World of Yesterday" backed by "Imitation Love." Fochtman explained how both cuts came to be written: "Harold Wilburn come to me with the words to the songs, and I set them to the guitar chords. We made several hundred of the records and sold them right off the stage." The records sold out quickly and today are difficult to find.

In 2008, Scot Wilburn and Wylie Gustafson approached Hal Cannon, director of the Western Folklife Center, with a collection of reel-to-reel tapes that Fochtman had made of the Sunshine Bar radio broadcasts. The tapes were a time capsule that preserved some of the best music ever played and performed in Missoula. As Cannon put it, "Most of the new popular country music [of the '50s] evaporated in the air never to be heard again. But with this [2008] recording of the live radio shows, we now have a little slice of history, a saved moment of the Wild West."

The repertoire included mainly covers of popular country songs of their own era. "The Golden Rocket," a 1950 smash for Hank Snow, was in regular rotation, especially since its opening lyric referenced the Treasure State:

From ol' Montana down to Alabama
I've been before and I'll travel again
You triflin' women can't keep a good man down
You dealt the cards but you missed the play
So hit the road and be on your way
Gonna board the Golden Rocket and leave this town.
(© 1950 Hank Snow, RCA-Victor 21-0400)

They also covered Hank Snow's "The Only Rose," as well as "Now and Then There's a Fool Such as I," written by Bill Trader but also rocketed to fame by Snow. Other contemporary hits they kept on their set lists included Lefty Frizzell's signature tune "Always Late (With Your Kisses)," a number-one hit he generated in 1951, and "Let Me Love You Just a Little," a Jim Reeves classic from 1953.

When Ruby took the stage, she would sing "Careless Hands" in a plaintive, clear voice. Her unadorned phrasing matched the mood of the lyrics and allowed the evocative melody to carry the song, making it one of the standouts in the Outlaws' set list. The tune had been written by Carl Sigman and Bob Hilliard and recorded in 1948 by Sammy Kaye, but was made into a huge smash by Mel Torme in 1949. Although it was originally a popular song in the big-band idiom of the day, country musicians quickly adopted it, illustrating a key aspect of a musical ethos inherited from the old-time dance bands that preceded them: while traditional fiddle tunes and Childe ballads formed the core of the old-time repertoire, local musicians frequently adopted and adapted contemporary hits into their set lists, and occasionally those tunes would become part of the country canon. Old "Grange" songbooks from the era attest to this practice, as does the ever-expanding repertoire of the old-time fiddling community (see chapter 5).

The Outlaws also wrote several original numbers that matched the rest of the material in tenor and mood: "My World of Yesterday" proved popular with the crowds, as did their "Imitation Love." They also made older, traditional material a key part of their program, a practice that reinforces another of the key elements of Americana as a musical form. The Grayson and Whitter song "Wreck of the Old '97" and the fiddle tune "Devil's Dream" connected them to a hillbilly and rural country music tradition that stretched back into the nineteenth century, where the roots of country found purchase in the musical bedrock of the nation. Similarly with the cowboy ballad "Streets of Laredo," a tune that first appeared in print in John Avery Lomax's *Cowboy Songs* (1910), although musicologists seem to agree that the tune derives from the much older "Unfortunate Rake" of English origin.

Even Jimmy Widner would sing a tune now and then. He enjoyed doing his take on Carson Robison's 1942 hit "Don't Let My Spurs Get Rusty While I'm Gone," delivered with sincere abandon and punctuated with his flashy western fiddle breaks. The title of the song itself weaves together perennial Americana themes, including the romance of the cowboy and the inevitability of death.

The Snake River Outlaws provided a bridge between an old-time music tradition that reached back into the early nineteenth century and the more modern country music sound that emerged after the 1960s, which influenced country rock by way of the folk revival. The Outlaws also anticipated, if they did not inaugurate, a sort of local, homegrown emphasis on music that would be the hallmark of many Montana bands, including such nationally recognized acts as the Lil' Smokies, the Mission Mountain Wood Band and Rob Quist and Great Northern.

The brothers Wilburn proved to be the most stalwart and devoted members of the Snake River Outlaws. Long after Widner and Fochtman departed from the band, Harold and Vern kept the Outlaws alive and working through the 1950s and '60s, adding Larry Caldwell on guitar and moving Vern over to fiddle. Jesse Ramirez joined them on drums, along with Les Skramstad, who sang and also played guitar. Richie Pierre joined the band on steel guitar, until the band fired him and replaced him with Rusty Wheeler. According to Scot Wilburn, "Richie Pierre was an amazing steel player, but he had a little drinking problem," a common enough affliction among musicians. "He would often hock his steel for money to buy booze, and then the rest of the band would have to all throw in together to get his steel back so they could do a gig."

Having to pool their pocket money to get his steel out of the pawnshop was inconvenient, but Richie's talent made it worthwhile, at least for a while. Eventually, however, the band decided that it could not abide a steel player who went missing altogether. "The reason they finally fired him was kind of a funny story," Wilburn explained. "[Country legend] Hank Thompson was in town playing, and Richie knew the Bob Marshall [Wilderness Area] pretty well and promised to take Hank on a trail ride. It was actually a poaching trip on horseback, as there were no game wardens to speak of in those days.

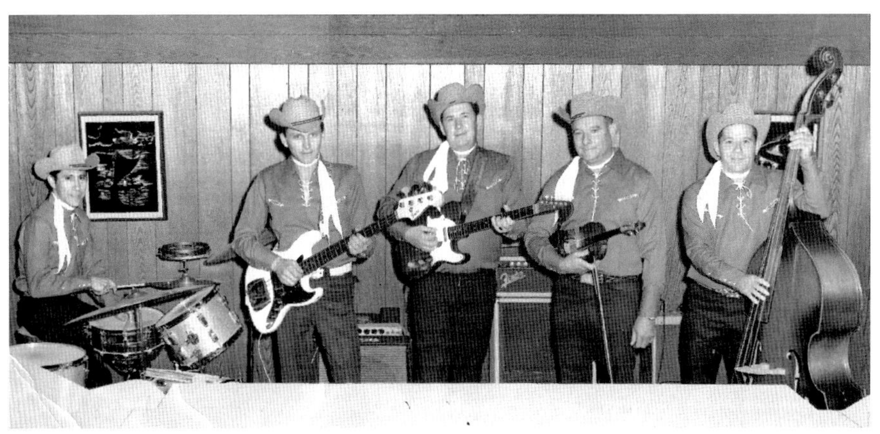

Although Orval Fochtman and Jimmy Widner left the Snake River Outlaws in the late 1950s, brothers Harold and Vern Wilburn carried the band on with various lineups until 1968. *Courtesy of T. Scot Wilburn.*

Anyway, Richie took off for a ten-day trail ride to guide Hank Thompson and was fired when he returned."

The band even had a weekly television show in 1957 and 1958 in Missoula on KGVO (Channel 13). As the 1960s drew to a close, the Snake River Outlaws were still playing six or seven nights a week in Montana, mostly in towns far north of Missoula like Kalispell and Libby. They still drew enthusiastic crowds, but the glory days of the Sunshine Jamboree were behind them and the youthful buzz surrounding the band had faded. The bloom was off the rose in other ways as well: the country had changed considerably from the tranquil days of the postwar 1950s and was now mired in endless tension over civil rights issues and bitterly divided over the war in Vietnam. Meanwhile, thanks to Elvis and the irresistible appeal of the backbeat, rock-and-roll had conquered popular music, relegating country music to regional markets and all but condemning bluegrass and old-time to the woodshed, at least until the folk music revival of the 1960s.

For the humble country outfit from Weiser, Idaho, changes in personnel brought changes in the sound—the pleasant frenzy of a hillbilly fiddle and banjo had given way to a more staid and conventional country sound with a steel guitar and a snare drum for rhythm. It wouldn't be long before the remaining original members decided to call quits on the tough and demanding life of the traveling band. The Wilburn boys had a great run, carrying on the Outlaws for a decade after the departure of Orval and Jimmy. Nothing could ever match the joyous energy of the early years anyway—those few golden years after the war when fortunes were high and everyone was young and in a mood to go down to the saloons along the railroad tracks in Missoula and listen to honest country music played by real fellows from an honest country town over on the other side of Lolo Pass. That sense of feeling flush and infallible, poised for a future filled with spaceships and robots, hit Montana as much as it did the rest of the country, providing a brief and fertile flash in time for country music to emerge from the old-time seeds sown during the Depression. For a decade, it felt as if the entire country had struck it rich and spent ten years celebrating in bars and nightclubs.

But eventually, complacency set in, and the party wound down into the reality of realpolitik and bomb shelters and an entirely new soporific: television. As Widner put it in an interview with Nashville songwriter Stephanie Davis in 1980, "TV changed the night life in Missoula, and although we still drew a crowd, the night life was fizzling out." Upon reflection, though, he realized that blaming technology entirely was perhaps a little unfair. After all, he noted, "We all got married, and if anything is bad for a band, it's getting married." Orval Fochtman expressed similar sentiments fifty years after the fact. In 2015, he reflected on the 1954 demise of the original lineup: "We all went our ways about that time. We all got married, and I come back to Idaho. Anyway, the six nights a week was over when we left Montana."

The Outlaws were hardly the only country band to take the stage in Montana in that halcyon era. Dozens of other country music outfits flourished in Montana in the 1950s and 1960s, some of whom sound surprisingly contemporary. One good example is a band called Boone and the Buckskins, who recorded four songs in 1968 on an EP at Valtron Recording Studios down in Helena. Hailing from Belt, Montana, about twenty miles east of Great Falls, the band played shows all over north-central and eastern Montana, routinely going up even into Canada. The four songs showcased on that 45-EP would not constitute an especially remarkable demo but for the pedal steel guitar work of Tom Gliko, which features some strikingly innovative licks and a unique, almost frenetic technique.

In addition to Tom on steel guitar, the band consisted of Dan Gliko on guitar and a third brother, Tim, on drums, with Jerry Marn playing bass. Dan Gliko, ostensible band leader for the Buckskins, still lives in Belt, where he continues to front a working country band (called Boone Country) and operates a state-of-the-art recording studio. Now seventy-three, Gliko still regularly plays and records music, much of it in conjunction with Nashville

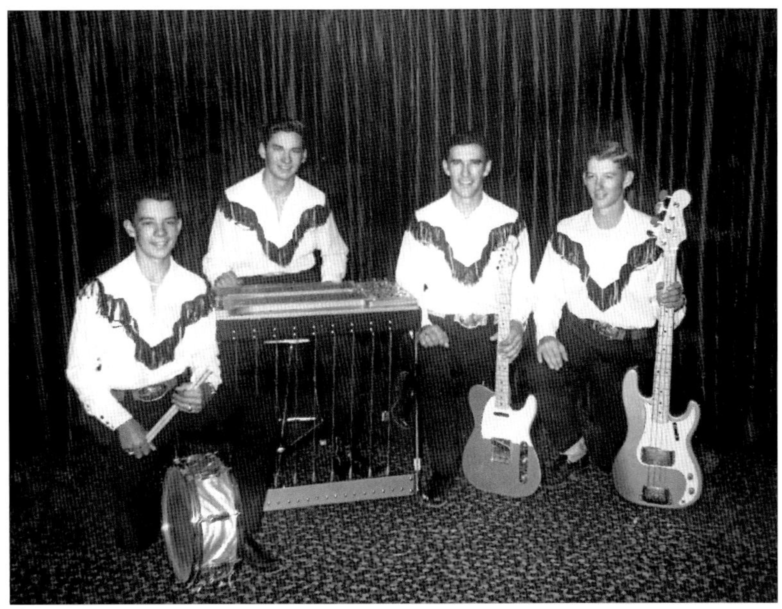

Boone and the Buckskins circa 1965. The Buckskins played rock-solid country music in the Bakersfield vein, featuring the steel work of Tom Gliko. *From left to right*: Tim Gliko, Tom Gliko, Dan Gliko and Jerry Marn. *Courtesy of Dan Gliko.*

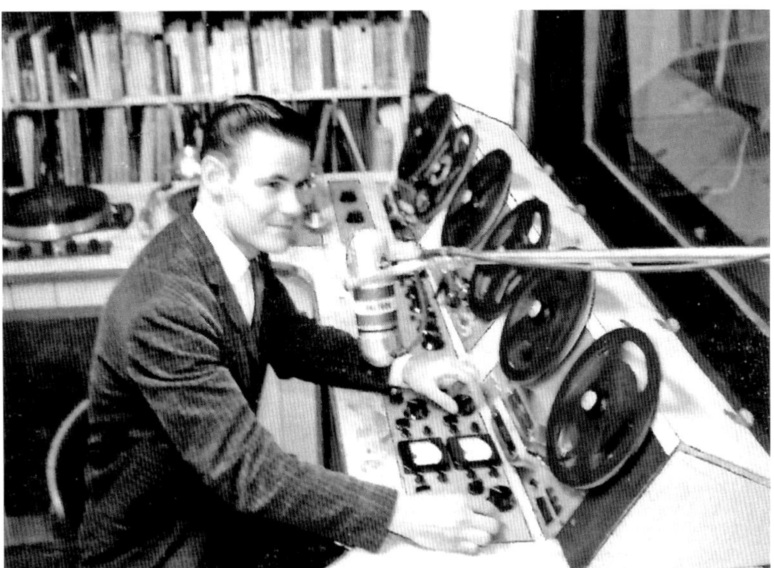

For much of the 1950s and 1960s, Valtron Studios in Helena, Montana, was the only recording studio between Seattle and Minneapolis endorsed by the Federation of Musicians Union. Pictured here is longtime owner and engineer Les Liedle. *Courtesy of Mike Liedle and Valtron Studios.*

studio musicians. "We can e-mail tracks back and forth now," he explained. "So really, I can have just about anybody you want throw down a part."

While Boone and the Buckskins members always hung on to some sort of day job to make ends meet, performances were a big part of their life in the 1960s. Gliko went into the flying business in the 1960s, and still flies planes and helicopters, the latter for firefighting and telephone and power pole installation. "We played all over, at clubs and fairs and all that. But I had the aviation business here for over forty years, which helped pay the bills," Dan said. "The helicoptering really helped pay for the recording studio."

Other country singers also gathered notice in the Montana newspapers following the reign of the Snake River Outlaws, including several women whose recordings still sound surprisingly fresh. Betty Jo Starr, for example, eponymous star of the Betty Jo Starr Show, played venues throughout the state in the 1950s and '60s, recording hit songs on the Four Star Label, including the popular "Montana Waltz."

In the eastern part of the state, around Miles City, Lindy Ness and his band the City Dudes recorded songs on the Vega label and even backed up Patsy Cline when she played a show in Miles City. Their own recordings, however, were met with a tepid response in *Billboard*. One notice (September 19, 1953) dismissed his release of "Saddle Leather" backed with "My Heart's in Montana" rather abruptly: "The warbler tries his best to put over this new effort, but his performance is listless." As for the B-side, a terse "Not much here" ended further speculation. Ness toured around Montana and the West for at least a decade, playing the Miles City clubs regularly—the Red Rock Inn, the Crossroads and Leon Park—when not out on the road. He settled down to farm in the 1960s and passed away in 2012.

The story of "Country Girl Kay" Whittaker (1923–2002) offers a spooky corroboration of Oscar Wilde's dictum about life imitating art, as it resembles something taken right from the Louvin Brothers' album *Tragic Songs of Life*. Country Girl Kay recorded more than eight sides at Valtron Studios in Helena, Montana, in the mid-'50s and was a regular performer at various venues throughout the state. Although she had an alluring and melodic voice and a talent for writing original country songs, she vanished from the spotlight following the shocking murder of her husband in 1964.

Born Helen Evelyn (Kay) Smith in Missouri in 1923, Country Girl Kay married Carson Jack Whittaker from Livingston, Montana, in the 1940s, and together they began recording EPs and singles at Valtron Studios in an effort to launch her career. Kay wrote songs and sang them in a clear, slightly wan

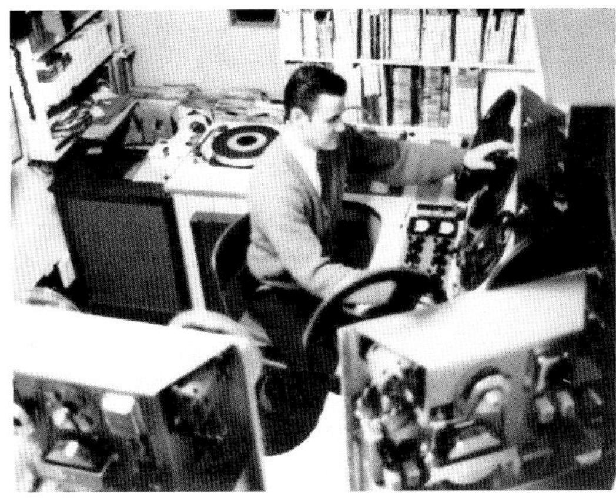

Les Liedle in the 1960s, Valtron Studios. *Courtesy of Mike Liedle and Valtron Studios.*

voice, often overdubbing a harmony on a second track with a slight delay that lends a haunting, forlorn feel to the finished product.

According to her obituary in the Buffalo, Missouri *Buffalo Reflex* of April 3, 2002, Helen Evelyn Smith "was a country musician at heart" who could play guitar, mandolin, banjo, fiddle and accordion by ear. She and her sister, Wanda, both "performed with traveling country bands in the 1940s." According to country music historian Lisa Wheeler, both were "regular performers on KWTO in Springfield, Missouri." Not long after Wanda married a singer named Ted Henderson, Ted introduced Kay to Carson Jack Whittaker, who happened to be looking for a woman with whom to sing duet material. According to Wheeler, Carson Jack and Kay toured throughout the United States, eventually settling down in Helena, Montana, where they recorded at least eight

SETTING UP FOR SESSION — Les Leidle, who owns the only American Federation of Musicians-authorized recording studio between Minneapolis and Seattle, sets up a boom microphone for a recording session. (Staff Photo by Ben Hansen)

Recording Is His First Love

Valtron article from the *Independent Record. Courtesy of Mike Liedle.*

sides in the early 1960s. It was around this time that she began to bill herself as "Country Girl Kay," and Carson Jack receded from the stage to focus on managing her career.

Unfortunately, just as her career was set to take off, tragedy struck: in July 1964, Carson Jack Whittaker was murdered just outside Afton, Wyoming, by a couple who picked him up as he was hitchhiking, apparently on his way to Bozeman, Montana. When the killer, Richard W. Kirk, was apprehended in Maine a few months later, a suitcase was discovered in his possession that contained a number of handwritten lyric sheets of Country Girl Kay's songs, an unusual form of evidence that contributed to his conviction. According to the *Montana Standard* of August 28, 1964, Kirk confessed to shooting Whittaker "point blank in the face." His accomplice, Shirley Brearley, was also charged in the death, although the charges against her were ultimately dismissed.

Richard Kirk was convicted and sentenced to death in December 1964 by Judge H.R. Christmas, presiding over the case in Kemmerer, Wyoming. By a dreadful twist of fortune, however, Kirk's conviction was overturned two years later by the United States Supreme Court. According to an AP newswire account on October 23, 1967, the opinion was issued by the court unsigned, although Justice Hugo L. Black did register a dissenting vote, unfortunately "giving no amplification of his views." The reversal evidently hinged on the status of Kirk's confession, which the ACLU persuasively argued had been inappropriately extracted. Kirk walked away a free man.

The odious crime cut short the life of Carson Jack Whittaker and halted the career of Country Girl Kay, who so far as can be determined did not record anything else after the Whitkay sessions in the early 1960s. Country Girl Kay eventually remarried, this time to a man named Bill Gardner, and the couple relocated to Cut Bank, Montana. After her husband passed away in 1975, Kay moved again to Kalispell, where she gave music lessons and occasional local performances. In 2002, Country Girl Kay died in a nursing home in Spokane, Washington. She is buried in Buffalo, Missouri.

Although once hailed by the *Independent Record* in Helena as "the Guitar-playing Burl Ives of Lincoln, Montana," Tiny Stokes is all but forgotten. In his prime, he was a successful musician, both as a performer and a songwriter, and he left behind an appreciable body of Montana music. Born Elmer Wayne Stokes on July 12, in Anna, Illinois, in 1917, "Tiny" made a name for himself playing music for Buck Jones cowboy films from the late 1930s to 1948, when Jones died. The most successful of his original compositions was a song called "Judy," featured in the film *Oklahoma Blues* (1948), starring

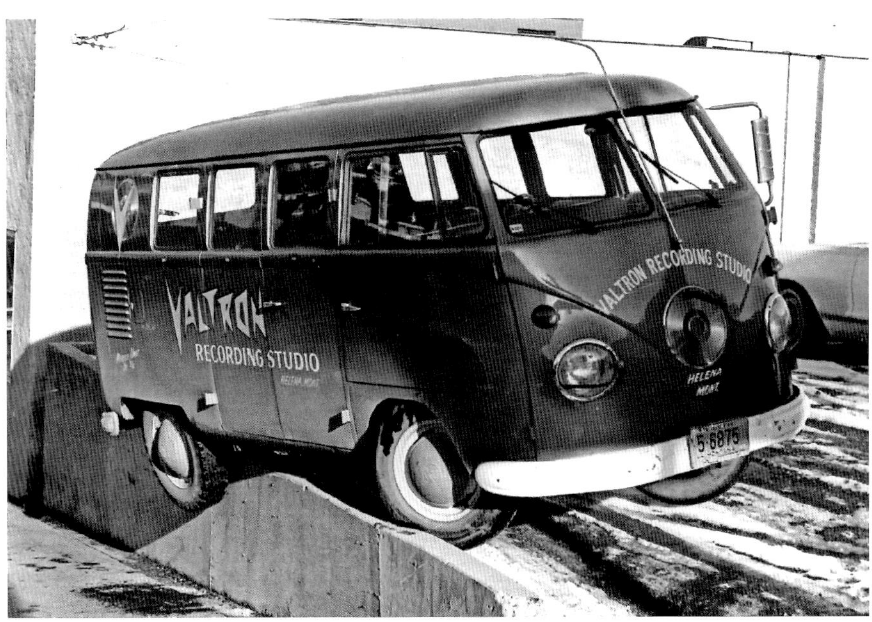

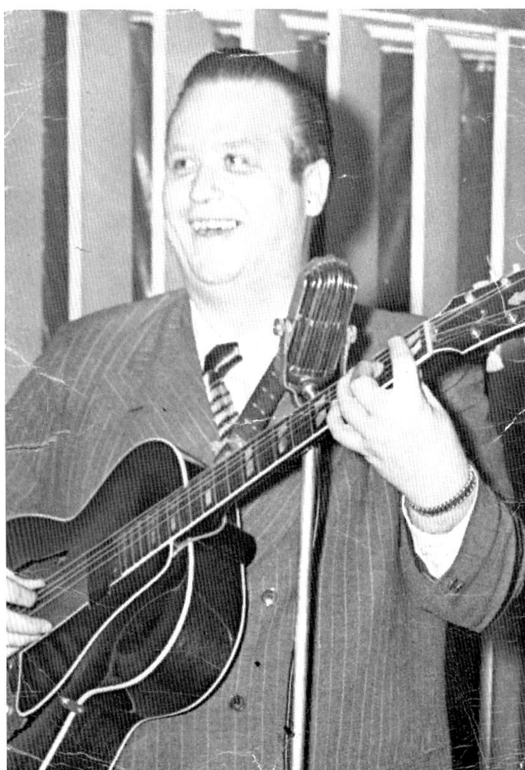

Above: Valtron's VW bus. Engineer Les Liedle had parked atop a snowbank when he arrived at the studio in the morning, but a Chinook blew in and melted all the snow, stranding the bus over a retaining wall. *Courtesy of Mike Liedle and Valtron Studios.*

Left: Tiny Stokes wore many hats. He was a consummate performer and songwriter, but he also taught music in Helena and was a DJ at KBLL for years. He also cut trees for a fencepost mill and ran a hot dog stand in downtown Helena. *Courtesy of Doug Stokes.*

country star Jimmy Wakely, who made the song a hit. It was later recorded by Hank Thompson and Marty Robbins, among others.

By 1951, Stokes was living in Helena, Montana, where he continued to record and write songs, although his income there could hardly match what he'd made in Hollywood. To augment his musical career, he gave guitar lessons out of Helena music stores and was a disc jockey for KBLL for twenty years. Like his contemporaries in the Snake River Outlaws, Stokes also worked as a timber cutter and a sawyer for a mill making fence posts. At one point in the 1960s, according to newspaper accounts, after suffering an injury in the sawmill, Stokes negotiated with the City of Helena for a hot dog franchise downtown, a kind of sinecure bestowed on the local character whose efforts to put Montana on the musical map did not go unappreciated.

A 1952 article in the *Great Falls Tribune*, in fact, described Stokes as "a big friendly fellow who has been entertaining people with his western singing the past 23 years." One of his cuts, recorded with his band the Frontiersmen, showcases some of the best hillbilly boogie to come out of the Treasure State, especially the standout tune "Blackfoot Boogie," a song that offered a veritable catalogue of Montana honky-tonks, as illustrated in these lyrics:

Well, I'm going on a tour of the Treasure State
Part of the towns we're gonna try to make
I'm gonna check the dance that's going around
Cause the doggone thing's about got me down
It's the Blackfoot Boogie and it's on the ball
Yes, they tell me that it started way up in Great Falls.

Well there's the Green Lantern and the H and J
The Ranger's Club is where they swing and sway
There's the Wagon Wheel they do mighty fine
Let me tell you man they have one big time
With the Blackfoot Boogie, Oh they're really living
Now hold on tight we're pulling into Billings.

There's the Beacon Club and the Big 4 Star
The Elmo Club is not very far
There's the Horseshoe Club where Pop and Dixie
Run the Seventeen Bar where they get their kicks
To the Blackfoot Boogie, they're counting coup
Now hold on tight, we're pulling into Butte.

Well there's the Rocky Mountain and the Forty Five
You done left here with Stake-Out jive
There's the big Red Rooster and the COD
Raymond's Club just smiling free
Do the Blackfoot Boogie it's here to stay
They do the Blackfoot Boogie till the break of day.

There's the Cajun club in Havre and the Northside Bar
The Sportsman up in Shelby then you jump in your car
Then Kalispell and Browning man they're really the towns
The nightspots there jump up and down
The Blackfoot Boogie they shout it up to the sky
Well the Blackfoot Boogie will get you by and by.

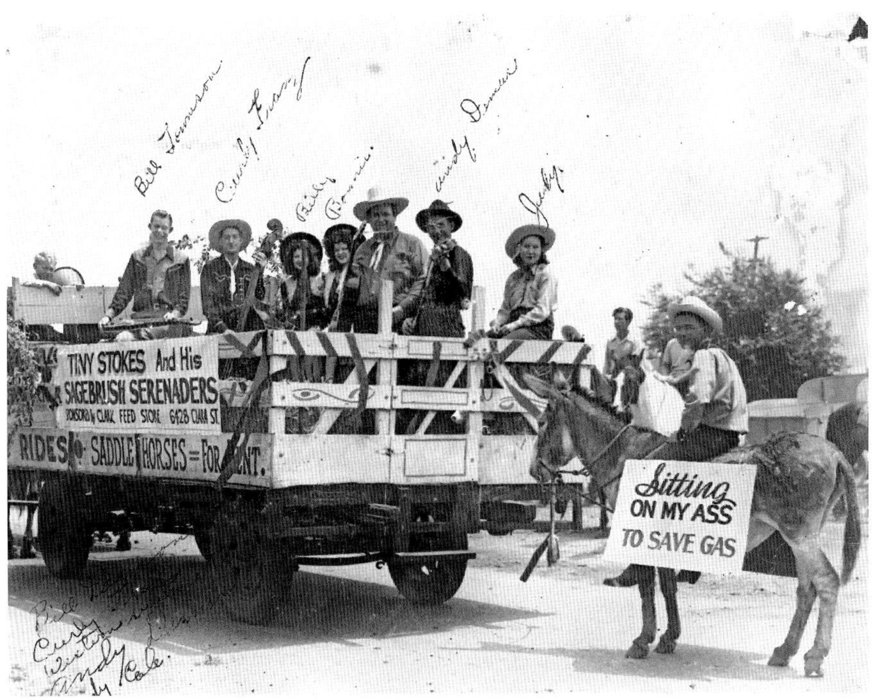

Tiny Stokes had a career as a musician in Hollywood providing music for cowboy films starring Buck Jones in the 1930s and 1940s. After Jones died, Stokes moved to Montana, where he continued to perform. He penned many songs about Montana, including "The Great Falls Waltz" and "The Blackfoot Boogie." *Courtesy of Doug Stokes.*

Then we go to Missoula and the Frontier Lounge
The Sunshine and the Maverick as you make your rounds
Helena is next to the big Night Owl,
Let me tell you man they jump and howl
To the Blackfoot Boogie, Oh they never stop
They do the Blackfoot Boogie till they blow their top.

There's Livingston and Lewiston, Columbus, and Glasgow
Miles City, Glendive, jumping like a beehive
Bozeman, Boulder, and Dillon too
Anaconda, Deer Lodge and Drummond to go through
To Hamilton and Polson and Whitefish and Libby
Right on down to diddy wah diddy
They're all doing the Blackfoot Boogie now.
(© 1953 Tiny Stokes, Big-T Music)

Stokes also made local news in 1952 when he worked out an arrangement with radio station KMON out of Great Falls, Montana, to donate all the proceeds from his song "The Great Falls Waltz" for the benefit of a youth program in the community. The key lyrics Stokes penned in praise of Great Falls emphasized its geographical location and good-natured people:

There are signs that read welcome at each entrance to town,
No friendlier city is there to be found
Mid high snow-capped mountains and wide rolling plains
They sing of her praises and shout of her fame
I may roam the world over by land or by sea
But Great Falls, Montana's where I want to be.
(© 1952 Tiny Stokes, Big-T Music)

According to his son, Doug Stokes, Tiny also recorded a side or two under name of "Yellowstone Chip" and briefly hosted a TV show in Missoula in 1956.

In his work as a disc jockey for KBLL radio in Helena, Stokes maintained his connections to some of the bigger names in country music back east. In 1962, Red Sovine and Red Foley played a show in Helena, for example, and Tiny Stokes introduced the two stars to a friend of his who worked at a local smelter and played semipro baseball for the local team, the East Helena Smelterites. The kid moonlighted as a country crooner in the local clubs

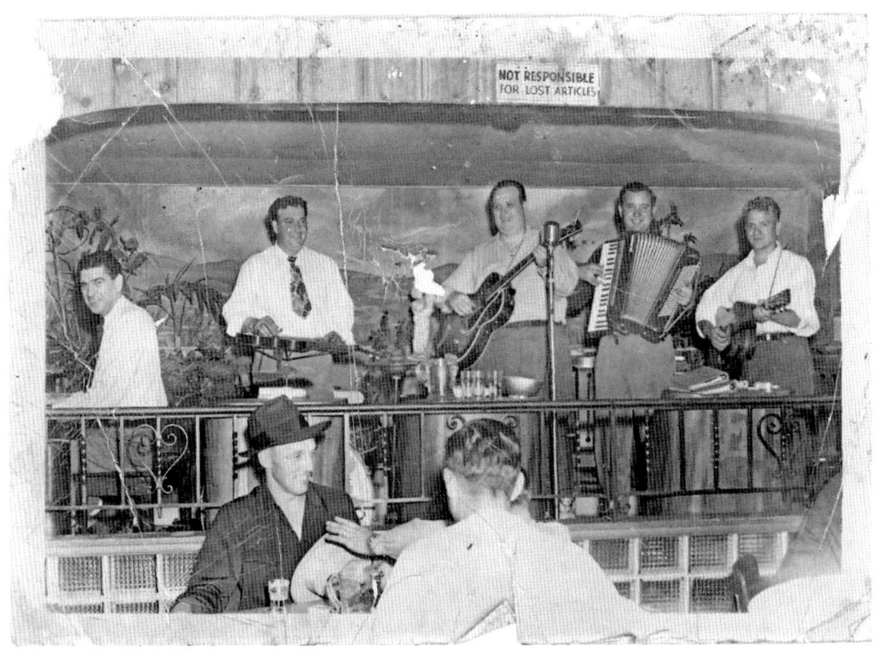

Tiny Stokes on stage, circa late 1940s. *Courtesy of Doug Stokes.*

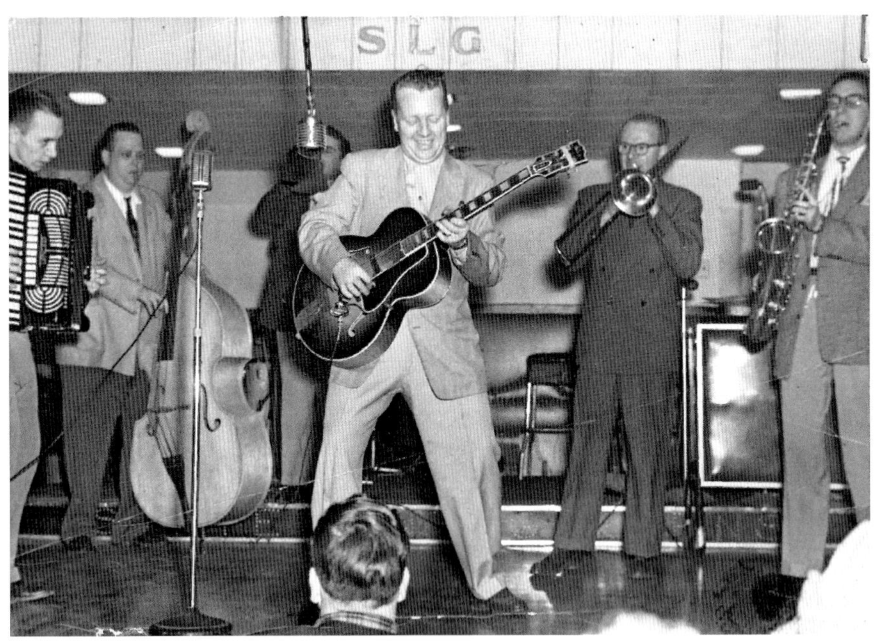

Tiny Stokes on stage in the early 1950s. Band members are unidentified. A trombone was an unusual instrument for a country swing ensemble. *Courtesy of Doug Stokes.*

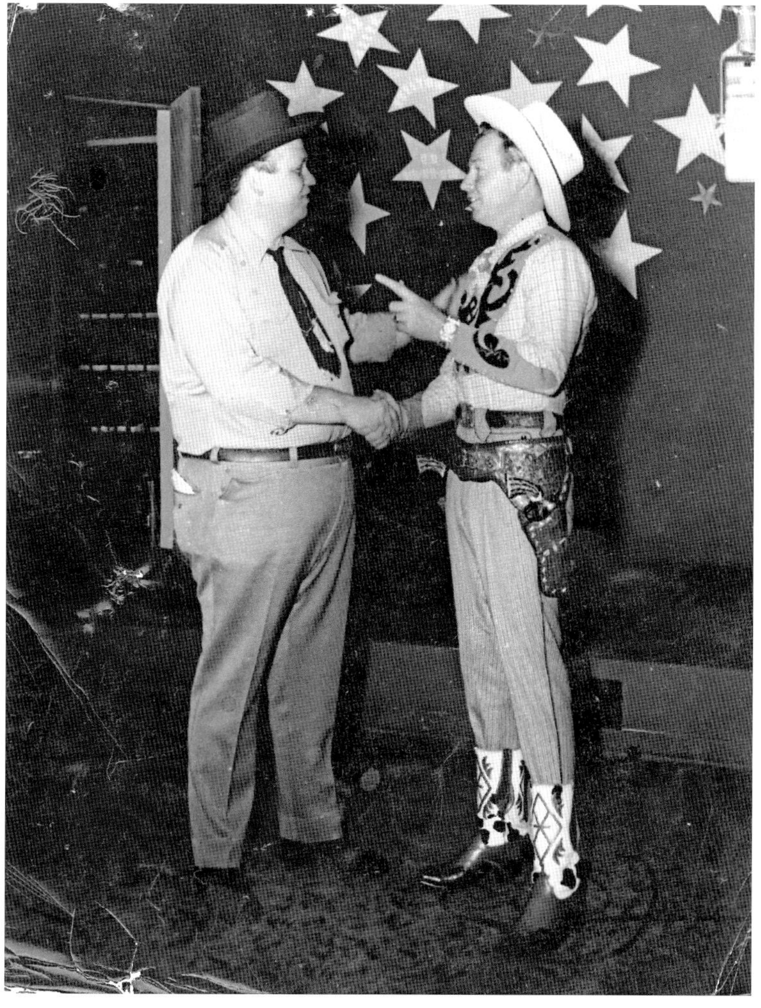

Tiny Stokes shaking hands with movie star Rex Allen, the "Arizona Cowboy." *Courtesy of Doug Stokes.*

around Helena, and Stokes recognized his ability and judged him to have talent enough to succeed in Nashville.

That kid's name was Charley Pride, and he ever afterward credited Stokes with his discovery. Charley Pride's musical career in Montana was brief but significant: when relieved from travel with the ball club, he would play around the state in various bars—especially Helena, Great Falls and Anaconda—developing his performance skills. His Montana fans have always been proud to point out that he got his start in Big Sky Country.

In 1963, while en route back to Montana after a failed attempt to make the cut for the New York Mets at spring training in Florida, Pride stopped in Nashville and went to Cedarwood Publishing, where Red Sovine had left him an open invitation. He was signed that week by Jack Johnson and went on to enjoy one of the greatest careers of any performer in country music, although his greatest success was still a few years off. In fact, Charley Pride lived on Peosta Street in Helena until 1967, still playing local nightclubs and working at the smelter after he had launched his career in Nashville in 1963.

Monty Cowles grew up in Helena and was playing in a band with Charley Pride as early as 1965. "I think I was fourteen or fifteen when I started. It was Jimmy Owen's band, he and his father, George," she said. "They had started playing with Charley, and they needed a drummer, so they called me." Longtime Helena musician Ron Darlington also recalled those years, noting that Jimmy Owens "owned the Country and Western scene in Helena in 1964." Darlington recounted a funny story about how his own rock-and-roll band was headlining at Matt's Club in downtown Helena and was drawing the country crowd away from Jimmy's band, who happened to be playing at another club called Tracy's. "He was so mad, he called the cops and reported us for being underage and being in a bar, which was true. Sure enough, the cops came and told the owner the only way it would work is if one of us had a legal guardian accompanying us." Darlington and his band

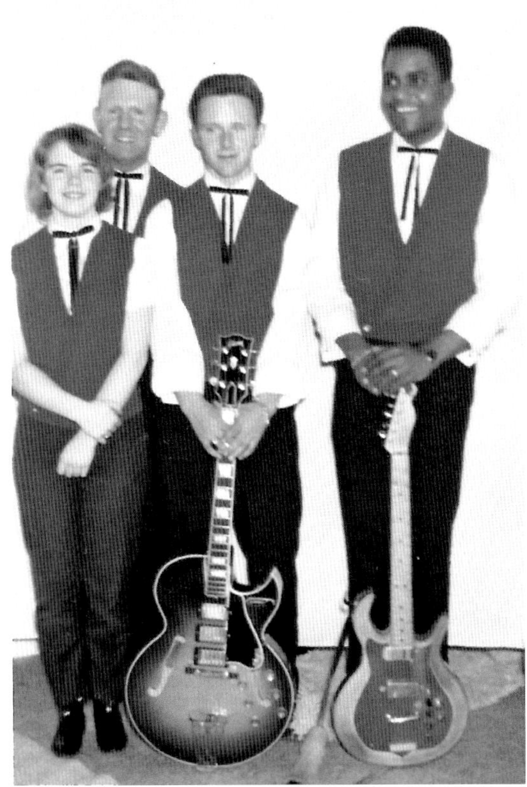

Long before he took Nashville by storm, Charley Pride got his start playing in Jimmy Owen's country band in Helena, Montana, in the mid-1960s. *From left to right*: Monty Cowles, George Owens, Jimmy Owens and Charley Pride. *Courtesy of Monty Cowles.*

were inventive: the following week, they had arranged for the nightclub owner to become the legal guardian of one of the band members, after which they never had a problem again. "Jimmy Owen and I were friends eventually, but we didn't play much together because we had our own bands." In any case, a year or so later, fifteen-year-old Monty Cowles was playing drums in Jimmy's band.

Many Helenans recall seeing Charley Pride playing in Helena, but not always in the nightclubs. "When I was a small child, my family attended the First Baptist Church up near the Cathedral," remarked poet and editor Rick Newby in Helena. "Quite often Charley would be up at the altar, playing gospel songs."

Charley Pride's years in Montana proved instrumental to his successful career in Nashville, and both he and his wife's understated success in bridging what many critics considered a formidable racial divide illustrates the power of music to transcend cultural prejudice. But Pride's seemingly effortless integration into a mainstream country music scene also showed that even if the usual demographic of country listeners perhaps tended toward the stereotypical southern redneck, the spectrum of actual fans happened to be more complex and surprisingly inclusive—a fact in part reflective of the complex and different multicultural streams of music that ran together to create what we now refer to as Americana. In a 1965 interview in the (Helena) *Independent Record*, Charley's wife, Rozene, made some interesting points about the civil rights movement and its impact in Montana: only once had she and her husband ever been refused service in Helena, she noted, but "there are thousands of Indians [in Montana] treated quite a bit like Negroes in the South."

Charley Pride dominated the airwaves between 1969 and 1971 with eight number-one country hits, all of which achieved notable success in the Billboard pop charts as well. As a consequence, Pride became credited as one of the innovators of the "countrypolitan" sound of Nashville country music that endured throughout the 1970s and that included such stars as Glen Campbell and the Billy Sherrill–produced stars George Jones and Tammy Wynette.

Many well-known Montana musicians are known more for their performances as working musicians rather than as recording stars, including, for example, Rex Rieke. Rieke made a living playing music in bars and clubs around the Treasure State for more than thirty years. He is currently among the most respected jazz musicians in Montana, but he is also adept at country music and has played with some legendary figures from the '50s and '60s.

"Hank Snow invited me to go out on the road with him sometime in the '60s," Rieke recalled, an offer he ultimately turned down. "I liked the

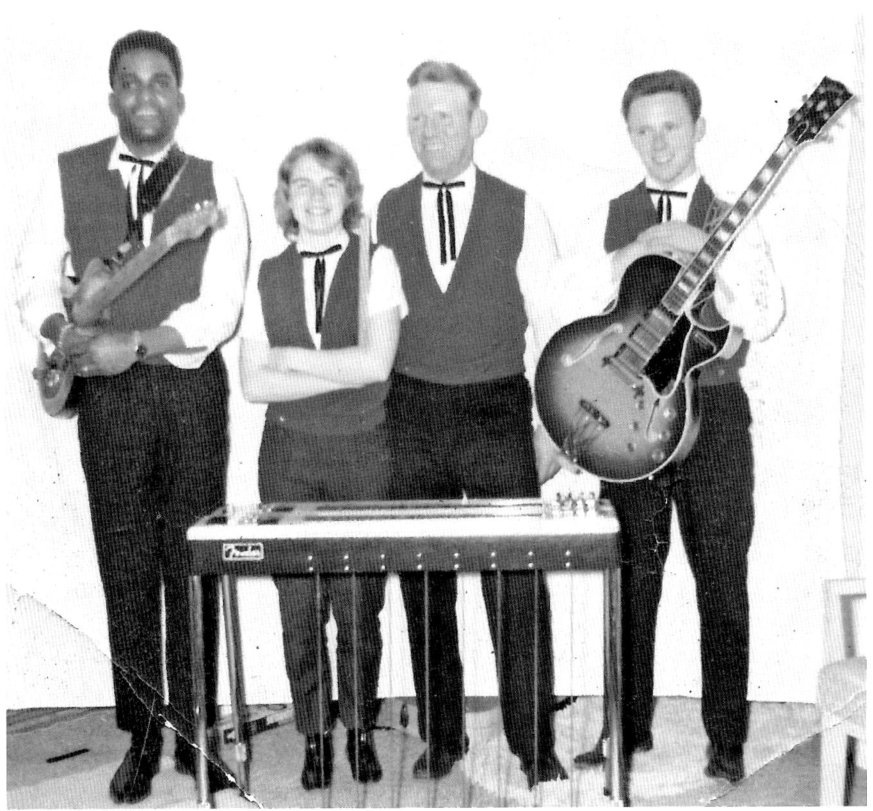

Not only was Jimmy Owens's country band unusual for having a woman (Monty Cowles) for a drummer, but she was also only fifteen when she joined the band. *From left to right*: Charley Pride, Monty Cowles, George Owens and Jimmy Owens. *Courtesy of Monty Cowles.*

idea, of course, but I was already making pretty good money playing in the house band at Duffy's in Great Falls. Snow understood." A piano player, Rieke also recorded with Kenneth "Thumbs" Carllile, the legendary guitar virtuoso who taught Roger Miller, among others, the idioms and techniques of country guitar. Like many Montana Americana musicians, Rieke chose fidelity to place over a perhaps promising career on the road back east. He now lives in the country outside Helena, retired but still playing regularly with jazz ensembles, and he occasionally holds court at the legendary country and western jam on Thursday nights at Scotty's Bar in Deer Lodge.

Another example is virtuoso steel guitar player Louis Armentaro, who holds one of the most unusual and probably unbreakable records in the *Guinness Book of World Records*. For the last sixty-five years, Mr. Armentaro has been the parade announcer at the Livingston Rodeo and Fair—that's *sixty-five* consecutive years. He just turned ninety-three and shows no signs of missing the rodeo or parade for the foreseeable future, so chances are his entry in *Guinness* is safe forever.

Louis Armentaro was born in 1924 in Livingston. During the Second World War, he enlisted and served in the Pacific Theater, seeing action in the Philippines. After V-J Day, he spent a year as part of the occupation force in Japan, where he found himself running sound for theaters and shows for the GIs. In 1949, he returned home and continued to run sound for whoever would hire him, launching a business he called Sound Over the West.

A guitar player since he was a young kid, Louis picked up the pedal steel in 1950 and decided that he wanted to start a country band. He recruited his brother and three other fellows and started a group he called the Rhythm Ramblers. The core of the band—Louis and his brother, Frank—still play occasional gigs around central Montana, making the Rhythm Ramblers a contender for one of Montana's longest-lived bands. "I've played all kinds of gigs over the years," Louis said. "I still play every week, but not out in the clubs as much, of course. I am ninety-three, you know." Armentaro played with many musicians over the course of his lifetime but managed to keep the Rhythm Ramblers a working concern for a half century. "We recorded some shows but never put out any records. We were a working band, for the most part."

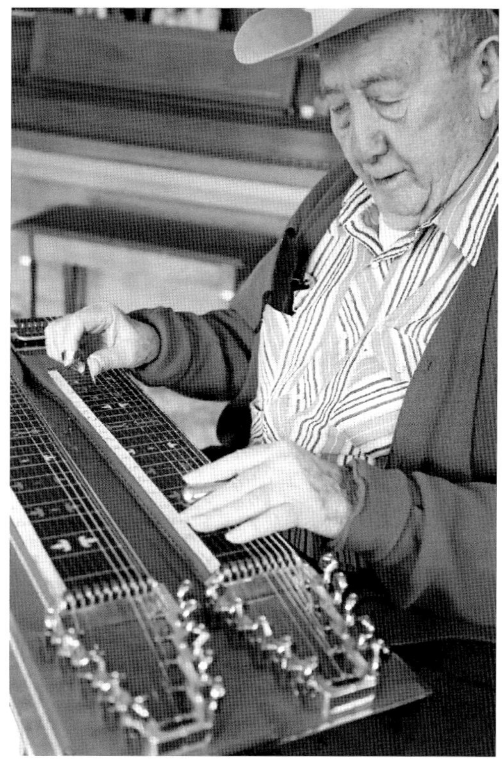

Louis Armentaro is almost certainly the world's oldest active pedal steel guitar player. He has been playing with the Rhythm Ramblers out of Livingston, Montana, for more than sixty years. *Courtesy of Seonaid B. Campbell.*

Armentaro is a respected elder statesman of the pedal steel in Montana, one of the definitive instruments of authentic, country Americana. And anyone of that brotherhood in Montana knows who Armentaro is and holds him in

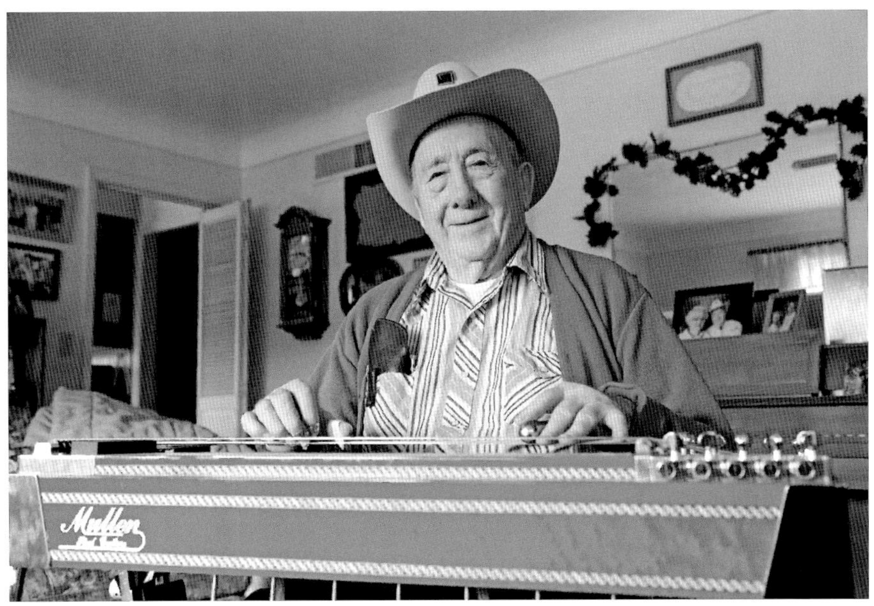

Louis Armentaro once remarked that the pedal steel is such a difficult instrument that "it might take you 'til you're ninety" to master it. *Courtesy of Seonaid B. Campbell.*

high esteem, including both Dave Martens of Havre (the Best Westerns) and Gibson Hartwell of Missoula (Tarkio, Stellarondo), who speak of him in reverent tones. Most people are amazed that Armentaro plays what most people consider an extremely difficult instrument at an advanced age. "Well, you got to play that steel a long time to get any good," he said. "It might take you 'til you're ninety!"

Louis Armentaro's early years in country music were closely contemporaneous with those of the Snake River Outlaws, although he seldom played over in the Missoula area, doing most of his playing in central and eastern Montana and the Dakotas. "If we crossed paths," he said, "I don't remember it, but there were lots of good bands in those days, and you could see good country music every Friday or Saturday night."

Louis Armentaro also holds the unofficial title of "World's Oldest Steel Guitar Player." "I regularly play the two-neck, twenty-string steel, with four pedals and knee levers going both ways," Armentaro said. "I've been playing so long now I can play anything, but I love that old western swing." For a pedal steel player who has lived in Livingston, Montana, for nearly a century, what may sound like a boast is in truth a pretty fitting grace note ornamenting a thoroughly musical career.

Armentaro is about the same age as the surviving Snake River Outlaws, Orval Fochtman and Jimmy Widner.* Although Jimmy and Orval were the first members to leave the band, eventually all the Outlaws found themselves married to wives who hoped that their husbands would find more conventional jobs and settle down—a not unusual development in the life of nearly every band. In Widner's case, an exit was inevitable, especially after he "got religion," although he continued to fiddle, playing mainly for a band called the Burrus Family, a gospel group out in the Bitterroot Valley. With the help of writer Tom Brown, Widner recounted his life story in a biography called *Fiddlin' Around the West*. After the Outlaws, Widner immortalized himself in the annals of old-time fiddling by winning the National Oldtime Fiddlers' contest two years in a row (1955 and 1956). Because Weiser, Idaho, happened to be the home of both the Outlaws and the national contest, the Snake River Outlaws will forever be entwined with the aura and mystique of Weiser itself and all it represents to fiddlers of all styles who converge at the edge of the little dusty town in the middle of summer to swap tunes and trade fiddle lore.

The Snake River Outlaws played their last shows in 1968, working seven nights a week at the Slipper Inn in Libby, Montana, during the peak of the construction boom between 1966 and 1972 as the Libby Dam went in on the Kootenai River. At the end of that run, the band packed it in for good, and Harold Wilburn, the erstwhile bootlegger who had been reluctant to join the Outlaws back in 1953, finally traded in his slacks and western shirts for dungarees and went to work in a sawmill.

Although the Snake River Outlaws were an outfit every bit as talented as the famous stars of the era—Ernest Tubb, Red Foley, Moon Mullican, Lefty Frizzell, Hank Penny and Ted Daffan, to name a few of their more successful contemporaries—they lacked the ambition or desire to leave the West for Nashville, which would have been a practical necessity for national fame. Instead, they chose to remain anchored in the West they loved, playing music in an idiom evocative of the locale in which they flourished. Their sound was simple but polished through practice, their vocals clear and unadulterated. Jimmy's prowess on the fiddle drove their sound without overpowering his rhythm section or making himself a flashy spectacle. Like Hank Williams and his band, the original Snake River Outlaws generated plenty of danceable rhythm without a drummer, which kept their music rooted in the fertile soil of a rich old-time music tradition that stretched back into the nineteenth century. Part of what made the Snake River

* Sadly, Jimmy Widner passed away just as this book was going to press.

Outlaws so legendary in Montana, in fact, was their working-class ethos and renunciation of going east "to make it big." Their music exudes the good-natured exuberance of youth out on the town, throwing down and having a good time.

In the liner notes to the one album of their music available on CD, Scot Wilburn adroitly captured the essence of the Outlaws: "There was none of, 'I'm more important than you are,' or, 'I'm the star and you're not.' They just loved being together, playing music. It was like, here's the roll of bologna, everyone make a sandwich, and we've all got a place to sleep tonight, and at the end of the night everybody got to do what they did best."

Chapter 2

Private Stash

The Mission Mountain Wood Band and Homegrown Music in the 1970s

The 1950s were a golden age for country music all over the United States, and the sound developed by bands such as the Snake River Outlaws and Tiny Stokes influenced the course that Americana music would take as it evolved in Montana in the 1970s and beyond. In the 1960s, dozens of bands around the state like Boone and the Buckskins helped solidify that country sound by cultivating the rich possibilities of the pedal steel guitar, which by the end of the 1960s had replaced the fiddle as the definitive "country" instrument.

Meanwhile, the folk music revival of the late 1950s and early 1960s was going on, primarily on college campuses across the country. On the one hand, that movement helped resurrect and preserve a host of Americana styles, including not only the Mississippi Delta blues, especially as played by Mississippi John Hurt, Skip James and Son House, but also the "old-time" sound created by fiddlers and ballad singers of Appalachia. On the other hand, purists and more authentic practitioners of those styles lamented how the "folk scare" often produced soulless, sanitized imitations of the source music, epitomized in the albums put out by the Kingston Trio and the New Christy Minstrels, for example, but imitated in the recordings of countless clones.

The Big Sky Singers, who put out a record (*The Big Sky Singers*) on a major label (Dot 3603) in 1964, would qualify as such a band. The album itself is standard late folk-era stuff, but this album retains some interest today because it featured liner notes by gonzo writer Hunter S. Thompson, who had yet to graffiti the walls of journalism. Bruce Innes founded the Big Sky Singers after touring with legendary blues singer Josh White. Innes had been in show business from the 1950s, and according to his website, he formed the group while attending Montana State University in Missoula (which became UM in 1968). The Big Sky Singers first met Thompson after a performance at the Gun Room of the Finlen in Butte. Thompson urged the band to try their luck in California.

After landing a contract with Dot Records in Hollywood, the band recruited Thompson to write the liner notes. "A couple of months ago in Bug Sur, Calif., the Big Sky Singers went up on a hill above the Pacific surf and posed for the photo that appears on the cover of their first record album," Thompson began. He recounted the their travails after leaving Montana, baldly describing the band as a "latterday Kingston Trio with a big swinging sound that comes from three guitars, three voices and a bass in the background."

This piece contains none of the over-the-top journalese that would become the trademark shtick of the Hunter S. Thompson of *Fear and Loathing* fame. On the contrary, Thompson's blurb here is a case study in feigned enthusiasm; his sentences of unspectacular prose read as if they were enlisted to fulfill an obligation: "[The Big Sky Singers] are making $1000 a week…and they've played or are booked in at such reputable Western clubs as the Exodus in Denver, the Red Fox in Spokane, the Red Onion in Aspen, Colorado, and the Troubador [*sic*] in Los Angeles."

In one brief paragraph toward the end, Thompson musters a feeble effort to capture the essence of the group, as he summarized the crew-necked folk "world" of that era and its elusive success stories overshadowed by predictable moments of failure:

> *There are two sides to that world. One side is the big rock candy mountain, where musicians hand out records like calling cards. Where all the audiences are standing-room-only and booking agents for big-time nightclubs always say "please." The other side is where you feel lucky to get $25 for a one-night stand at the Elks Club in Lewiston, Idaho, and where you have $6 to last until the next "gig" 1000 miles away and your agent calls to say it's been cancelled and you're out of work until further notice.*

Thompson recounted the Big Sky Singers' long climb from coffeehouse gigs on and around the old MSU campus in Missoula to playing more lucrative engagements at the Gun Room at the Finlen in Butte to ultimately becoming the house band at the Hacienda in Fresno, California. When that gig dried up, the Singers found themselves at a crossroads: either fade back onto the Elks Club circuit or record an album and drum up a new following.

Alas, the Big Sky Singers dissolved not long after their debut for Dot Records. In spite of positive reviews, the success of the album (and the band) came to an abrupt and tragic halt with the death of David Stiles, who had been the main singer for the group.

Nevertheless, the "folk scare" atmosphere of the early '60s did play an oblique role in the formation of one of Montana's most famous and well-loved bands—the Mission Mountain Wood Band—who would dominate the music scene a decade later in the era of the Aber Day Keggers in the 1970s.

Missoula, Montana, in 1971 was a pretty heady place. As the home of Montana's liberal arts university, the town offered about the only sanctuary in the state for anyone with long hair or a taste for intoxicants other than alcohol. Like many college towns of its era, it had a fair number of hippies, although in the Pacific Northwest, the longhairs tended to wear flannel shirts and hiking boots instead of madras shirts and sandals. The skid row district that the Snake River Outlaws had called home back in the '50s was still just about as run-down, although some of the bars had changed names and a few of the greasy spoon cafés had put dishes with alfalfa sprouts and herbal tea on their menus. Butterfly Herbs opened on Higgins Avenue, the main thoroughfare downtown, in 1972. It sold tea and incense and strange herbs from huge glass jars and exotic, French-pressed coffee at a bar in the back. A few years later, Bernice's Bakery appeared across the river, which served coffee so thick and strong that patrons would joke about going down there in the morning "to cut off a slab." A head shop called the Joint Effort might have started it all back in 1968, the first store of its type in the state, according to proprietor Bill Stoianoff, who was only twenty when he opened its doors.

The counterculture persisted for a decade or more in Missoula beyond the '60s expiration date elsewhere, preserved by the college atmosphere and the funky shops that routinely appeared downtown. Probably the best example was the world-famous music store Rockin Rudy's (opened in 1982), which offered locals and tourists alike quirky merchandise alongside its extensive music offerings. The logo on a T-shirt heavily marketed there in the 1980s summed up the town nicely: "Missoula: A Place, Sort of." Nowadays, Missoula making an appearance on every list of "the best places to live in the West" has become something of a cliché, but in the late '60s and early '70s, it was a remotely hip oasis surrounded by the conservative desert of the West.

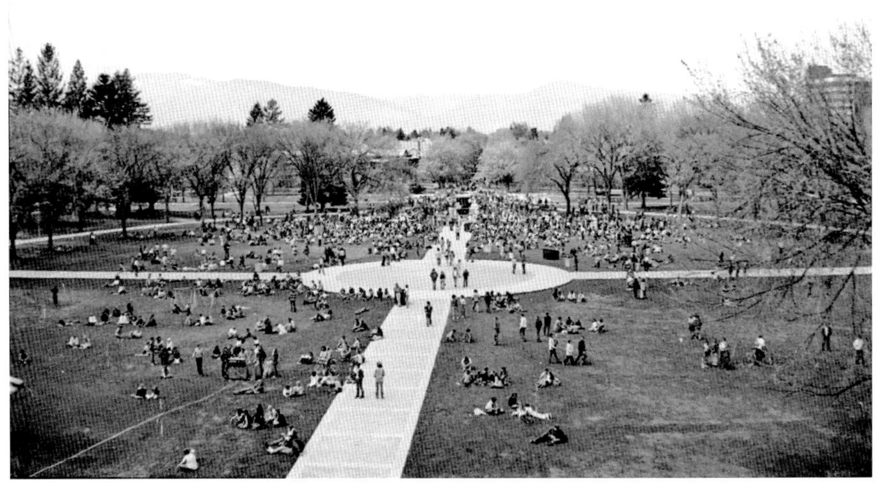

The Quad at University of Montana, 1974. *Courtesy of Archives and Special Collections, Mansfield Library, University of Montana.*

In 1971, one of the more dramatic chapters in Montana music history was opened when Rob Quist and Steve Riddle met each other in Missoula. Quist was a young kid from Cut Bank, Montana, way up on the high line, not terribly far from the Blackfeet Indian Reservation. Anyone driving into town on Highway 2 was greeted by a twenty-five-foot-high penguin bearing a cheery boast: "Welcome to Cut Bank Montana, Coldest Spot in the Nation." Compared to Cut Bank, Missoula might as well have been on a different planet. This brave new world had a lot of goodly creatures in it, including talented musicians from all over the state.

Steve Riddle, another Montana boy, was born and raised in Libby, up in the equally remote, very northwestern corner of the state. His father was sheriff of Lincoln County for fifteen years, and his mother ran the Dairy Queen down the street. During his sophomore year in high school, the family relocated to Missoula, where he attended and graduated from Sentinel High School. After high school, he enrolled at UM, since it was close and his mother was an alumna.

Steve and Rob wound up together in the university glee club, called the Jubileers. Like probably every other college glee club of the era, the Jubileers sang hackneyed folk material, and everything about them seemed

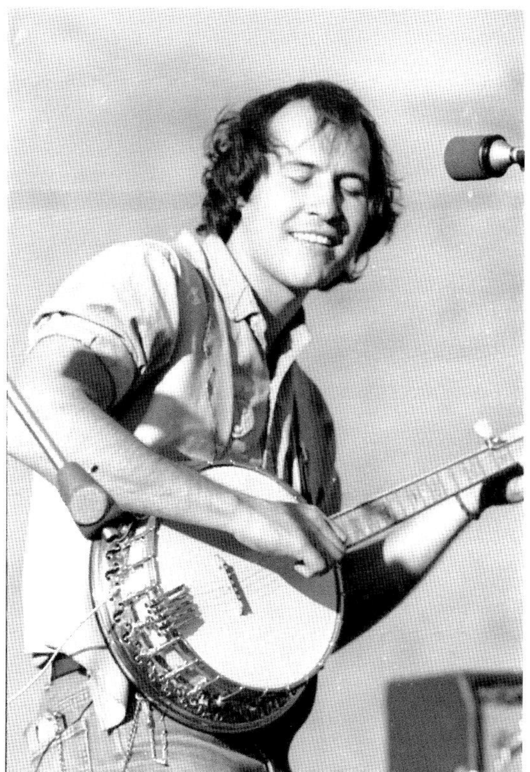

Right: Rob Quist having a good time at Aber Day, 1974. *Courtesy of Archives and Special Collections, Mansfield Library, University of Montana.*

Below: Steve Riddle strikes an emotional chord at an Aber Day performance, 1974. *Courtesy of Archives and Special Collections, Mansfield Library, University of Montana.*

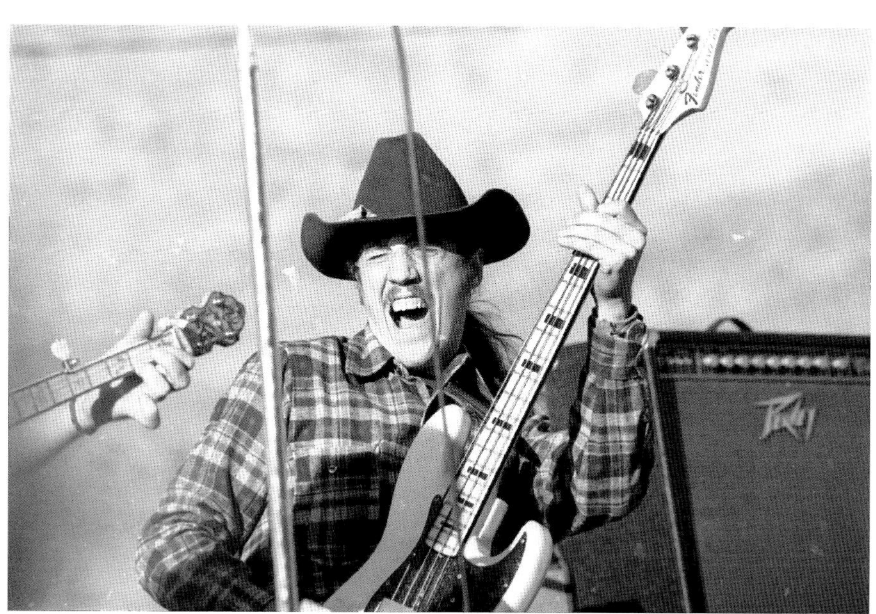

a hangover of the folk craze. "Robby was coming from that V-neck, crew cut chorus side of things, while I was coming from a more long-hair, rock and roll background," said Riddle. Still, they discovered they had a lot of musical tastes in common. "Jonathan Edwards was a big influence at the time," Quist said. "That style he played—a little country, very acoustic oriented—that inspired us."

Not long after Steve Riddle and Rob Quist found each other, they hooked up with another singer, Terry Robinson, who also strummed a guitar. "Terry tuned the guitar to an open chord and then just moved one finger in a bar up and down to make the chords," Riddle explained. (The great country singer Webb Pierce, famous for "There Stands the Glass" and "Slowly," played the same way.) Robinson also had been in a folk group in the early '60s, called the Greenwood Singers, yet another band cast in the mold of the Seekers or the New Christy Minstrels. Like those bands, the Greenwood Singers played the soulless folk that was all the rage in the early '60s, the stuff derided by purists as representative of the "folk scare."

The three of them decided to form a band and play the music they liked. Robinson brought a lead vocal strength to the band that significantly expanded the range of material they could perform, and everyone involved

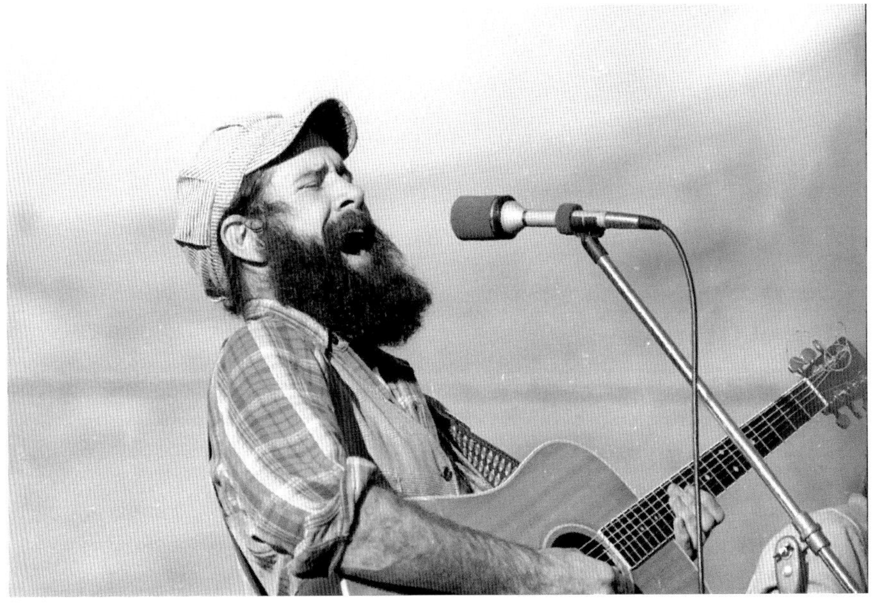

Terry Robinson belting out vocals at Aber Day, 1974. *Courtesy of Archives and Special Collections, Mansfield Library, University of Montana.*

with the band agrees that without Terry Robinson, the whole project might never have come off. "Terry was one of the 'good casting' cogs in the wheel that brought coolness to the band," Steve Riddle explained. "Neither Rob nor myself could rise to that level of lead vocalist." And it didn't hurt that Robinson was incredibly tall, handsome and personable. "Girls loved him, and guys loved him. Everyone loved the guy," Riddle said, an assessment echoed by nearly any one of the countless fans asked to recall their memories of the band.

Soon the three of them—Quist, Riddle and Robinson—were playing together as an all-acoustic trio around Missoula and also booking gigs throughout the state. After a few months, they realized that in order to take the sound where they really wanted it to go, they needed to expand the ensemble. They recruited Christian Johnson, an experienced rock-and-roll guitarist, and a drummer named Greg Reichenberg. Riddle emphasized that their synergy came in part as a result of what he calls "good casting": "Christian and Greg contributed elements to the band that the original three of us could not have covered." They also settled on a name, the Mission Mountain Wood Band, in honor of the impressive mountain range that rises along the eastern shore of Flathead Lake.

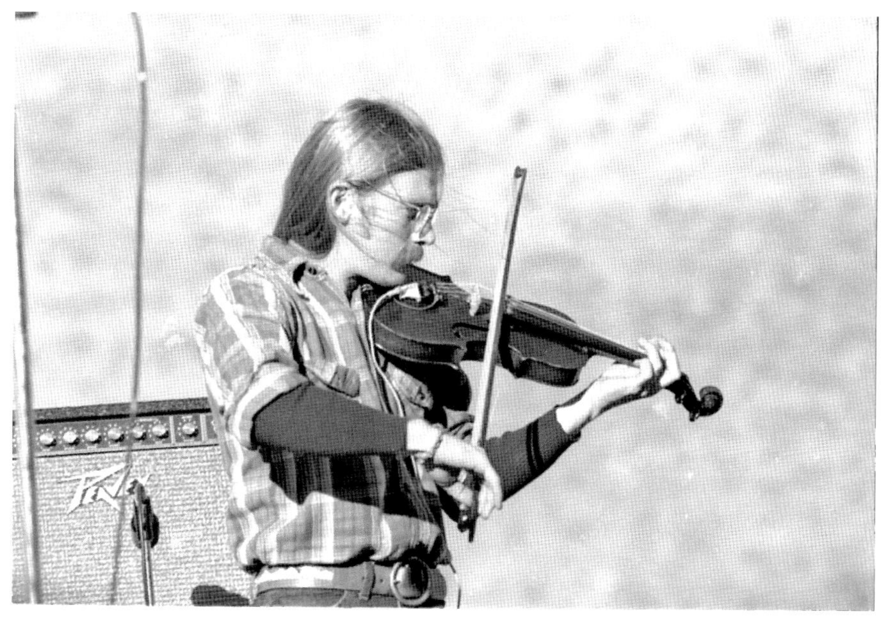

Christian Johnson sawing on the fiddle at Aber Day, 1974. *Courtesy of Archives and Special Collections, Mansfield Library, University of Montana.*

It so happened that Steve Riddle's older brother, Dick Riddle (fifteen years his senior, in fact), had himself worked in a Kingston Trio–type folk group in the early '60s called 3 Young Men from Montana, a band that had achieved enough success to land a recording contract in New York and to put out a pretty successful LP in 1962 on the Cameo label called *3 Young Men from Montana*.

As a consequence, by 1971, Dick Riddle was well versed in the realities of show business. He and his band had been regulars on the TV show dedicated to the folk revival called *Hootenanny* (1963–64) and had played on the Johnny Carson show almost a dozen times, and by the time he teamed up with the Mission Mountain Wood Band, it would have been difficult to find another Montanan so well connected to the New York music world. The elder Riddle listened to his younger brother's band rehearse one afternoon. He could see they were ambitious, if perhaps a little rough around the edges, but he recognized potential when he saw it. He therefore agreed to manage the band. The first thing he suggested to them was that they think about relocating to the east, to New York City, where all the action was.

His advice made sense. The band had put its dues in playing local shows and parties, and buoyed by their natural appeal and pleasant vocal harmonies, their quick rise to the top of the Missoula music scene suggested that they were capable of bigger things. In any case, Montana—with its population of 700,000 people—was hardly a mecca for show business.

Up to this point, Riddle and Quist had stayed enrolled in school and had also been singing in the Jubileers. The conductor, UM music professor Joe Mussulman, went on to publish an interesting and somewhat unconventional music textbook in 1974 called *The Uses of Music* (1974), which fused discussions of Mozart and Stravinsky with commentary on the Beatles and Paul Simon. The cover displayed a psychedelic rock band behind the title rendered in a typeface whose Jugendstil flourishes captured perfectly the loose and decorative ethos of the early '70s.* It's probable that the interactions Mussulman had with some of the Mission Mountain Wood Band members influenced the approach Mussulman took in his book, as he aimed for a slightly countercultural feel.

Just as the band was finalizing plans for leaving Missoula to chase the New York carrot that Dick Riddle had dangled before them, they got caught

* The name of that specific typeface, ubiquitous throughout the late '60s and '70s was called "Arnold Boecklin." In spite of its association with the hippie era, it was actually designed in 1904 by Otto Weisert, a conscious effort to reduplicate the finer points of the earlier art nouveau style. Much of the decorative style of the '60s and '70s visually echoed art nouveau.

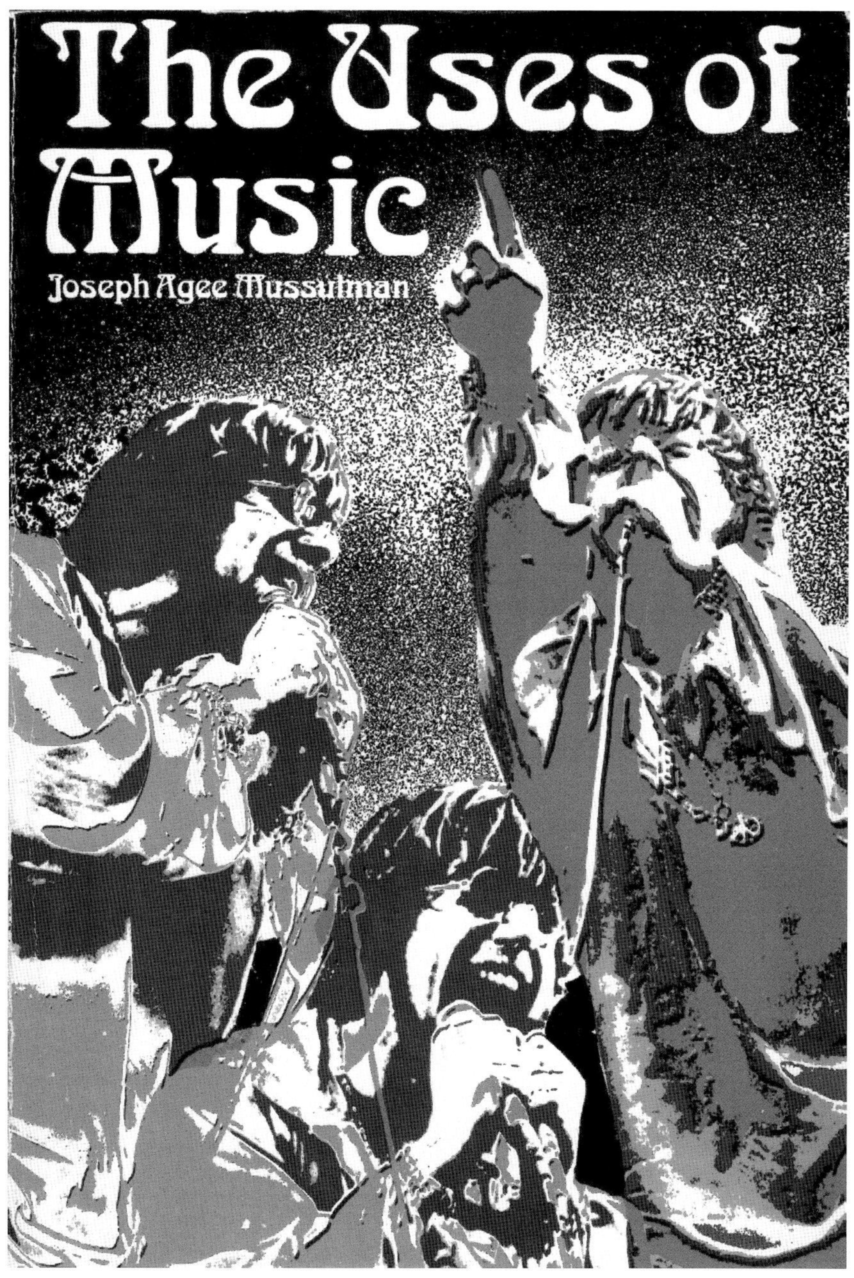

Joseph Mussulman was a professor of music at the University of Montana who also directed the glee club, the Jubileers, of which Steve Riddle and Rob Quist were both members before launching the Mission Mountain Wood Band. His 1974 book, *The Uses of Music*, sought to connect the hippie culture of which his erstwhile protégés were a part to the pleasures of classical music. *From the collection of Aaron Parrett.*

smoking pot. "We were getting real close to finishing school when we got caught," Quist recounted. "Things have changed nowadays, but this was a big deal then, and I found out I couldn't get a degree [from UM] if I had a record." Riddle explained that while their transgression was hardly a legal crisis, Professor Mussulman drew a line in the sand: "He told us we had to quit the glee club," Riddle explained. "He wanted us to go to the *Missoulian* and apologize to the community and to the university for getting caught with a little pot. Well, we couldn't do that and look at ourselves in the mirror, so we packed up and left town."

They started out sleeping on the floor of Dick Riddle's apartment in New York City. "We lived in Manhattan for three years," Quist explained, but "being the country boys we were, we periodically went to rural New Jersey to rehearse and write material." Thanks to Riddle's management, the band suddenly found themselves booked solid for two years out in an intense schedule that averaged out to more than three hundred shows a year. The touring took them all around the country, opening for acts ranging from the Grateful Dead to Elvis. "We played on local TV shows from Miami to Seattle, taping during the day and then playing a sold out show that night," Steve Riddle recounted. In fact, from the luxury of historical perspective, it seems that the greatest contributing factor to their enduring legendary status in Montana was that the Mission Mountain Wood Band achieved national prominence making music so intimately connected to their home state. Their success in New York and their constant touring schedule for two or three years—arranged by virtue of Dick Riddle's connections to booking agents and industry people—gave them legendary cachet back in their home state.

The also band played many of the happening nightspots of New York, including the legendary club CBGB (which few people remember originally stood for "Country, Bluegrass and Blues"—the very essence of Americana music). One of their most memorable performances while in New York happened to be a boat party for the outlaw motorcycle gang Hells Angels—the infamous "Hells Angels Pirate Party" held on September 5, 1973, on a boat called the SS *Bay Belle*. The Mission Mountain Wood Band opened that show, which featured later performances by Bo Diddley and the Jerry Garcia Band. A 1983 film directed by Richard Chase, Leon Gast, Kevin Keating and Lee Maden called *Hells Angels Forever* documented the bands' performances and immortalized the event on celluloid.

In 1974, they even played a fundraiser for Max Baucus, an aspiring politician running for the U.S. House. He won, and a few years later, he traded in his House seat for one in the upper chamber. Baucus remained

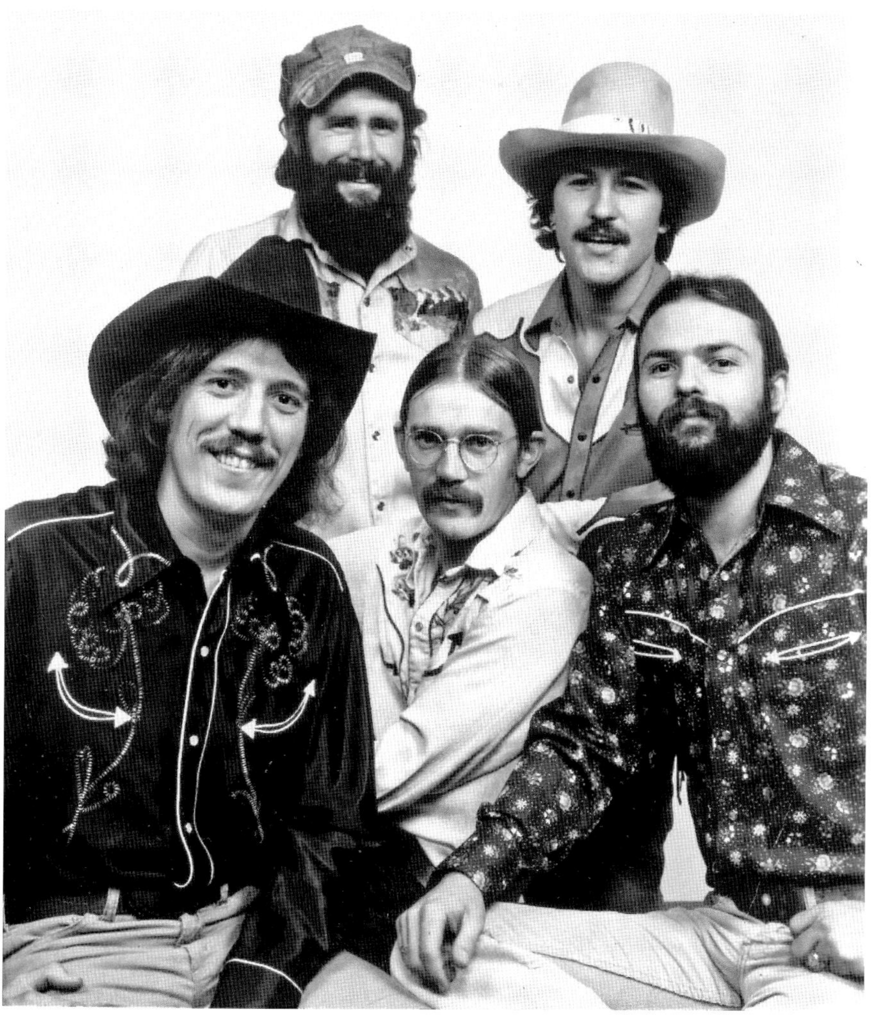

Mission Mountain Wood Band promotional photo by Dick Rubin. *From left to right*: Steve Riddle, Terry Robinson, Christian Johnson, Rob Quist and Greg Reichenberg. *Courtesy of Steve Riddle.*

a lifelong fan of the band and even introduced them to his Congressional colleagues and the rest of the country from the floor of the Senate, waving to them as the entire band sat in the balcony. After a long career in the Senate, Baucus took a post as U.S. ambassador to China.

Like the Snake River Outlaws, who had held court in Missoula twenty years earlier, the Mission Mountain Wood Band made their reputation as a performing band rather than a studio group. "We played hundreds of shows every year," Quist recalled. "One year we played 350 shows—a show every night of the year except for a couple of weeks at Christmas when we went home for the holidays."

In fact, they were so dedicated to their live performances that they did not actually release their first studio album until 1977. The band recorded the record in New York City at the Chelsea Sound Studios. It arrived to great fanfare in Montana and received a good response, although many critics noted that it failed to capture the true essence of the Mission Mountain Wood Band, which really only emerged in their charismatic live show. They titled the record *In Without Knocking*, after a painting by Montana's most famous western artist, Charles M. Russell, an image of which graced the cover. They called the label M2WB and assigned OU812 as the album catalogue number—a joke the heavy metal band Van Halen would imitate ten years later.

By far the most played song off the record was their signature song, "Take a Whiff on Me," an old American folk song about cocaine that musicologist Alan Lomax first brought to light when in 1934 he recorded Leadbelly playing a version. The song has hence been recorded by a host of artists, including the Byrds, the Flying Burrito Brothers, the Memphis Jug Band and Woody Guthrie, though often under the title "Cocaine Blues." The Mission Mountain Wood Band turned their take on the tune into one of Montana's most popular and beloved party anthems. It opened the album and set the tone, starting with someone taking an audible sniff followed by a crackling riff of banjo and mandolin roughly together in a brisk 2/4 time, clocking in at a rollicking 220 beats per minute. The provocative lyrics drove the song:

Cocaine Bill and Morphine Sue
Storming the avenues two by two
Oh Lord, Honey take a whiff on me
Said Sue to Bill won't do no harm
To take this one little shot in the arm
Hey hey, honey take a whiff on me.
(© 1977 Traditional Mission Mountain Wood Band arrangement, OU812 Music)

Other highlights from the album included "Mountain Standard Time," a catchy number with a hint of barbershop that still gets airplay and remains one of the band's most recognized tunes. Another song from the album that many Montanans associate with the band was "Sweet Maria,"

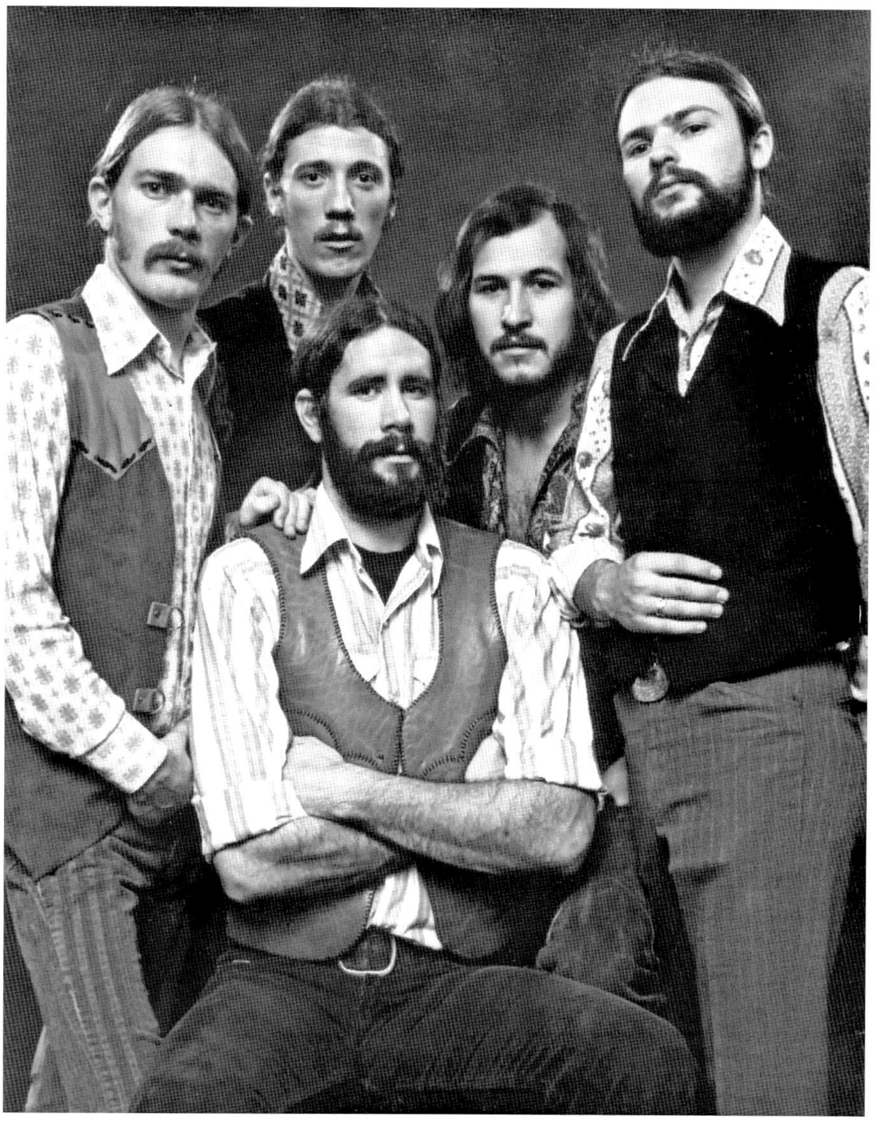

Early promotional shot of the Mission Mountain Wood Band. *Back, from left to right*: Christian Johnson, Steve Riddle, Rob Quist and Greg Reichenberg. Seated is Terry Robinson. *Courtesy of Steve Riddle.*

their version of the Jonathan Edwards's song "Athens County," which had come out on his debut album *Jonathan Edwards* (1971). The chorus featured a tagline that became the title of a documentary about the band: *Never Long Gone.*

The intensive tour schedule and constant coaching from Dick Riddle and other New York veterans gave the Mission Mountain Wood Band a stage show that was finely tuned and, by the end, automatic. "It was a science," Steve Riddle remarked. "From the perfect casting of each member in his role on stage to the tightly arranged order of the songs and the stage banter—we perfected the art of 'planned spontaneity,' as I called it." The Mission Mountain Wood Band shared stages with such illustrious acts as the Allman Brothers, the Bonnie Raitt Band and the Ozark Mountain Daredevils—many of the biggest names in rock. They were featured performers on national TV specials, including one hosted by Cheryl Ladd, and in June 1979, they even made an appearance on the popular country-music oriented television show *Hee Haw*, the footage of which is included in the box set *Private Stash*.

The band toured the country in a Greyhound Scenicruiser Bus that became almost as famous around Montana as the band itself. "It also had OU812 painted on the side of the bus," Quist mentioned, laughing at the memory of the band's best inside joke. Quist theorized that part of what made the band work so well was that each member of the band had his own bedroom on the bus. "It allowed us to stay somewhat sane

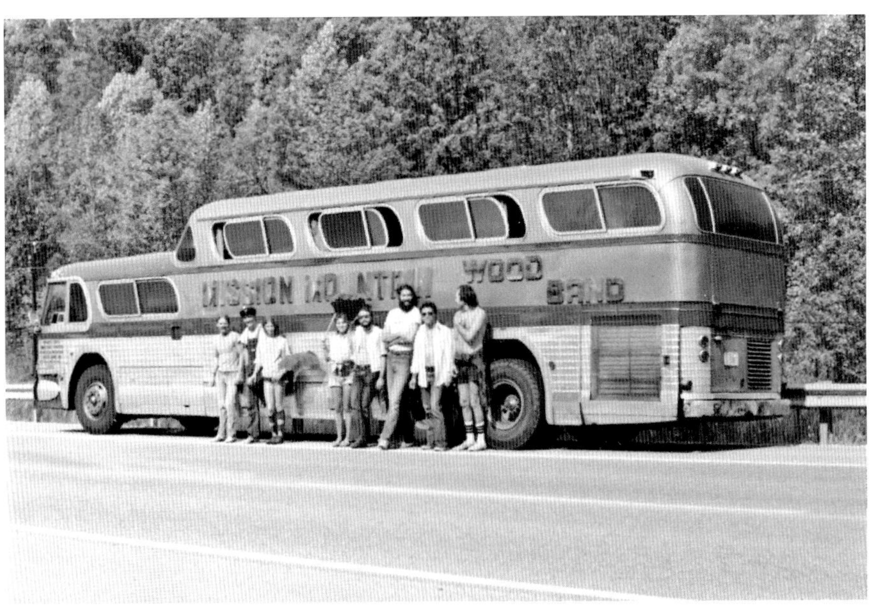

Mission Mountain Wood Band in front of their famous Scenicruiser traveling bus. It had actual wood lettering on the side and "OU812" on the license plate. *Courtesy of Steve Riddle.*

while being in such constant close proximity." Since the band played more than three hundred shows a year in the late '70s, they put on a lot of miles on that bus.

The Mission Mountain Wood Band, like many successful and popular bands, illustrated the principle of the whole being greater than the sum of the parts. None of the players was a virtuoso, but together they generated an infectious energy that produced what ordinarily might have been run-of-the-mill local country rock. Add in a few positive externalities like constant partying and charismatic stage presence and you suddenly have a musical ensemble naturally poised to produce what amounted to the basic soundtrack for the 1970s Missoula zeitgeist.

For example, mention the Mission Mountain Wood Band among people of the appropriate demographic even today, and it's likely the conversation will segue automatically into reminiscences about the famed Aber Day Keggers (1972–79). The most ambitious of these happened in 1978, when one thousand kegs of beer were consumed—a Guinness World Record that the band says is still on the books. Musician, Havre native and Chester resident Philip Aaberg (who played piano for Elvin Bishop in the 1970s) recalled racing from a gig in Bozeman to Missoula

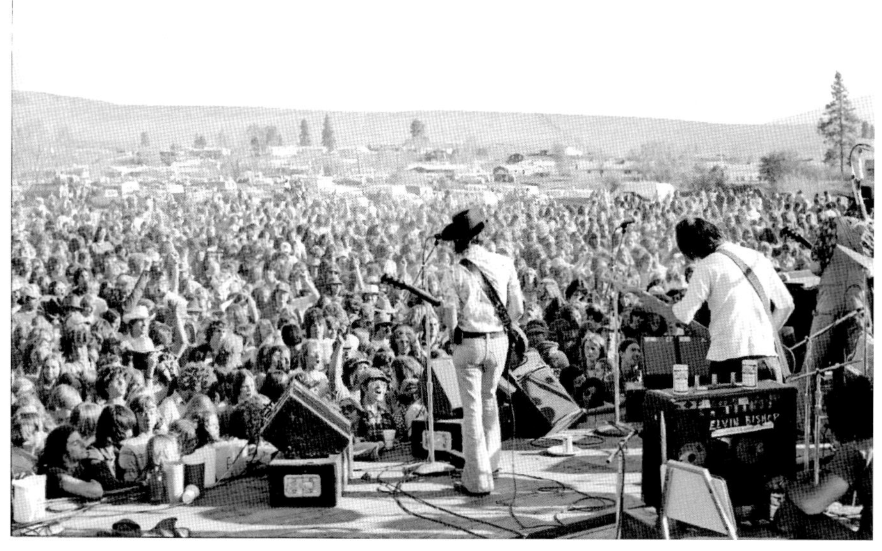

Elvin Bishop, 1974 Aber Day. *Courtesy of Archives and Special Collections, Mansfield Library, University of Montana.*

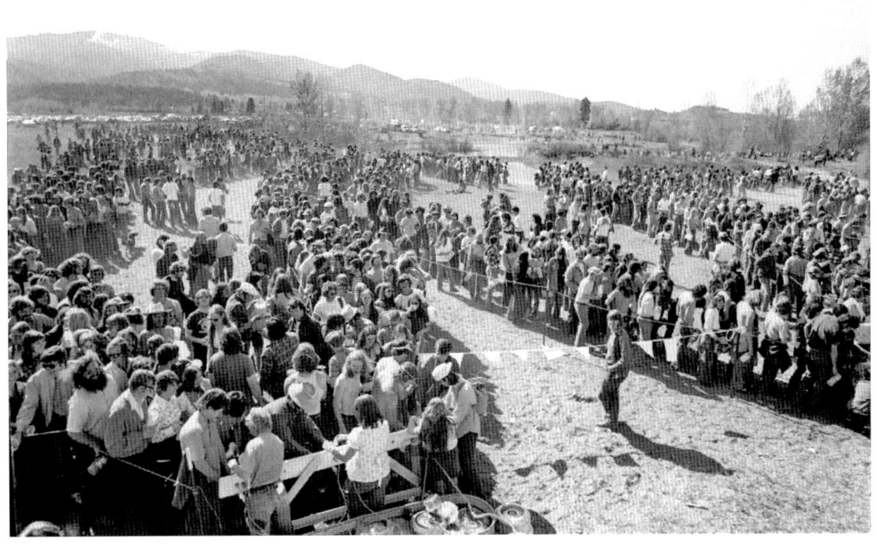

The beer line at the Aber Day Kegger, 1974. *Courtesy of Archives and Special Collections, Mansfield Library, University of Montana.*

with the Elvin Bishop Band to make their Aber Day appearance. When they got to Missoula, the bus driver asked Phil how to get to the festival grounds. "Just look for the cloud of dust," Aaberg quipped.

According to longtime Missoula musician and music promoter Rick Ryan, the famed Aber Day Keggers emerged from an assignment that popular UM professor Marty Baker began giving his classes in 1972. He specifically wanted students to design "a practicable project from which some social benefit could be derived." Not surprisingly, some of the more enterprising students decided to capitalize on the keg parties that had long been a staple of college life by simply charging admission for them and then donating the proceeds to charity.

In 1975, one group brought that idea home by organizing a massive party with hundreds of kegs to raise money that would directly benefit the school itself—the university had already begun construction of Mansfield Library but had run short of funding to complete the job. All over campus, rumors circulated to the effect that the school would lose its accreditation if the library could not increase its holdings. The students arranged the date of their kegger party that year to coincide with a university holiday called Aber Day, in honor of William "Daddy" Aber,

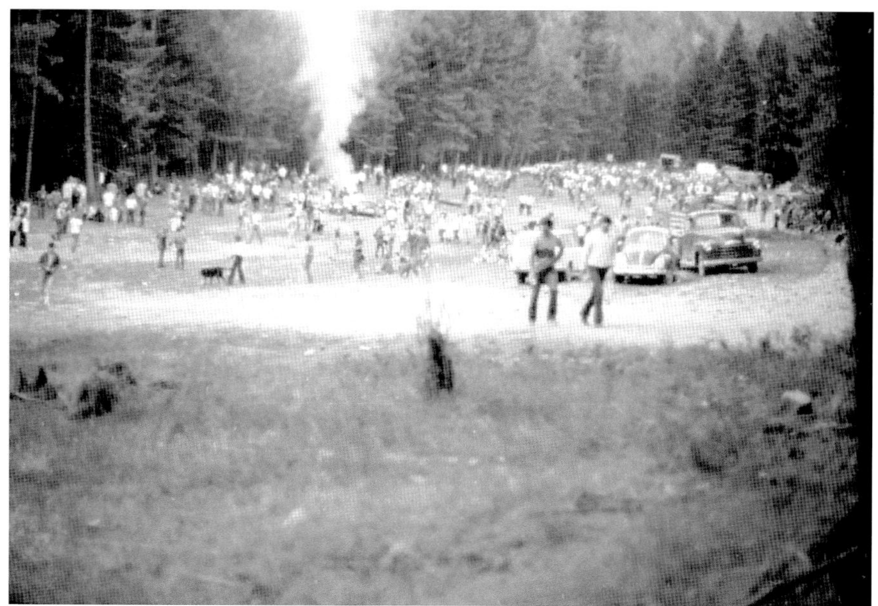

The crowd begins to form at an Aber Day Kegger, 1972. *Courtesy of Archives and Special Collections, Mansfield Library, University of Montana.*

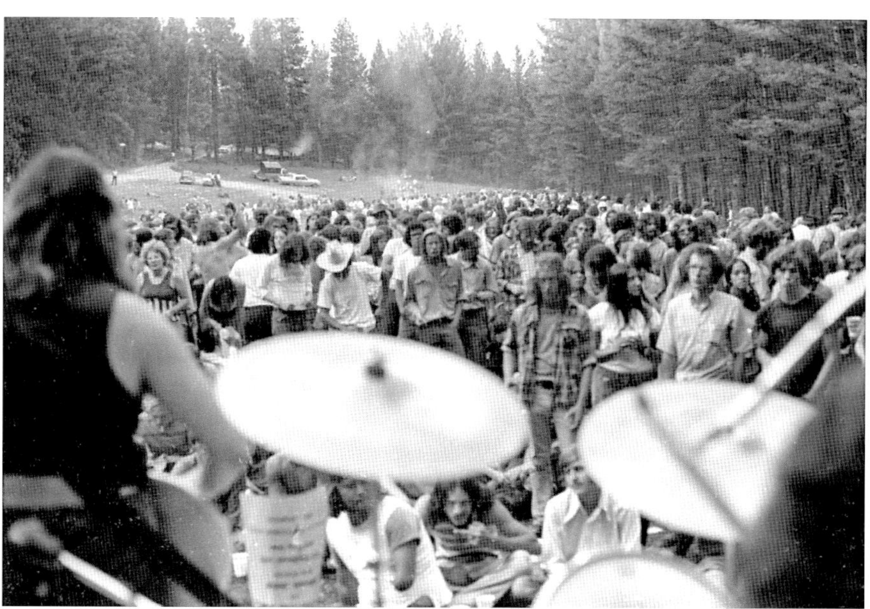

Aber Day crowd, 1972, taken from stage. Photographer unknown. *Courtesy of University of Montana Archive.*

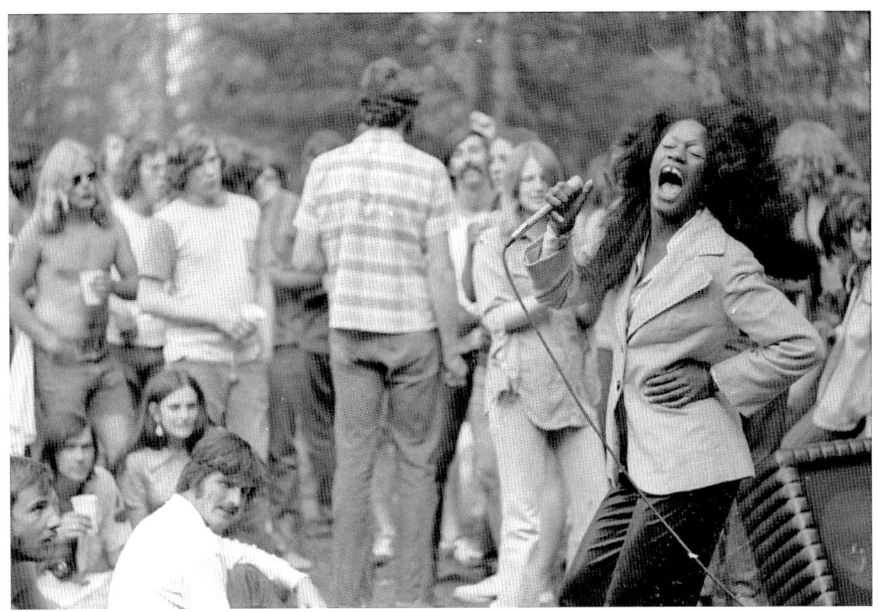

Goldie Ritchie of the Weston Davis Group, a band from Spokane, Washington, performing at the Aber Day Kegger, 1972. *Courtesy of Archives and Special Collections, Mansfield Library, University of Montana.*

one of UM's most beloved professors and one of the original five faculty members hired when the school was founded. The price of a ticket for "all the beer you could drink" was only eight dollars. Professor Baker's progressive experiment in civics and magnanimity had come to maturity, and the Aber Day Keggers became one of the most definitive features of the 1970s Missoula sound and landscape.

The Aber Day Keggers featured well-known national acts such as Jimmy Buffett and the Nitty Gritty Dirt Band, as well as popular Montana bands. The darlings of the festival, of course, were the Mission Mountain Wood Band. The massive party that the Keggers involved became a sort of Montana version of Woodstock or Monterey, smaller in scope and attendance but paralleling the sense of youthful optimism and unified purpose. As Bob Barrett (one of the organizers) remarked in the documentary film *The Kegger: A Film by Robert P. McCue*, "It was as if you lifted up a little section of Berkeley and gave everyone a cowboy hat and some waffle stompers" and set it down in Montana at the lower end of Miller Creek.

In the view of Ryan and many of his contemporaries, two things happened to converge at the end of the 1960s in Missoula that laid the groundwork for

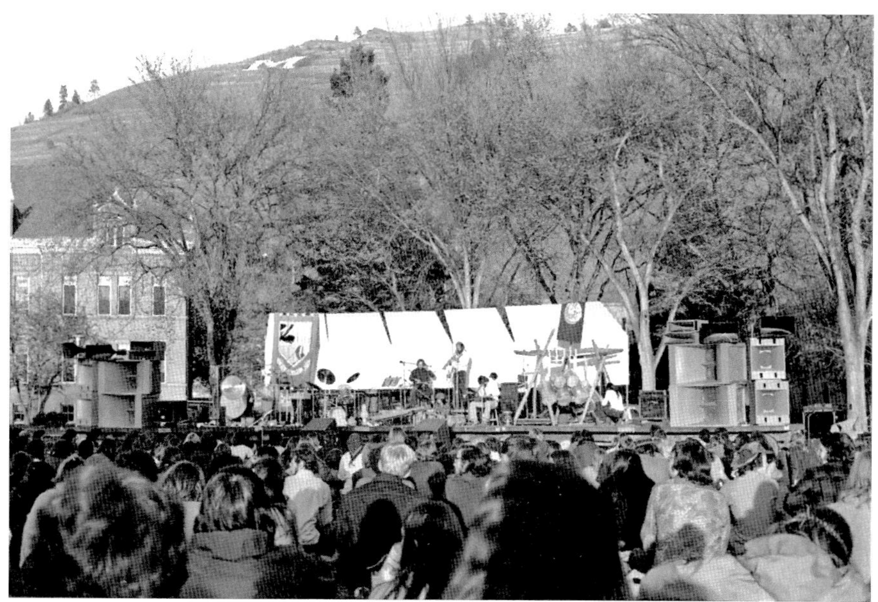

Aber Day in the University of Montana Oval, 1974. *Courtesy of Archives and Special Collections, Mansfield Library, University of Montana.*

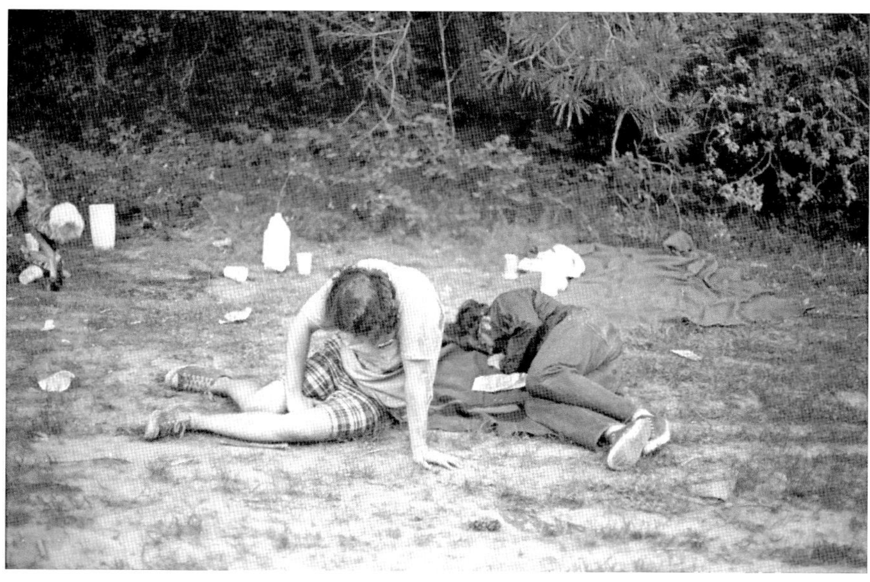

According to surviving members of the Mission Mountain Wood Band and the documentary film *Kegger*, the Aber Day Kegger of 1978 still holds the record for the most kegs of beer consumed at an outdoor party at one thousand. These two unfortunates appear to have imbibed more than their share, 1972. *Courtesy of Archives and Special Collections, Mansfield Library, University of Montana.*

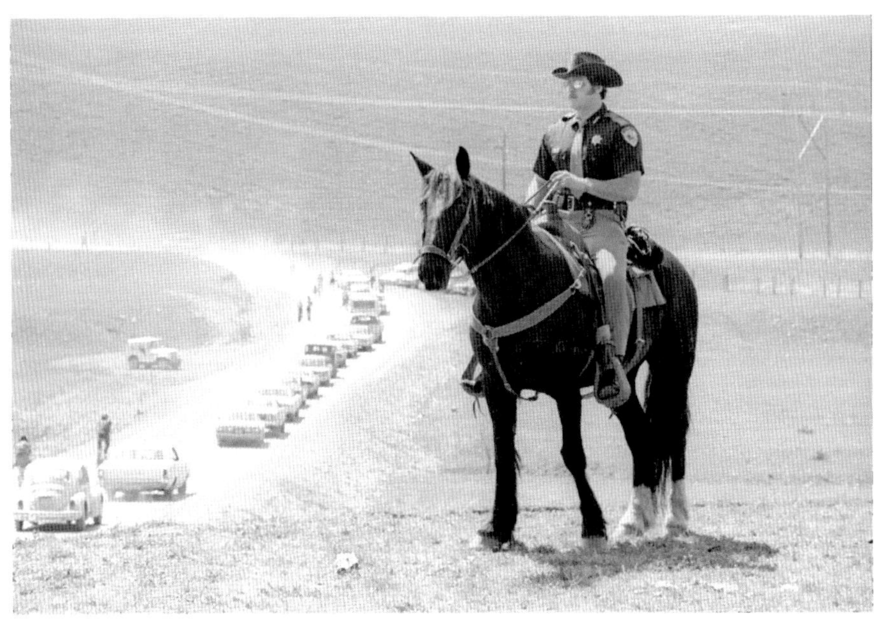

Crowd control, Montana style, 1975. *Courtesy of Archives and Special Collections, Mansfield Library, University of Montana.*

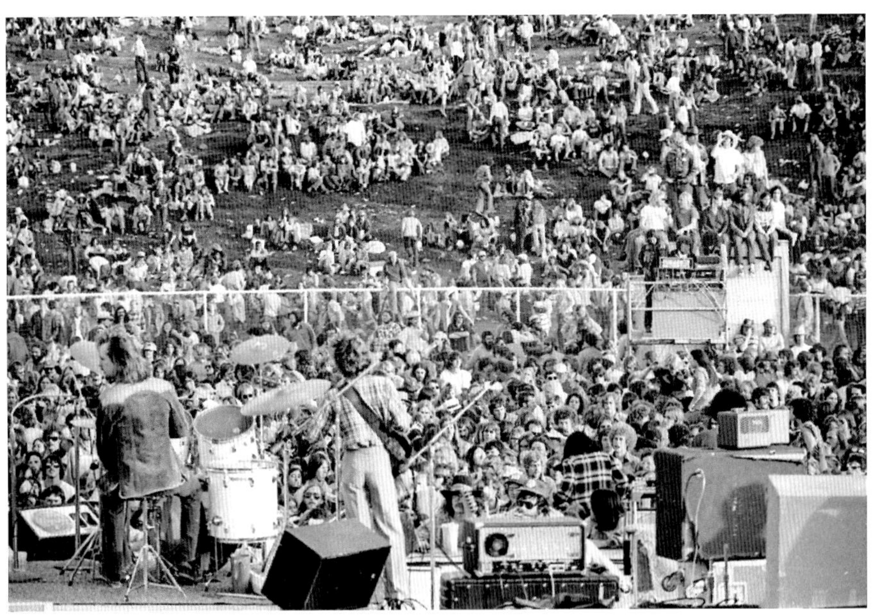

Great crowd shot from stage, 1975. *Courtesy of Archives and Special Collections, Mansfield Library, University of Montana.*

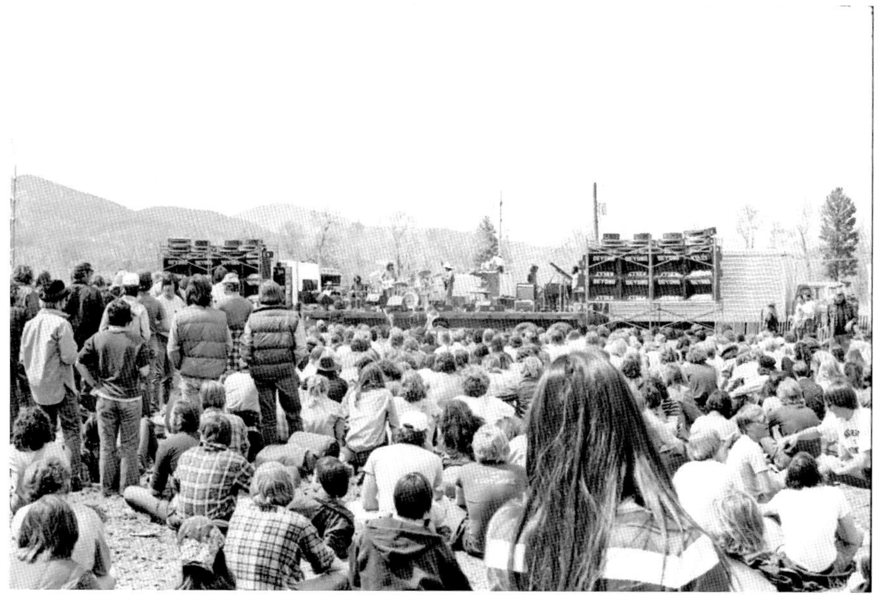

Crowd watching the stage at Aber Day Kegger, 1974. *Courtesy of Archives and Special Collections, Mansfield Library, University of Montana.*

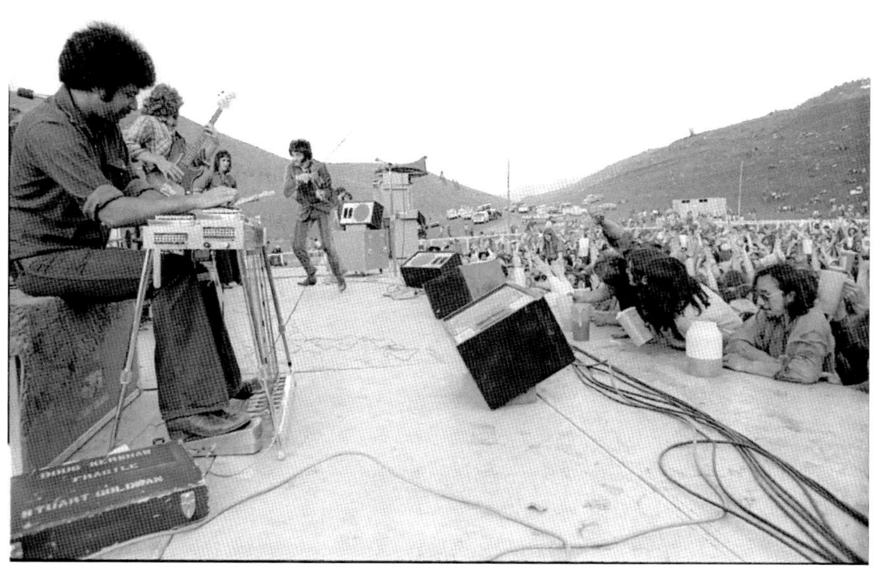

Doug Kershaw (fiddle) and Stuart Goldman (steel) in 1975. *Courtesy of Archives and Special Collections, Mansfield Library, University of Montana.*

the music scene in Missoula that would culminate in the Aber Day Keggers. The first was something that began back east when the promotional genius and Smithsonian folklorist Ralph Rinzler responded to the so-called folk scare heralded in bands like the Kingston Trio by parading Lester Flatt and Earl Scruggs around the country, both on television (*The Beverly Hillbillies*) and in live performances on college campuses everywhere. Rinzler deserves considerable credit for promoting an original and authentic form of bluegrass and folk music as played by its legitimate masters: his promotion of bands like Flatt and Scruggs amounted to a kind of counterassault against the crusade of anemic imitators sporting pinstripes, crewcuts and long-necked banjos who had begun to overwhelm the airwaves in the early 1960s.

But the other thing was the sudden availability (and popularity) of marijuana. The secret ingredient that only a few of the most hip jazz musicians and beat writers enjoyed in the 1950s was suddenly available on college campuses everywhere, even in Montana. "You put those two things together—pot and traditional bluegrass and old-time music—and you more or less have the essence of Missoula in the late '60s and early '70s," concluded Ryan.

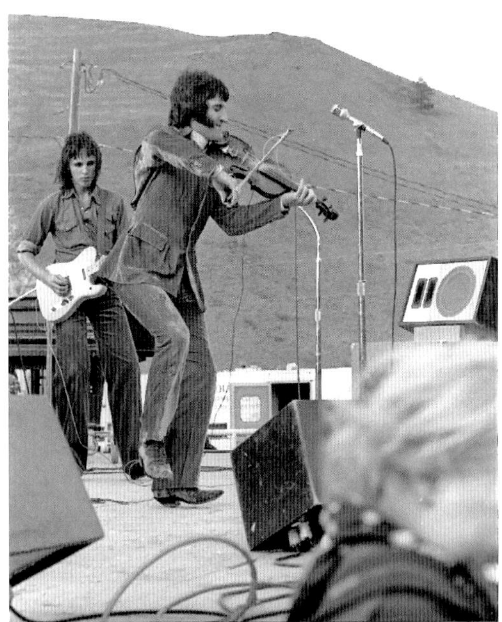

Doug Kershaw at the 1975 Aber Day. *Courtesy of Archives and Special Collections, Mansfield Library, University of Montana.*

Although the Mission Mountain Wood Band's signature brand of Montana music may not have been brilliantly executed hardcore bluegrass or country, it was undeniably rooted in it, and at the same time the band fully embraced the more relaxed attitude about getting high that had come to characterize Missoula. Audiences loved the Mission Mountain Wood Band because, more than anything else, they were a great party band who prided themselves on providing an experience in which everyone had a good time.

If television and a changing approach to evening entertainment signaled the demise of the Snake River Outlaws in the 1950s, a similar shift—this time embodied in the return to conservatism highlighted in the election of Ronald Reagan in 1980—spelled the end for both the Mission Mountain Wood Band and the Aber Day Keggers for which they had been the local star performers.

The reign of the Mission Mountain Wood Band and their days of holding court over the Keggers came to an end in 1981. In 1978, a staunch Missoula Mormon named Barbara Evans ran for a seat on the Missoula County Commission, running a campaign whose central message voiced vehement opposition to the Aber Day celebrations. As Ryan put it, "Barbara Evans opposed on principle the very idea of a university being

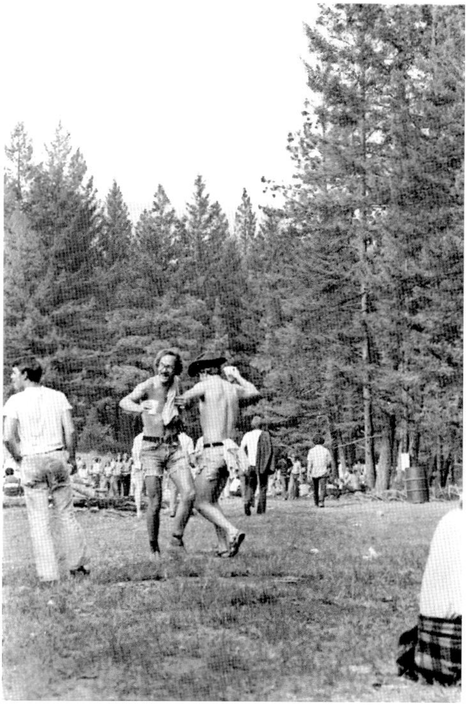

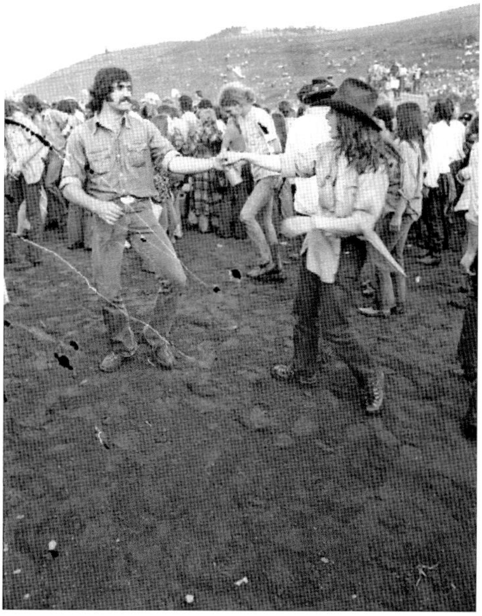

Top: Two men dancing, Aber Day, 1972. *Courtesy of Archives and Special Collections, Mansfield Library, University of Montana.*

Right: Couple dancing in the mud at Aber Day. *Courtesy of Archives and Special Collections, Mansfield Library, University of Montana.*

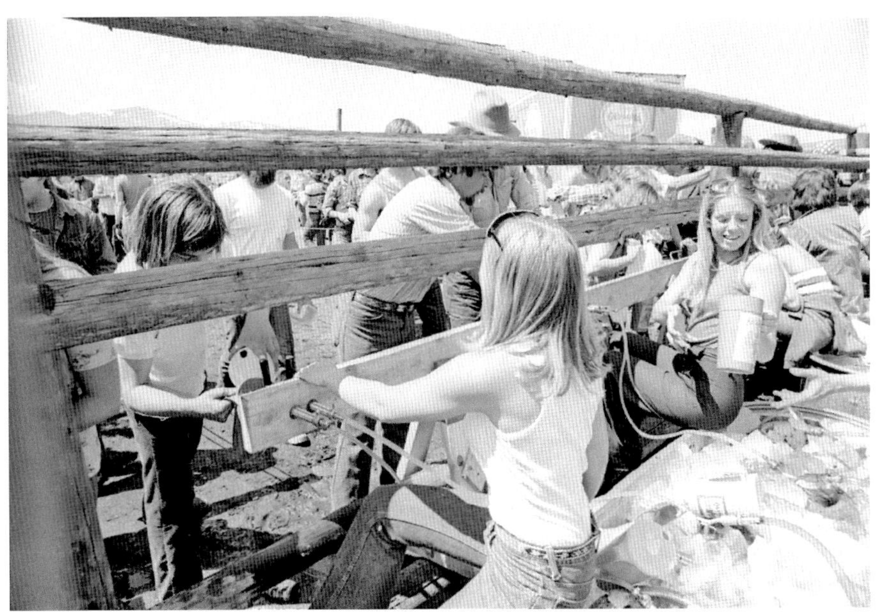

Aber Day beer line, 1975. *Courtesy of Archives and Special Collections, Mansfield Library, University of Montana.*

connected to a party involving one thousand kegs of beer." With the help of Ted Parker, UM physical plant director and fellow Mormon, who was sympathetic to her cause, she pressured the UM administration at every turn. After contentious negotiations, she succeeded in her goal, and the organizers agreed that the 1979 Kegger was to be the last big party.

Still, the Aber Day event and the fate of the Mission Mountain Wood Band seemed tied together. "The end of the dream really came in 1981, when the Mission Mountain Wood Band tried to resuscitate the event," Ryan said. In lieu of the outdoor festival, they worked very hard, in spite of others' misgivings, to arrange a stadium concert at Adams Fieldhouse on the UM campus. That stadium seats more than six thousand, but organizers of the show sold only 1,000 tickets, and even though 1,400 additional tickets had been given away, the fated event marked a clear end to the glory days of both Mission Mountain Wood Band in Montana and the Aber Day celebrations. The cultural significance of that auspicious partnership is difficult to downplay. The Aber Day Keggers mark an unparalleled series of musical events in Montana history that paved the way for the success of the contemporary Red Ants Pants Festival, for example. For those who lived through the era, the Aber Day Keggers and the presence of the Mission Mountain Wood Band coalesce into a prominent landmark on the cultural horizon, evoking powerful emotions in the hearts of Montanans.

Like nearly every one of his generation who spent time in Missoula in the '70s, for example, Montana writer Matt Pavelich—author of acclaimed novels including *Our Savage* (2005) and *The Other Shoe* (2012)—has an Aber Day Kegger story to tell. An avid flyer of hang gliders in his youth, Pavelich routinely took flight from Mount Jumbo or the South Hills to fly down into an intramural field near just north of the campus. One year, he decided to crash the Aber Day party going on out at the old rodeo grounds on lower Miller Creek. Coming in a little fast, he clipped a power line and crashed his glider. The music instantly stopped because he had cut the line supplying power to the stage. "Hell, I don't think the crowd really noticed much, to be honest," he said. "But I figured I was going to get in considerable trouble, so I recruited a friend who happened to be nearby to help me." Pavelich quickly disengaged the sail from the aluminum frame and then yelled to his friend, "OK! Let's roll her up!"

As it happened, an especially festive young woman within earshot took his cry as an invitation and dove into the sail cloth as if it were a bed. "She was topless and covered with mud from the waist down," explained Pavelich. "Under other circumstances, it might have led to an entirely different conclusion, but I was expecting security to come nab me at any moment, so we had to wave her off." In the end, he made his way out of the festival with no one noticing, although as he drove away with his glider

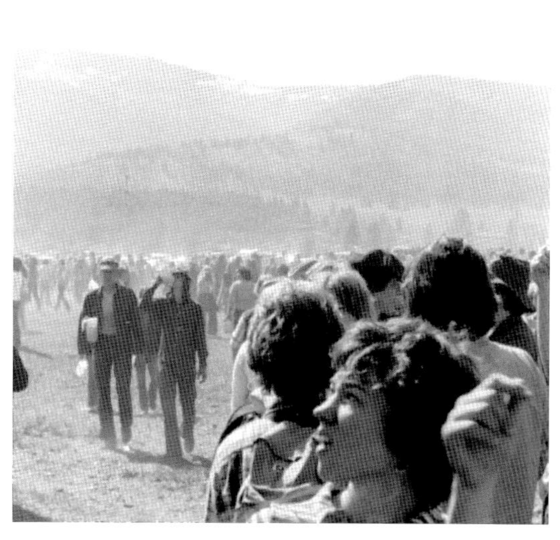

A paraglider comes sailing into Miller Creek, 1974. *Courtesy of Archives and Special Collections, Mansfield Library, University of Montana.*

in the back of his truck, the power at the festival had not yet been restored.

The demise of the keggers happened to correspond to the dissolution of the Mission Mountain Wood Band. "We were no longer in our twenties, and some of us were falling in love and getting married and having children, and we were feeling that need to become better husbands," Riddle observed. After they called it quits in 1982, three of the members of the Mission Mountain Wood Band—Terry Robinson, Rob Quist and Kurt Bergeron—put together the Montana Band, which also received some national attention, although it never achieved the homegrown notoriety of its predecessor. As it happened, Quist left the Montana Band not long before one of the worst tragedies in the history of Montana music befell the band.

To the devastation of many fans, all the members of the Montana Band were killed in 1987 when the Beechcraft-18 plane they were in crashed near the site of their final performance, just hours after they had left the stage and as they were en route to another performance in Coeur d'Alene, Idaho. At the time, it constituted the worst private plane crash in Montana history, producing ten casualties, including the band and flight crew. Among the victims were Terry Robinson and Kurt Bergeron, formerly of the Mission Mountain Wood Band.

After the breakup of the Mission Mountain Wood Band in 1982, Steve Riddle returned to New York and pursued a successful acting career that took him to Broadway. Greg Reichenberg relocated to Atlanta, Georgia, and continued to play music, although he devoted most of his attention to establishing training schools for future building inspectors. Christian Johnson is a sound engineer in Kalispell, where he gives music lessons and continues to play music. Rob Quist has pretty much devoted his whole life to music, and in the thirty-five years since the Wood Band called it quits, he has maintained the same heavy concert schedule, mostly with his band Rob Quist and Great Northern but also with other musicians and bands, including Jack Gladstone. Three of the surviving original members—Rob Quist, Steve Riddle and Greg Reichenberg—continue to make music together and keep the torch of the Mission Mountain Wood Band lit and burning.

In fact, over the years, the surviving members of the Mission Mountain Wood Band have reunited to perform some memorable concerts. One example is the celebrated 1992 reunion concert in Polson, in which Bruce Robinson sat in for his brother, Terry. In the last few years, the reunion concerts have become even more frequent, culminating in a sell-out reprisal of the Aber Day Kegger in Philipsburg, Montana, in

August 2015.*

In 2008, the Mission Mountain Wood Band released their entire discography as a box set called *Private Stash*, which featured a bonus DVD with concert footage. For the cover art, they commissioned world-renowned Missoula artist Monte Dolack, another veteran of the era and a graphic artist for many of the other bands who played in Missoula in the 1970s. Riddle guessed that over the course of their career, the band "moved 400,000 units" of *In Without Knocking*, but their more recent issues of unreleased and released material, including *Private Stash*, have been, not surprisingly, great successes.

While the Mission Mountain Wood Band certainly dominated the music scene in Montana in the 1970s, plenty of other talented bands made a living playing music and released albums of enduring quality. Not that it was a contest—one thing that seems to define the scene in the '70s was the intense camaraderie among musicians. Many of them, in recalling those years, describe the Americana scene as operating something like an intimately connected, extended family. The Mission Mountain Wood Band was a national act by 1975, certainly providing inspiration for other bands, but at the same time leaving a local vacuum to be filled by groups with similar appeal and a kindred sense of the age and its music. Among them were the Lost Highway Band and the Live Wire Choir.

Michael Purington and Phil Hamilton started the Lost Highway Band in 1974. The two of them shared a sort of communal house in lower Miller Creek (rent at eighty dollars per month!) and spent most of their time playing music together in the living room. Eventually, they teamed up with another pair of talented musicians, Chojo Jacques and Price Quenin, and in 1974, the four of them formed the Lost Highway Band, taking their name from the old Hank Williams song. Michael Purington described the advent of the band thusly: "We were all really into the 'outlaw sound' coming out of Texas at the time—Willie Nelson and Waylon Jennings had had a big article in Rolling Stone, I think—and we all looked at each other and said, 'Hey! Let's go to Austin.' So we piled into an old International Scout and drove down there."

Purington described the Lost Highway Band's early sound as "bluegrock," a term that conflates bluegrass and rock but also hints at the verb *grok*, a word the sci-fi writer Robert Heinlein coined in his groundbreaking novel *Stranger in a Strange Land* (1961) to describe a sort of telepathic mode of understanding beyond language. That verb captures the sort of intuition each player brought to the band.

* In fact, the great success of that reunion has prompted a repeat of the event, scheduled for August 20, 2016.

"We had a term for our approach," Purington explained. "From the very beginning, the thing we were pursuing we summarized as 'the original idea,' which was 'to explore music and be real.'" As a result, the various members of the Lost Highway Band all communicated musically with one another on stage or even in rehearsal without having to dispute over the basic aim or purpose of the band. In terms of genres, they could blend styles instinctively, without a lot of theoretical posturing. "We did play bluegrass," Purington acknowledged, "but we played it with a real strong emphasis on the fourth beat, more like rock-and-roll."

In Texas, the band hooked up with Augie Meyers, a lieutenant of Doug Sahm (of the Sir Douglas Quintet), who quickly became enamored of the sound of this band from Montana and agreed to produce the band's first single and album on the Austin-based Re-Cord label. The single featured two originals, "I Wish You Were Mine," backed by "I'm All Out of Time." The band called the album, released in 1976, *Travelin' Light*.

Although they enjoyed their sojourn in Texas, the band missed their home state, and with their record pressed and ready to sell, they returned to Montana. Through most of 1976 and after, they spent a considerable part of their time playing what today might be considered an unusual circuit: the Black Angus Supper Clubs scattered around Montana and neighboring states. "It was a great, interesting gig," Purington recounted. "We played six nights a week for a pretty solid paycheck, which in those days just couldn't be beat." The band also traveled a fair amount, and between Black Angus engagements, they played the usual clubs of the Montana circuit whenever they could, especially the Park Hotel and the Top Hat in Missoula. Especially memorable was a coffee shop show in Seattle graced by Bruce Springsteen in 1975, when he was at the very pinnacle of his career. "We crossed paths with him and his band somewhere in Seattle," Purington recalled, "and we invited them to our show. They all smiled at that, but I'll be damned if Bruce did not show up by himself about halfway through our set and get up to play a few songs with us."

"You know, that was an era that could never happen again," Purington said. "In Missoula in those days, you had the Mission Mountain Wood Band on the national scene, and around town you had six or eight clubs with live music six nights a week. The Lost Highway Band played six nights a week pretty much from 1976 to 1985." The band released a second album in 1979 called *Play Something We Can Dance To* on the Ball of Wax label at Backstreet Recording in Missoula. That record clearly showcased the band's eclectic influences and undeniable talent and remains probably the best sonic portrait of one of Montana's best Americana bands. Although everyone in

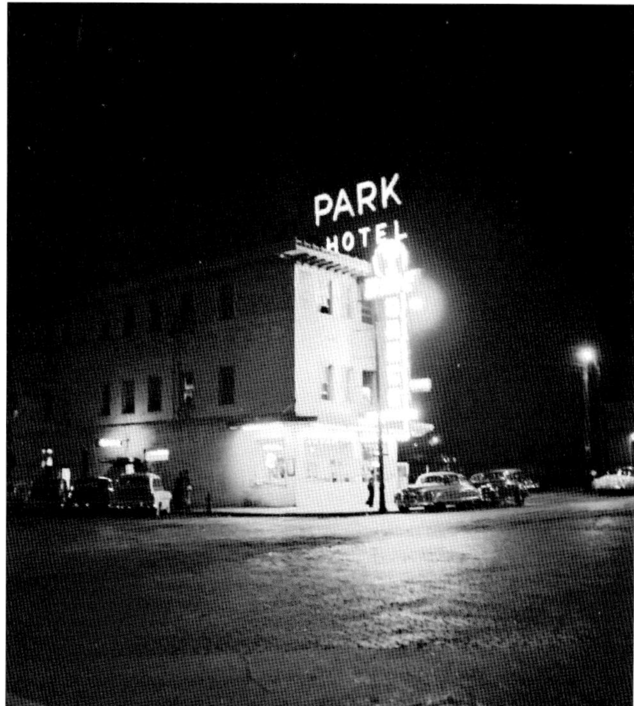

In the 1970s and 1980s, the Park Hotel on North Higgins was among the hottest venues for live music in Missoula. *Photo by Stan Healy, courtesy of Archives and Special Collections, Mansfield Library, University of Montana.*

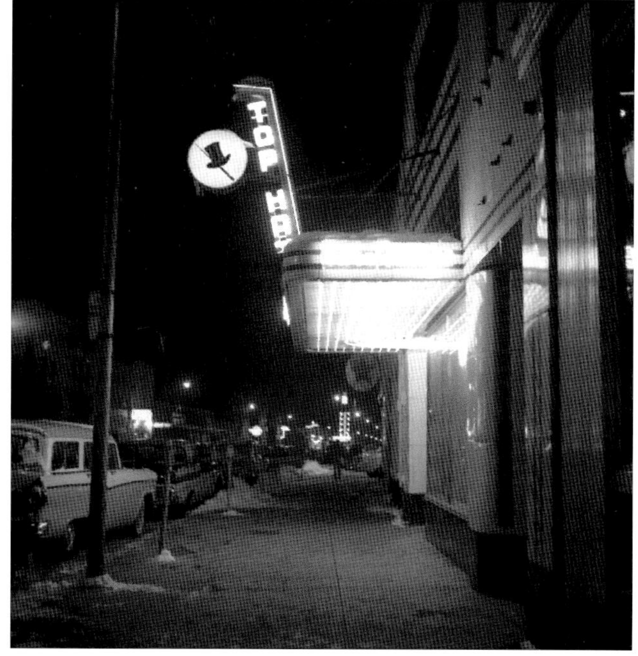

The Top Hat has long been a Missoula institution and a leading venue for live music. Here pictured as it was in 1957, the newly renovated venue continues to showcase some of Montana's finest Americana musicians. *Photo by Stan Healy, courtesy of Archives and Special Collections, Mansfield Library, University of Montana.*

the band parted ways in 1985, they reunited that summer for a few shows, one of which was recorded for posterity, though not released until 2010, as *The Lost Highway Band Live*.

"We didn't realize what we had at the time we had it," lamented Purington. "That's the way it is when you're in your twenties. But we never lost sight of what we called 'the original idea.'" For more than a decade, the Lost Highway Band did, in fact, adhere to the principle of playing music and being real.

After the Lost Highway Band, Purington became legendary for another musical enterprise. Under the name Rafe and the Scum, Purington and some friends recorded an underground classic album of hard-drinking songs infused with a post-punk feel and a healthy dose of ribald humor. The title of the one of the songs gives a good indication of the album's overall content: "If You Don't Like Me the Way I Am, You Can Go Fuck Yourself." The album is a highly sought-after artifact of underground Americana from Missoula, as it was released only furtively on cassette and in a small original run. Purington also wrote a regular column in the *Missoulian* during the Lost Highway years under the banner "Montana Music," which profiled local and regional musicians, especially rock-and-roll bands most people had never heard of. Purington continues to play music today, although nowadays his focus is music exclusively devoted to sobriety.

Purington encapsulated the 1970s scene with a nice contrast between two of the best bands to emerge from that era. "The Mission Mountain Wood Band was a great act," Purington explained. "They had an amazing stage presence and a rehearsed show. But Lost Highway Band was a great band. We were musical explorers, playing everything from hardcore bluegrass to country blues, folk rock—a bunch of different styles."

Meanwhile, sometime around 1976, a band of hippies in South Lake Tahoe in California who called themselves the Live Wire Choir were playing a high-energy amalgamation of bluegrass and swing music that listeners flocked to with rapt enthusiasm all over the Northwest. At a show at Harrah's in Reno, Nevada, one night, they shared a bill with a band from Montana called the Mission Mountain Wood Band, who loved their set. At an afterburner back at the commune where the Tahoe band was staying, the Mission Mountain boys encouraged them to come play some shows up in Missoula. And so they did.

The Live Wire Choir had played for responsive audiences before, but in Missoula it was like they were the Grateful Dead returning to Haight-Ashbury for Old Home Week. They'd never experienced anything like it. The band and the town were all on the same wavelength, as someone might have remarked in the idiom of the time.

The Choir would eventually play countless shows at the old Top Hat Bar down on Front Street and at the Park Hotel between Spruce and Alder, a venue that was to '70s Missoula what the Sunshine Bar had been to the '50s. "It was a sort of seedy old hotel next to Double Front Chicken that was the very last stop on Higgins," recalled Richie Reinholdt, who played guitar and banjo in the Live Wire Choir from 1976 to 1979. "That place was classic Missoula—a rough-and-tumble bar with an unpredictable clientele, and the crowds were there to get rowdy and dance. Upstairs there were some pretty low-rent rooms."

The rest of the band consisted of Rick Waldorf on bass guitar, Frank Chiaverini on guitar, Oakley Cassaboom on steel guitar, Don Townley on drums and David Swayne on fiddle. In the autumn of 1977, Gene McGeorge, owner of a folk music store in Missoula called Bitterroot Music, approached the band and offered to foot the bill for an album, which he released on his own label, simply calling the record *Live Wire Choir*. Against the blue backdrop was a distinctive logo designed by a then-unknown artist named Monte Dolack. "I think he charged us $200 for the logo back then," Reinholdt recalled. "Try getting an original Monte Dolack anything for that price now."

The record came out in the spring of 1978, just in time for the band's debut appearance at that year's famed Aber Day Kegger. They shared the bill with Elvin Bishop, the Dirt Band and, of course, the Mission Mountain Wood Band. "It was pretty cold and rainy that year," Reinholdt remembered. "We had to play our show wearing coats. I was shivering the whole time. When we got through, we got right back on the tour bus." Along with most of the other bands of the era, especially the Mission Mountain Wood Band, the Live Wire Choir shared a taste for marijuana, possession of which in those days was still considered a relatively serious offense by the authorities. "The bands all had busses back then, and there was a reason," Reinholdt said. In retrospect, he acknowledged that partying had been a primary impetus for the music, and the music certainly facilitated the partying. "I think I missed out on a lot of other stuff going on in those years because I was all about a cute chick and a bag of weed. We sort of lived in a bubble, traveling everywhere on a bus with a driver, showing up to play the show and partying afterward, and then the next day it was on to the next place. It was a kind of whirlwind for two or three years there."

The band also played the Aber Day Kegger the following year (1979), this time on a bill with the New Riders of the Purple Sage and Lamont Cranston.

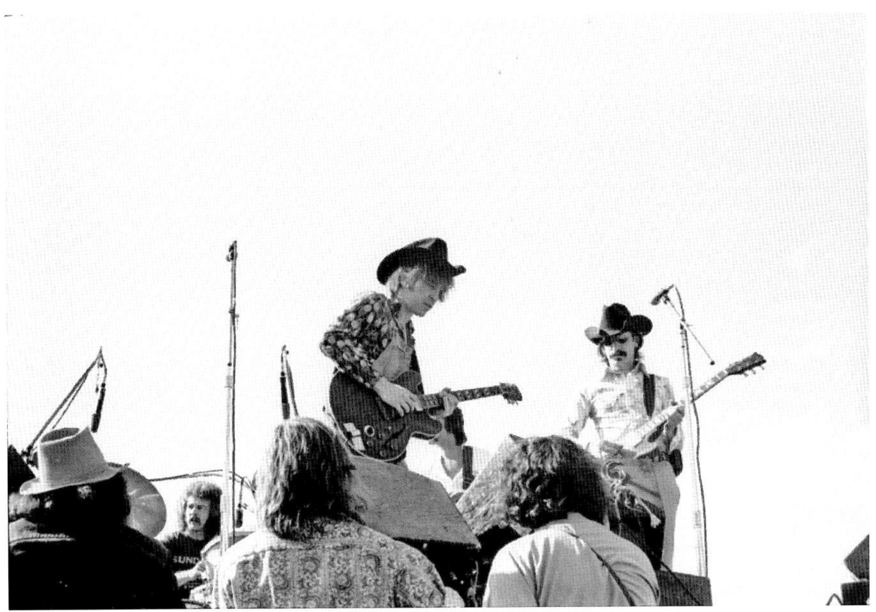

Elvin Bishop, 1974 Aber Day. *Courtesy of Archives and Special Collections, Mansfield Library, University of Montana.*

But the band members themselves had started to drift apart. Reinholdt and a few others had relocated to Missoula permanently, for starters. "The people in Missoula loved the band, and we loved the town, so I could never understand why we didn't do it earlier." But the change in scenery and tension over the second album, called *Topsy*, led Reinholdt to part ways with the band altogether, and before long they all found themselves involved in other projects. "We all went on to do other stuff, but I mainly wanted to play hardcore bluegrass, and Frank and Oakley wanted to play more swing. For a few years, it was a pretty magical band with some great sounds, but toward the end I was just swatting a guitar when I was really wanting to play Monroe-style bluegrass."

Reinholdt got his wish, eventually playing in some of Missoula's most acclaimed bluegrass outfits, including what must be one of Montana's longest-lived bluegrass ensembles, Pinegrass, a band that held court on Tuesday nights at the Top Hat in Missoula for almost two decades (although Reinholdt stopped playing with Pinegrass almost ten years ago). In fact, Montana turned out to harbor a considerable number of bluegrass musicians in the 1970s, a select few of whom would become nationally known as songwriters like Stephanie Davis (who wrote Garth Brooks's hit "Learning to Live Again") and John Lowell

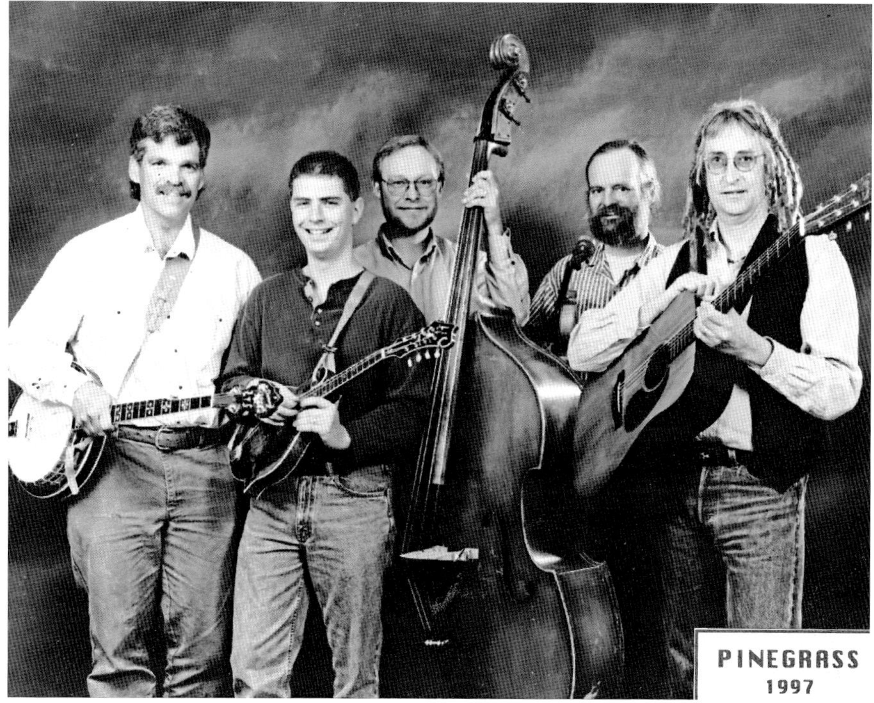

Formed in 1991, Missoula band Pinegrass is one of Montana's longest-running bluegrass outfits. Pictured here is the original lineup. *From left to right*: Jack Mauer, Bill Neaves, Rick Ryan, John Joyner and Richie Reinholdt. *Photo by Mark Hefty, courtesy of Bill Neaves.*

(author of the bluegrass hit "Sarah Hogan").

Jane Horton, another veteran of the Mission Mountain Wood Band era, has been inseparable from a guitar more or less since she was fourteen. "I discovered Joni Mitchell early on, before she became a household name, and I absorbed everything she did," she said, flashing a smile indicative of her stage presence.

Born in Bozeman, Horton grew up on a ranch in the Gallatin Valley. She played her first solo gigs around Bozeman—lots of covers of the Beatles, Judy Collins, Joan Baez and her favorite musical mentor, Joni Mitchell—while she was still in high school. Since her older sister had dated Terry Robinson of Mission Mountain fame when Jane was still in high school, she became pretty close with the players in that band as well and even sat in with them on vocal harmonies at shows or played between sets on the summer *Retta Mary* boat rides on Flathead Lake. "I always love singing harmony with Robbie [Quist] and never pass up the chance even today to sing with him when the occasion arises," she said. "We played a wedding together years ago, which was a great experience." She also went to college at MSU but left in 1975 to try out the music scene in Los Angeles. She played stages during that short period away from Montana, experiencing amazingly appreciative audiences, especially at the famous Troubadour.

After discovering she wasn't especially fond of city living, Horton didn't stay away long before getting back to Montana and spent a decade playing in various bands, the most successful of which was a hardworking, hard-traveling band called Avalanche Rose. That six-piece band was a full-time job for all the members, Horton explained. "We didn't have day jobs—we all made our livings playing music for those years. We had a van and traveled all over to college towns and ski towns—from Whitefish to Bismarck to Jackson Hole to Sun Valley, and all points between. We were regulars at the Top Hat in Missoula and places like the Outlaw Inn in Kalispell." The band also regularly appeared on the bill at the Sundance in Bozeman, the Shady Lady in Jackson and the Bierstube in Whitefish. They played the skiing circuit around the West in the winter, as well as clubs and weddings in the summers.

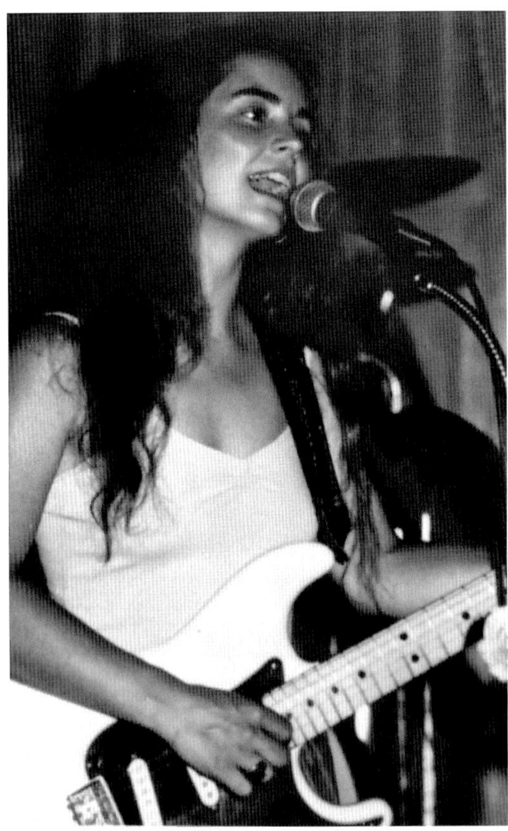

Jane Horton on stage with Avalanche Rose. *Courtesy of Jane Horton and Doug Holly.*

Avalanche Rose was known for their intricate harmonies and complex song arrangements, which raised them head and shoulders above the "three-chords and a cloud of dust" approach so typical many country-folk bands and which was practically a point of pride for those promulgating the "folk scare." Avalanche Rose's arrangements by contrast emphasized complicated passages of passing chords,

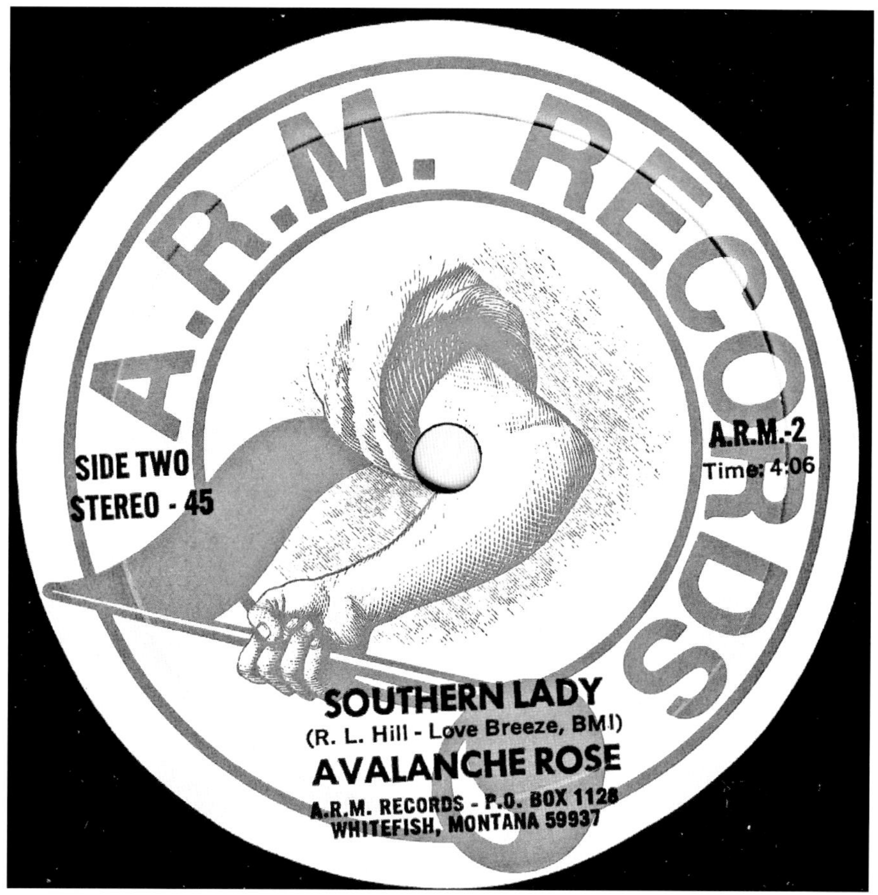

Avalanche Rose's unique ARM (Avalanche Rose Music) record label, designed by Christie Pearson. The record was 45 rpm. *Courtesy of Jane Horton and Doug Holly.*

often backed with solid swing rhythm. "It really was good, hard work, but it was also a lot of fun. We crossed paths with so many great local musicians and got to know so many wonderful folks across the region that loved to dance to our music," Jane said. "We devoted a lot of time to our sound and the music we performed. For about four years, we really made it work. We shared stages with some eminent musicians and bands including David LaFlamme, Asleep at the Wheel and Vassar Clements."

Avalanche Rose divided their sets between cover material and original songs. The band had four talented writers in Christie Pearson, Stephen Majstorovic, Tom Bernstein and Jack Purdy. The music was well supported in the main by virtuoso musician Majstorovic, who played everything

Avalanche Rose was a hardworking traveling band in the 1970s and 1980s in Montana. *Back, left to right*: Tom Bernstein, Stephem Majstorovic, Marc Taylor and Jack Purdie. *Front, left to right*: Jane Horton and Christie Pearson. Not pictured: Gregg Alexander (sound man). *Courtesy of Jane Horton and Doug Holly.*

from banjo to pedal steel, and "Tennesee" Tom Bernstein's guitar leads. The rhythm section consisted of Jack Purdy on bass and Mark Taylor on drums. With flute or guitar in hand, Christie Pearson shared vocals with Horton, who also played guitar, and the two women together worked out what one fan recalled as "simply gorgeous duets." Jane and Christie had brought to the band their sound from their previous folk-oriented duo, Wild Roses.

Like the Lost Highway Band or the Live Wire Choir, Avalanche Rose was fundamentally a working band, which meant that if you added up the time of rehearsals and traveling and actually performing their sets, the band was working the equivalent of a full-time job. "It was probably more than forty hours a week," Horton said. "And sometimes it did feel like a job." But as jobs go, it was pretty good time, and it was without question the sort of job you look forward to going to.

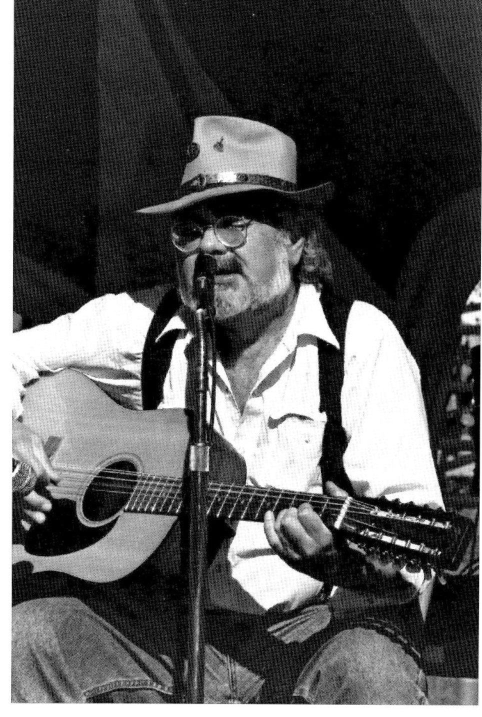

Artist Jay Rummel was also a well-respected folk singer and performer. *Courtesy of Timothy Irmen.*

As with other bands of the era, the members began to pursue other interests over time, and the band eventually came to an amicable demise. After Avalanche Rose split up, various combinations of the group's members worked in different bands for a while, but eventually Horton went back to college, getting a PhD in range science and natural resource ecology. Nowadays, Horton keeps her chops and calluses playing in a long-lived Irish traditional music session in Helena.

One of the more colorful personages to emerge from Missoula in the 1970s was celebrated artist and musician Jay Rummel (1939–1998), who distinguished himself also as a key figure at the periphery of the bluegrass and country scene in Montana, writing songs such as "The Butte Cowboy," "The Lady from Missoula" and "Montana Blue," among others. He also ran an open mic night at Luke's Bar on Front Street in Missoula in the 1980s called "Ace Wheeler's Talent Showcase." Luke's was a world-famous biker bar—named for Hank Williams's alter ego, "Luke the Drifter"—and had graffiti on its walls inscribed by such legendary figures as Buddy Reed, George Thorogood and Utah Phillips. In true gonzo style, Hunter S. Thompson one evening scrawled "Death to the Wierd!" for posterity, misspelling the key word.

Rummel integrated his graphic art with his musical tastes, producing iconic posters of American musical history, often in wall-sized prints that hang in homes, bars and galleries all over the state. In fact, Charlie B's bar in Missoula—cultural heir to Eddie's Club and Luke's Bar—has devoted

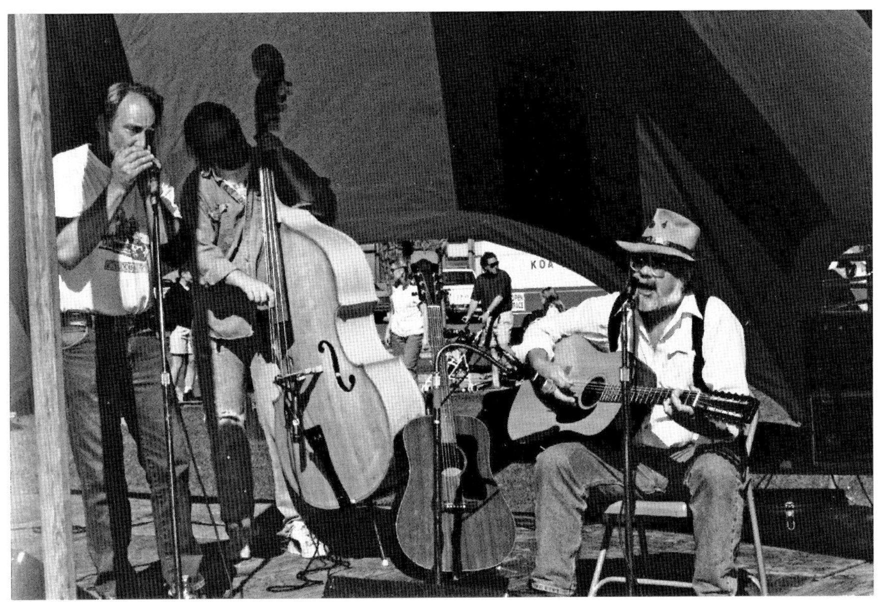

Jay Rummel performing with Michael Story at Caras Park in Missoula. *Courtesy of Timothy Irmen.*

one whole wall to some of his finest work. Also an accomplished potter, Rummel also made huge ceramic plates decorated with his homages to Jimmie Rodgers and Hank Williams.

The curator of a show of his work at the University of Montana Museum noted that his "contemporary vision of Montana" embraces a "strong narrative of allegory and parable," which nicely summarizes the talent Rummel had for illustrating the position that Montana's own singers and musicians maintained in the pantheon of America's great country artists. His graphic art was heavily influenced by his deep respect and admiration for the iconic figures of early Americana, as well as later artists who he felt continued to carry forth the tradition. In an artist's statement, Rummel himself said that "I feel a direct relationship between folk/country music and the narrative direction of my visual art."

Rummel was perhaps best known for his song "The Butte Cowboy," a tale of a hitchhiker traveling through the state, with the chorus an amalgam of catch phrases from old folk standards like "When the Work's All Done This Fall." He also penned a half dozen songs for a 1979 album recorded in Seattle by erstwhile Missoula musician Jim Finneran called *The Road Ain't No Place for a Lady.*

Rummel threw himself into his music the way he threw himself into his art,

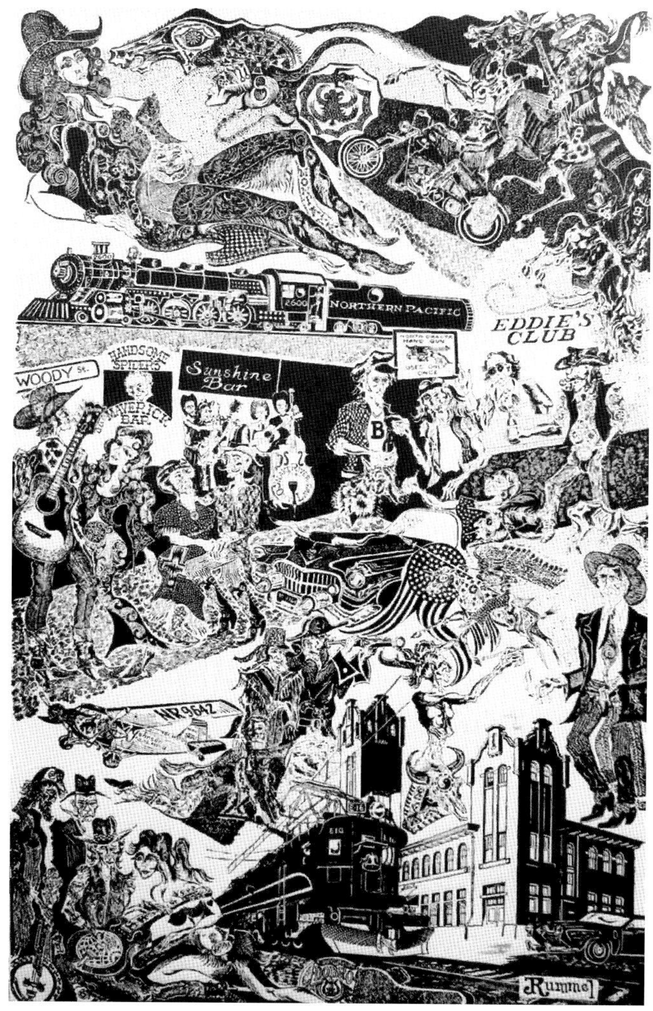

Although he was loved all over Montana as a singer of folk and country music, Jay Rummel (1939–1998) is best known for his phenomenal artwork, most of which celebrated the musicians and venues he admired and connected Montana to Americana in a profoundly visual way. His artwork adorns many famous Montana musical establishments, including Charlie B's bar in Missoula. Jay Rummel, *Lady from Missoula County*, from *The Five Valleys* triptych, 1995, offset photo-lithograph, 35.5 x 22.5 inches. *From the Missoula Art Museum Collection, courtesy of the artist's estate.*

keeping long hours and stretching the nights into mornings with energy more suited to a teenager. Anyone who ever met him or played a tune with him recognized that he was the very antithesis of a poseur. He could be irascible,

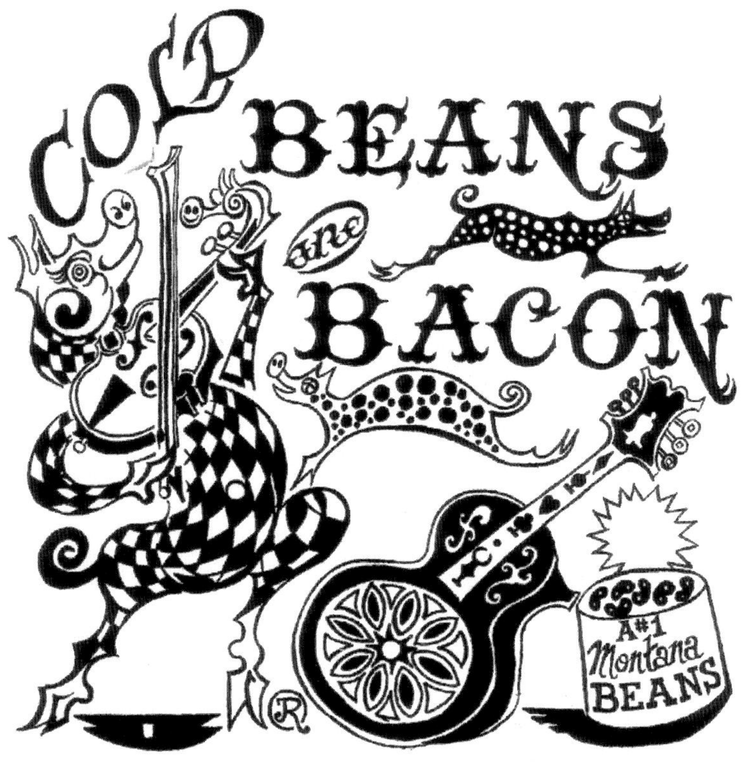

Folky Missoula Americana band Cold Beans and Bacon commissioned Jay Rummel to do the art for their only release (1995 self-titled album), described by Missoulian music critic Erica Parfit as "hotter than a torched campfire hot dog [and] funnier than that time a cue ball landed in your jambalaya, jettisoning a crawfish tail into the bartender's hair." *CD from the collection of Aaron Parrett.*

but he had paid his dues, and the music and art he made ran bone-deep and cut like a March wind along the highline. His prints endure as artifacts of the era of Missoula in the 1970s, but they also express a deep reverence for "the weird, old America" and the annals of storytellers, drifters and eccentrics who inspired the musicians who forged the music that became Americana. Even more, he connected Montana both musically and conceptually to the country as whole by showing in both in his songs and his prints how rural folk invariably turn to music to tell their story.

The versions of Americana in Montana played by the generations of musicians who came of age in the 1970s helped cultivate an optimistic environment in places like Missoula and Bozeman in which new generations could incubate new musical ideas and hatch fresh variations on an established theme. The days of the Aber Day Keggers may have passed into the annals of fond memories, but the legacy of a Big Sky music scene has endured—carried on, for example, by the musicians profiled in the next chapter.

Chapter 3

"Changing Shades"

Bluegrass and Folk Music in Montana

No one in Montana will dispute that the Mission Mountain Wood Band were one of the most popular Americana bands to ever grace a stage in the Big Sky State. Still, a few local critics begrudged them a little for all the media attention and critical acclaim they gathered while other bands with more accomplished players, such as the traditional bluegrass band Poor Monroe (also based in Missoula in the 1970s), seemed to go relatively unappreciated. "It often seems that with folk music, the bands that get the spotlight are not the best or most pure examples of the genre," observed longtime Missoula music promoter and bluegrass musician Rick Ryan. "The Mission Mountain Wood Band had an aura and stage presence that could never be rivaled, and it was great that they popularized that style of music, but it happened sort of in the way that the Kingston Trio had popularized folk and old-time music ten years earlier."

Ryan's point cuts to the heart of one of the inevitable frustrations of putting together a survey of Americana music in Montana: with such an amazing wealth of musical history to draw from, it is difficult, if not impossible, to do justice to many obscure bands and musicians who failed to achieve great notoriety in spite of having accomplished great things musically. The curse of obscurity inevitably haunts bluegrass and old-time Americana musicians, in part because their approach resembles a pastime or hobby more than the sort of all-encompassing and consuming lifestyle that one associates more with rock-and-roll, for example. At the same time, playing music that is definitively acoustic means less bother in setting up to perform, so that folk and bluegrass bands can more easily make their musical interest at least a part-time paying job, which paints their whole approach a slightly different color as well. What bluegrass and "folkies" sometimes lack in cultural cachet, they make up for in actual "gigs"; the average rock-and-roll band, for example, has a limited number of venues to work in a small town and can't easily land jobs playing low-volume dinner music. And because the big bands with the busses get the press, for the most part, the working bands—often flaunting oodles of talent—often go unappreciated, at least in the media if not the memories of listeners. The examples are legion, starting with Poor Monroe and myriad other top-notch bluegrass and country outfits that have emerged from around Montana, especially from smaller towns in the days before the Internet helped level the playing field. From having YouTube for hosting self-made music videos, Bandcamp for audio files and iTunes and CD Baby for actually selling merchandise, it's hard to image how anyone nowadays loses out on their fifteen minutes of fame. Even as recently as thirty years ago, about the only chance any aspiring musical artist had was to get out and perform in any venue that would have them. For hard rock musicians, especially in Montana, the options are perforce limited. But bluegrass is another story.

From the mid-1980s to the present day, for example, the Top Hat Bar down on Front Street regularly hosted a bluegrass jam on Tuesday night that served as a kind of informal training camp for a surprising number of Montana pickers, many of whom moved on to accomplish impressive feats in the bluegrass and folk world. Ivan Rosenberg, winner of the Bluegrass Song of the Year honors at the International Bluegrass Music Association awards in 2009 for a song he cowrote with Chris Stuart called "Don't Throw Mama's Flowers Away," is one example among many. "A lot of people came through that jam at the Top Hat," Rosenberg said. "There was really nothing like that anywhere else in the West." He noted that for some unfathomable reason, Montana collects bluegrass and old-time musicians at a rate that far outstrips its modest population. "I'd argue that that style of music is an intimate part of the culture," he explained. "It's not just the cowboy thing, though that's there too. But I played hundreds of weddings and unusual gigs in Montana that sort of revealed how much a part of the whole state's 'ethos' is wrapped up in the music. I mean, we played for fly-fishing expeditions regularly and ultimate Frisbee tournaments and for the

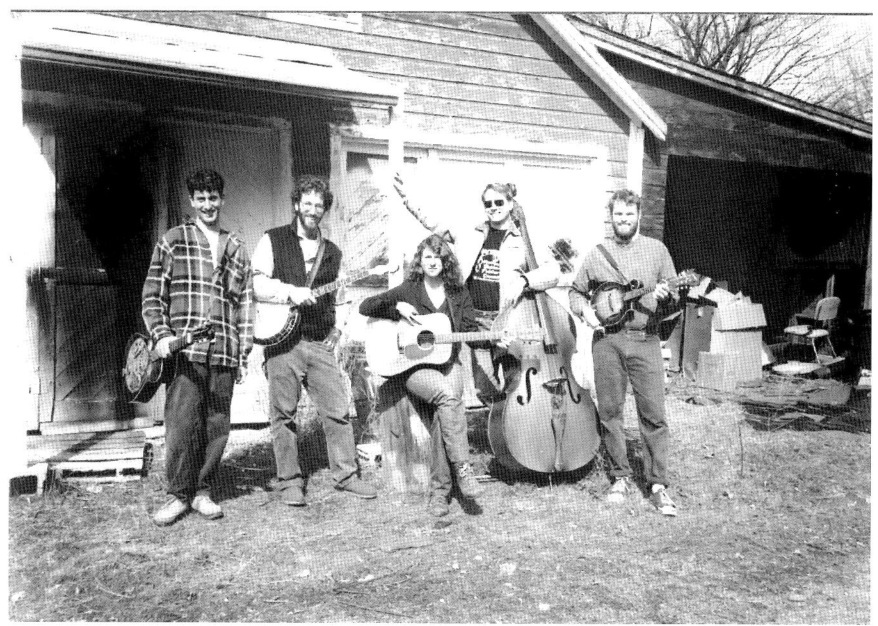

In 1996, Ivan Rosenberg played in the Crazy Water String Band, along with future stars of old-time music Thomas Sneed and Martha Scanlan of the Reeltime Travelers. *From left to right*: Ivan Rosenberg, Jake Schepps, Martha Scanlan, Danny Pearson and Thomas Sneed. *Photo by Gillian Ehrich, courtesy of Ivan Rosenberg.*

smokejumpers and a lot of gigs at the ski resorts—it's like every element of what people do in Montana that makes the place it is invites this kind of music along as the soundtrack."

Rosenberg started playing music in his early twenties in Missoula but then left to finish college in California. "When I graduated, I knew I wanted to move back to Missoula—for the sole reason of playing bluegrass music, which I knew was just *there*." Rosenberg played in dozens of bands and then began touring with some of the best musicians in contemporary American bluegrass: Jonathan Reischman, Chris Stuart, Chris Jones and April Verch, among others. Along the way, he ran his own recording studio for a while and wrote music for films and television, including the Emmy Award–nominated Drury Gunn Carr and Doug Hawes-Davis film *Libby, Montana*. He's released a dozen CDs of his own music and played on hundreds of others as a studio musician.

Rosenberg noted that few towns the size of Missoula can boast as many bluegrass and old-time and folk musicians, many of whom do double duty in rock-and-roll or more mainstream country outfits. Off the top of his head, he named three Montana Dobro players, for example, who are all phenomenal

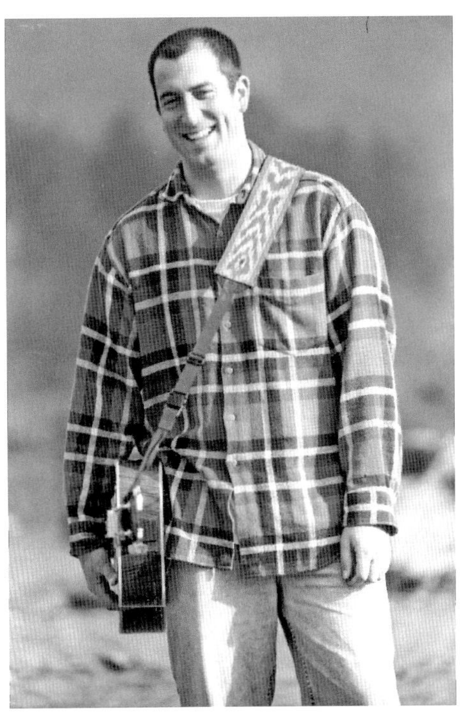

One of the country's premier Dobro players, Ivan Rosenberg started his career playing bluegrass in Montana, where he played in various bands over a dozen years. *Photo by Patrick Satterfield, courtesy of Ivan Rosenberg.*

instrumentalists: Jack Mauer, a forty-year veteran of bluegrass who plays banjo and Dobro in Pinegrass, one of Montana's most venerable bluegrass bands; "Dobro" Dick Dillof, the legendary writer and raconteur from Livingston who used to pal around with Richard Brautigan in the 1970s and is well-known throughout the Pacific Northwest as a demon of the C6 neck; and Tim Ishler (1959–2008), one of Montana's most beloved and talented musicians, who earned enduring fame as the seventeen-year-old kid who actually "won" *The Gong Show* in 1976 by playing "Dueling Banjos" by himself on the banjo and the Dobro.

Rosenberg eventually left Montana to pursue musical opportunities that a state with such a modest population cannot easily provide. "On the one hand, I could scratch out a living there because there just were always fifty- or hundred-dollar gigs to be had. But on the other hand, Montana is not really close to anything else—even Seattle is seven or eight hours away." He continues to write music for movies and television and plays in a half dozen different musical ensembles, but his tour schedule has slowed down now that he's a family man. He plays a lot of festivals and even directs a bluegrass camp in Canada every summer.

Meanwhile, Missoula (and, to a lesser extent, its rival city across the divide, Bozeman) continues to produce astonishing talent in the bluegrass world, including a band called the Lil' Smokies, winners of the 2015 band contest at the Telluride Bluegrass Festival. That particular contest happens to have launched the careers of an impressive slate of Americana musicians: previous winners include the Dixie Chicks (1992), for example, and Greensky Bluegrass (2006).

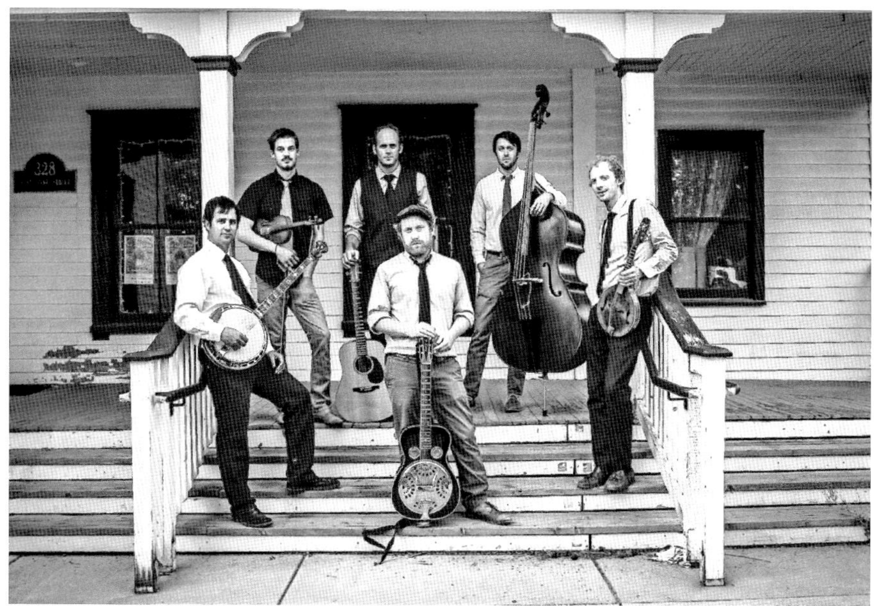

In 2015, Montana's premier bluegrass band, the Lil' Smokies, won the prestigious band contest at the Telluride Bluegrass Festival in Telluride, Colorado. *From left to right*: Matt Cornette (banjo), Jesse Brown (fiddle), Pete Barrett (guitar), Andy Dunnigan (Dobro), Scott Parker (upright bass) and Cameron Wilson (mandolin). *Courtesy of the Lil' Smokies.*

June 20, 2015, was a beautiful day for the Forty-second Annual Telluride Bluegrass Festival band contest—bright sunshine in the high mountains, with the temperature reaching almost eighty degrees at the festival grounds. The Lil' Smokies, relatively unknown and not nearly as seasoned as some of the other entrants, were nervous. "Nervous? Hell, I was terrified!" Matt Cornette said. "Not that I doubted our ability—we knew our material, we were well-rehearsed. It was more the fear that something technical would go wrong—like maybe my picks would fall off my fingers." They had traveled a long way from home, but the humble band from Missoula, Montana, wowed the crowd with their enthusiastic performance, and in spite of their jitters, they impressed the band contest judges, too: the Lil' Smokies took top honors.

From what started modestly as just a bunch of guys living in Missoula who liked to pick together, the band had evolved in the previous year or so into a full-fledged bluegrass outfit along the lines of the Infamous Stringdusters or even the Newgrass Revival. Matt Cornette's melodic banjo rolls certainly echoed elements of his predecessor Courtney Johnson's signature contribution to the more hippie-friendly version of bluegrass that emerged in the 1970s. Dobro player Andy Dunnigan's strong songwriting meanwhile

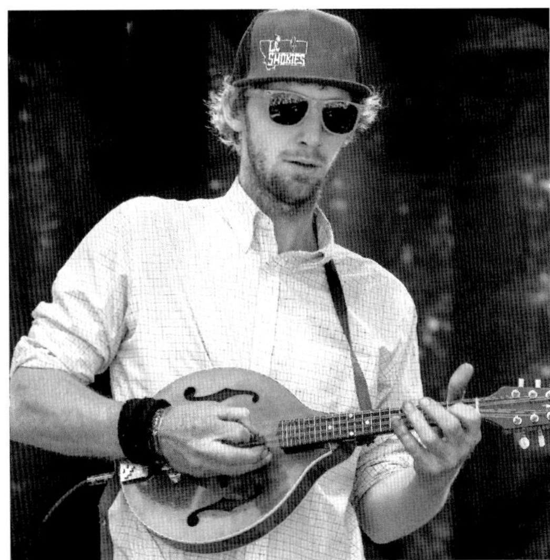

Left: Cameron Wilson from the Lil' Smokies. *Courtesy of the Lil' Smokies.*

Below: The Lil' Smokies, promo shot at sunset in Missoula. *Courtesy of the Lil' Smokies.*

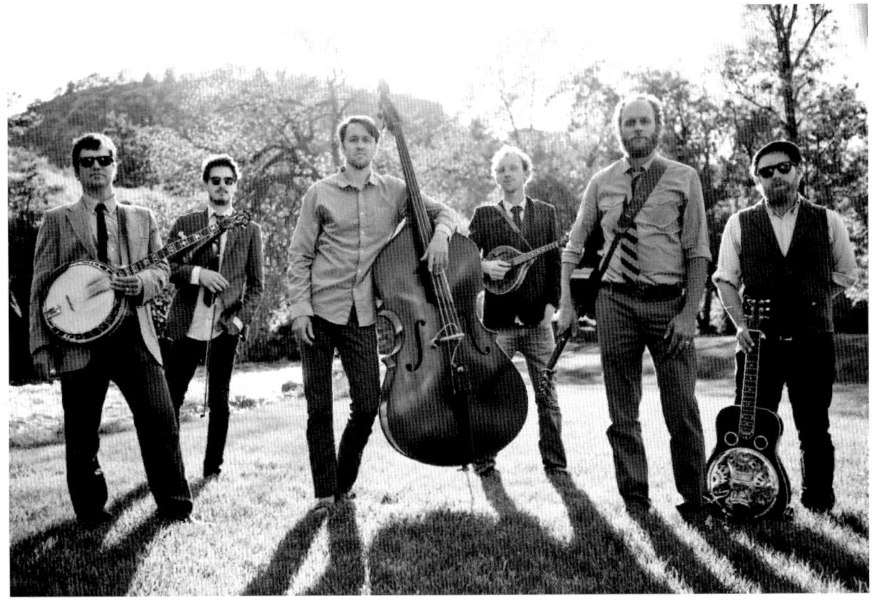

fueled the band's homegrown aura, and his vocal style drew comparisons to Curtis Burch, bandmate of Courtney Johnson and one of the godfathers of the newgrass sound.

At the same time, the band brings a distinct old-time sensibility to the bluegrass format. "When I was learning, I spent a fair amount of time hanging out with the Missoula old-time crowd—Brian Herbel and those guys," Cornette said, "and I definitely liked that vibe better, where everyone is always engaged with the tune, as opposed to the 'Hey, look at me taking this wicked solo' approach in bluegrass."

Now here they were at the premier bluegrass festival in the West. "On Friday, we watched Jerry Douglas take the stage, and a couple of us almost went into a panic attack," recalled Pete Barrett, guitarist and de facto front man for the band. "We were thinking, 'Wow. We're gonna have to get up on that stage?'" But when their moment came, not one bead of sweat marred a flawless performance, and the band tore up the stage just the way they had all over the Northwest in the previous few months, mixing originals with unique renditions of classic rock songs like Led Zeppelin's "Going to California" and Dire Straits' "Money for Nothing." Not only could Dunnigan whip out a torrent of slide licks like a card sharp hiding a sleeve full of aces, the guy could sing as well—fans too young to remember Curtis Burch compared him to the Punch Brothers' Chris Thile in a slightly lower register.

Dunnigan hails from a musical family: his father, John Dunnigan, is a well-known musician in the Flathead country and palled around with the Mission Mountain Wood Band back in the day. "Jack Gladstone used to babysit me," Andy said. His father encouraged but never pushed his son into music, however. "I came to it organically, I guess you would say." Dunnigan started out playing guitar and tried a banjo for a while but then spent a lot of time with an electric, pursuing the Hendrix muse. In about 2006, he picked up a Dobro, and suddenly a lot of musical doors were unlocked. He found he could get sounds that were completely unique. Moving to it from the electric guitar also provided a little more focus. "I started out in that mode of three hours of jamming a solo on 'All Along the Watchtower,'" he said, "which is a long way from focusing on a tasteful break."

For years, he focused on learning the instrument, and it wasn't until he went through a difficult breakup with a woman that he started writing songs: "Suddenly the floodgates were open. It was therapeutic." Before long, his songs were making up a substantial portion of the Lil' Smokies' sets. Like his bandmate Matt Cornette, Dunnigan envisions the sound the Lil' Smokies are after as something steeped in traditional bluegrass but somehow having evolved beyond it. "I think of the phrase 'Changing Shades,'" he said. "It suggests various things, but bluegrass comes in different shades. Traditional bluegrass can be pretty stringent, and I see us as breaking away from that and trying something different." The phrase also recalls the name of Cliff Waldron's band from the 1970s, the New Shades of Grass, which similarly pushed the genre envelope. Cornette put it a little less abstractly: "I think of

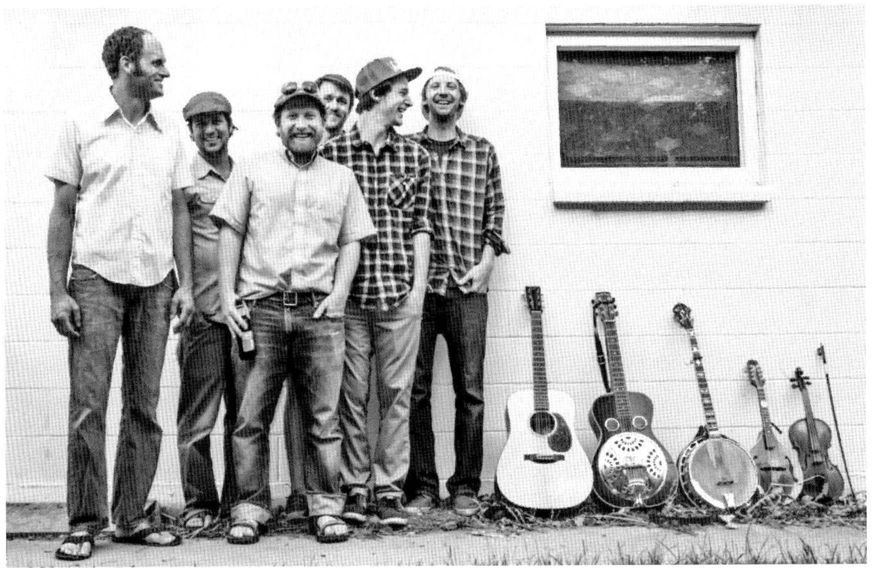

Lil' Smokies hamming it up. *From left to right*: Pete Barrett, Matt Cornette, Andy Dunnigan, Scott Parker, Jesse Brown and Cameron Wilson. *Courtesy of the Lil' Smokies.*

us as a bunch of guys playing rock-and-roll music on bluegrass instruments." The "rock-and-roll" part of the show the Lil' Smokies bring to the stage is the raw energy of the presentation as opposed to the material or format, which remain more in line with new acoustic music, but his point isn't hard to follow.

The Lil' Smokies embody a long-standing association between the city of Missoula and bluegrass-oriented music. And although its "scene" has never achieved the notoriety of, say, Fort Collins, Colorado, something about the proximity of the college, the mountains and the casual availability of "kind bud" have since the '60s tended to coalesce into the perfect environment for the proliferation of precisely the sort of music with which the Lil' Smokies rev up crowd after crowd.

The Mission Mountain Wood Band forty years earlier had found a way to inject a hint of authentic bluegrass into the more familiar and accessible rock-and-roll band format, a feat probably first performed by the Byrds (especially under the influence of Gram Parsons in 1968), although many other groups quickly caught the buzz, leading to more attenuated strains in bands like the Marshall Tucker Band and the Eagles.

By contrast, bands like the Lil' Smokies have kept the bluegrass vibe a

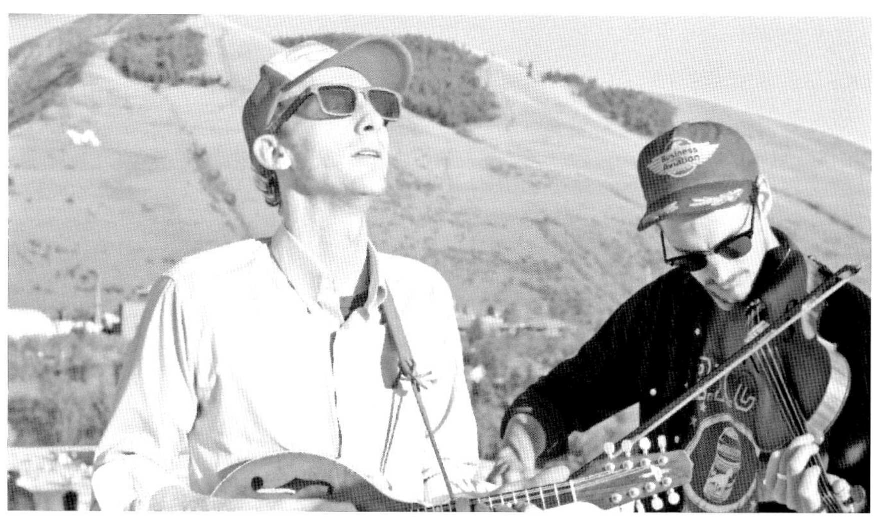

The Lil' Smokies' Cameron Wilson and Jesse Brown playing against the backdrop of Mount Sentinel in Missoula, Montana. *Courtesy of Noise Motion Productions.*

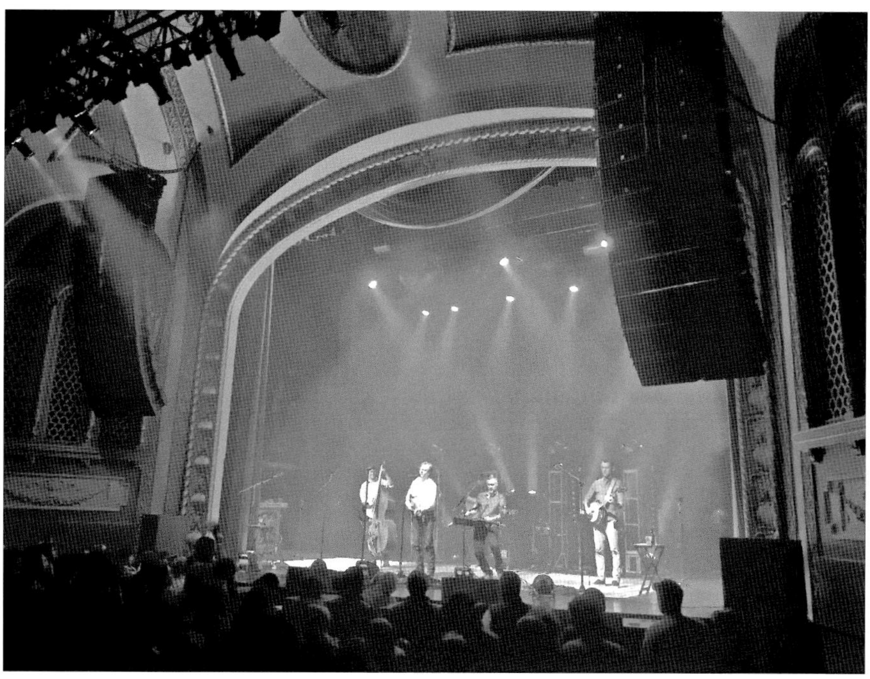

The Infamous Stringdusters at the newly renovated Wilma Theater in Missoula, where the upgraded sound system reportedly cost just under $1 million. *Courtesy of Walker Scarborough.*

little closer to the bone: for starters, as with traditional bluegrass, they have no drummer, and aside from using pick-ups for their instruments, they are entirely acoustic and can generate that front porch or living room picking party sound into a megawatt format. Having cut their teeth on the old-school Bill Monroe repertoire of bluegrass numbers, they can turn to that material as the occasion suits, but like their predecessors in newgrass, they're more interested in generating something new out of the old lonesome sound. The result resembles the tight, accomplished orchestration of a band like the Infamous Stringdusters much more than the loose carelessness of a band like the Yonder Mountain String Band, whom Missoula writer John Rimel once described as "one part bluegrass, one part Grateful Dead, and then shaken—not stirred."

Lyrically, Dunnigan's songs tend to be a little more imagistic than standard bluegrass fare and have a quiet subtlety that seems missing from a lot of more newgrassy stuff. For example, his song "Decades," the first cut from the Lil' Smokies' second album, has a decidedly pensive feel:

Wood smoke, thick pungent air,
she wipes her eyes and turns away,
and briefly forgets how far it is
back to the mountains and the cool streams she missed.
(© 2013 Andy Dunnigan)

While the Lil' Smokies leave plenty of breathing room in their songs for improvisation and showcasing the talent of the various pickers on stage, both Andy Dunnigan and Matt Cornette don't hesitate to distance themselves from the label of "jamgrass." They do see what they are bringing to the traditional bluegrass sound as something far less rigid and constrained than what might be called "traditional." They can play convincing renditions of the old standards in requisite three-part harmony, of course, but their hearts lie open to a much broader field of music. The band plans to record an album in the spring of 2016 in Portland, Oregon, at Hallowed Halls Studios. Like a lot of other young musicians and new bands, they're taking the DIY approach, even though in the aftermath of the Telluride triumph, they were offered a record deal. They turned that offer down, but they did land an agent and manager, which has freed up some creative space for honing their new songs and integrating their newest member, Matt Reiger on guitar, into

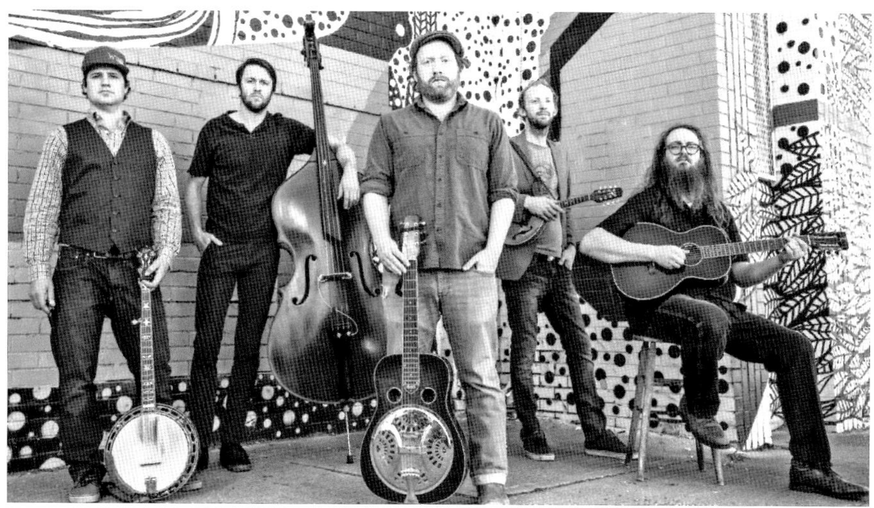

The Lil' Smokies welcomed new guitarist Matt Reiger in 2016. *Photo by Kristen Cohen Photography, courtesy of the Lil' Smokies.*

the band.*

Hang out with country musicians in pretty much any Montana town and the name "Gibson Hartwell" will eventually come up. He's an accomplished guitarist, having made his bones in Missoula bands with his pal Colin Meloy long before the latter went on to Decemberists fame. "We played acoustic stuff around Missoula in the early '90s," he recalled. "Coffeehouse junk, mostly." But eventually they hit their stride in a full-fledged Americana band called Tarkio. "It was in the vein of Uncle Tupelo and other stuff that was popular at the time." Tarkio was one of the most popular bands in Missoula in the mid-1990s. Their first recording was a cassette tape—probably among the last mass-produced to appear in Missoula. It was a demo, recorded on a 4 track. A year later, they put out the CD by which they are best known, *I Guess I Was Hoping for Something More* (1996). At that point, the band was beginning to realize that their talent and ambitions had outgrown Missoula, and the members were slowly, if affably, drifting in different directions. Their last effort was an EP with the Decemberists-sounding title, *Sea Songs for Landlocked Sailors* (1997).

Hartwell went on to play key roles in some of Missoula's most energetic

* Shortly after Telluride, Pete Barrett announced his (amicable) departure from the band in order to start a family. He did return to play a sell-out show at the newly renovated Wilma in Missoula on New Year's Eve 2015, and after several auditions for his replacement, the Smokies have welcomed Mr. Reiger, a Seattle-based musician.

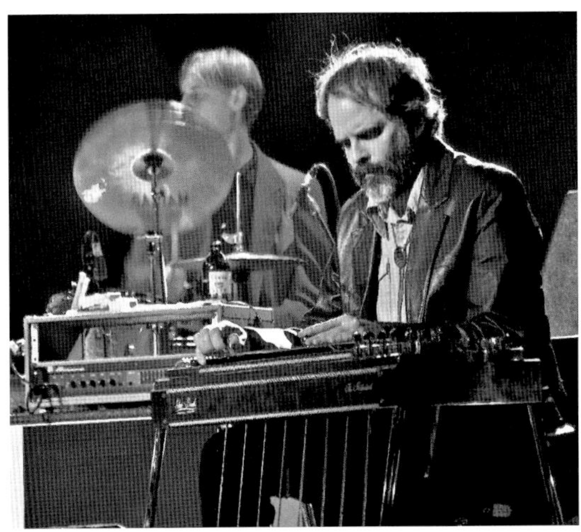

Gibson Hartwell is a longtime fixture of the Missoula music scene, having started his career with Colin Meloy (of Decemberists fame) in a band called Tarkio in the 1990s. Now known as one of the state's premier pedal steel players, he plays in half a dozen bands, including Stellarondo and the Idle Ranch Hands. Mark Dixon, photographer. *Courtesy of Mark Dixon.*

and fondly remembered Americana bands of the 1990s and 2000s—the Hayrollers, for example, but also Bob Wire and the Fence Menders, as well as a ten-year stint with Tom Catmull and the Clerics. He also played in Oblio Joes, Shodown and Churchmouse. He earned a degree a few years ago in natural resources from WSU, so between shows and practice sessions on the steel, he tries to squeeze in a little environmental consulting when he can.

Lately, his main gig has been manning the pedal steel in the Idle Ranch Hands, known for "dropping serious twang," as one of their posters advertises, but he also plays various instruments in the quirky improvisational and spoken-word band Stellarondo (whose CDs and live performances often involve the Yaak Valley writer Rick Bass reading his stories). Last year, he traveled to Paris to record with Oliver Night, and he recorded with Shiveries in Missoula for an album due out in 2016. He plays in half a dozen bands around Missoula, all mostly side projects, but each one pushing the vernier of Americana along unusual axes.

Like his friend Gibson Hartwell, Dave Martens is also pedal steel player. Martens plays in one of the most original country bands to emerge from Missoula in decades, the Best Westerns. It's a little misleading to call the Best Westerns a "Missoula band," since only one or two of the original members still lives in town. Nevertheless, the band released their impressive debut LP *The Best Westerns* there, and they maintain a committed following in their old stomping grounds.

Martens has come up with the phrase "dirt wave" to describe the Best Westerns' sound, a nod to both their unrehearsed rawness as well as an

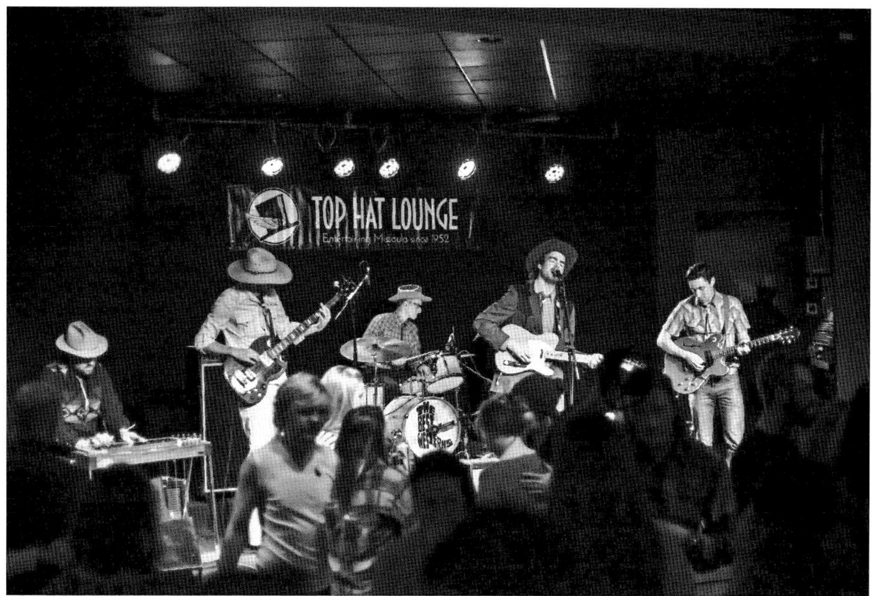

Lead singer and songwriter for the Best Westerns, Isaak Optaz. *Photo by Abi Baumann, courtesy of Dave Martens.*

acknowledgment that, like anything "new wave," the roots beneath it stretch back pretty far and lie deeply entangled with music that bands were making before anyone in the Best Westerns was even alive. The main creative force behind the band is Izaak Opatz, who writes most of the band's material and sings in a convincingly gritty, soulful country rumble. But "dirt wave" also seems to conjure an almost scruffy looseness that matches the band's own conception of itself—as Martens put it, the band often carries on as a "play when we can" kind of ensemble, especially since Opatz has moved away from Montana, first to Nashville and, more recently, to Los Angeles, in an effort to promote his work—but even their impressive debut album gives a sense that part of the band's charm is a certain aimlessness in approach. Whereas a lot of bands adhere to Bob Dylan's unspoken principle of avoiding rehearsal in order to foster spontaneity, very few are able to take that approach and walk out of the studio with demos that are anything other than unfulfilling sonic mush.

But it works for the Best Westerns. One gets the sense from listening to their LP that six more weeks of working with the songs might have tightened the seams but would not have improved the way the sound fits so cunningly together. As it is, the Best Westerns have a sound entirely unique and compelling: the rough gloss and looseness of the rhythm section provides

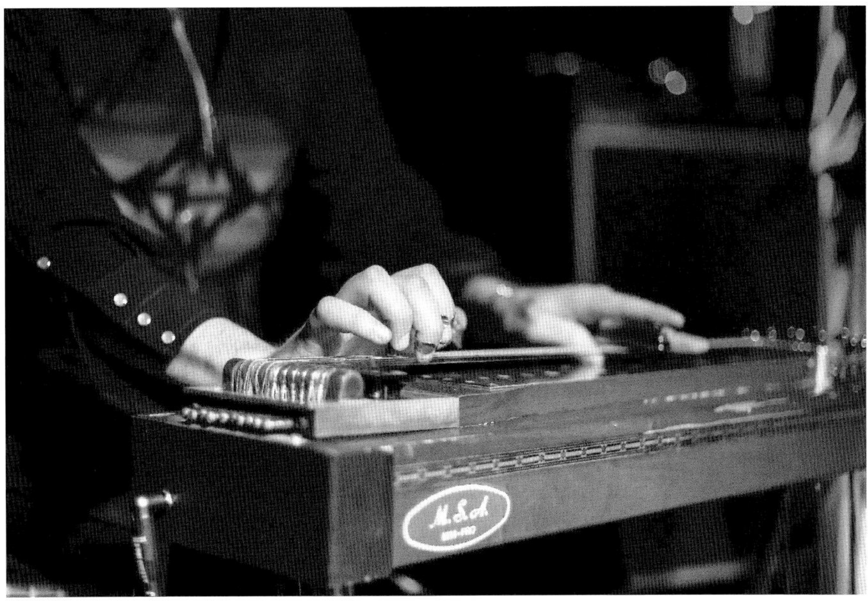

Pedal steel for the Best Westerns, Dave Martens. *Photo by Abi Baumann, courtesy of Dave Martens.*

the perfect background for Opatz's singing and Martens's soaring steel. Odd segments of banjo in the mix lend a quirky touch that hints at the old-time sound without pushing the whole thing too far down the hipster slope. It's incredibly difficult for any band to pool their talents and generate a collective sound that listeners won't immediately identify as somehow "derivative," but the Best Westerns have done it—and what's more, they've done it in a casual, almost offhand way, a pleasant reminder to anyone who slaps the LP on their turntable that the main point of making music is always to have fun.

A great example is their song "Backsliding" on *High Country*. This peppy country number has a quirky, unpredictable chord progression, and Opatz packs a surprising number of syllables into each line as casually as a trail boss might roll a cigarette. The catalogue of double entendres is tightly wedged between descending cascades of electric guitar notes, the whole effect a seamless sonic vignette that tells an age-old story in a clever way:

I don't hold anything against you now but I sometimes wish I did
I don't have a jealous bone in my whole body but I might have some jealous cartilage
I don't want to be the enemy so I guess I could give you a call

When I hear your voice it's like I don't have a choice
Nothing's really changed, nothing's really changed at all
Backsliding…it's so easy to do
Backsliding…I bet you never thought it would happen to you.
(© 2014 Izaak Opatz/Best Westerns)

Dave Martens now lives in Havre, where he curates a website of "lost" Montana music (see discography) and continues to unveil the secrets of the pedal steel. Both he and Hartwell agree that pedal steel guitar attracts a distinct subculture of those dedicated to its arcane mysteries. In bluegrass circles, the banjo seems ready-made for caricature as the hallmark of hillbilly buffoonery, but among musicians of almost any style, the pedal steel evokes an aura of almost wary awe. "Lots of people ask me things like, 'Oh you play the steel? What kind of handgun are you packing?' It's strange," Hartwell said. "Another I heard the other day at the Southwestern Steel Guitar Convention in Phoenix: some [steel player] said, 'I can't tell if I like doing this or if it's just a good outlet for my OCD.'"

Like Martens and Hartwell, longtime musician Russ Nasset has a solid connection to Missoula. Nearly every musician in western Montana knows, or knows of, Nasset. He's among the most admired and respected working musicians around. A plainspoken and unaffected man, Nasset has managed to make a solid living and raise a family playing no-frills, danceable roots-rock and country. "I ain't rich," he said, "but I don't feel poor, and I'm doing pretty good, all told." Nasset was born and raised in Shelby, Montana, but after a few inauspicious years at UM, he left for Oregon in 1968. While bands like the Mission Mountain Wood Band, the Lost Highway Band and the Live Wire Choir were busy forging the musical zeitgeist of 1970s Missoula, Nasset was touring the Northwest in a working band out of Oregon called Ramblin' Rex. In 1986, he returned to Missoula and continued to ply his trade, working four or five nights a week playing honest and unpretentious Americana music, most of which he wrote himself. "I do mostly originals, but I'll throw a Bob Dylan number in the mix or some old country blues. Depends on the venue, the show, what the crowd is after." And Nasset draws a crowd: he's known for his authentic vocal delivery and solid guitar work, and he knows how to make a band work. He's put out several albums over the years, most notably *Russ Nasset and the Revelators* (2003), *Blue Highway* (2010) and a solo album of acoustic country and country blues Americana that came out in 2014 called *Human Tongue.*

Over on the other side of the divide, listeners can find a host of professional songwriters, many of whom have achieved a permanent place in the record

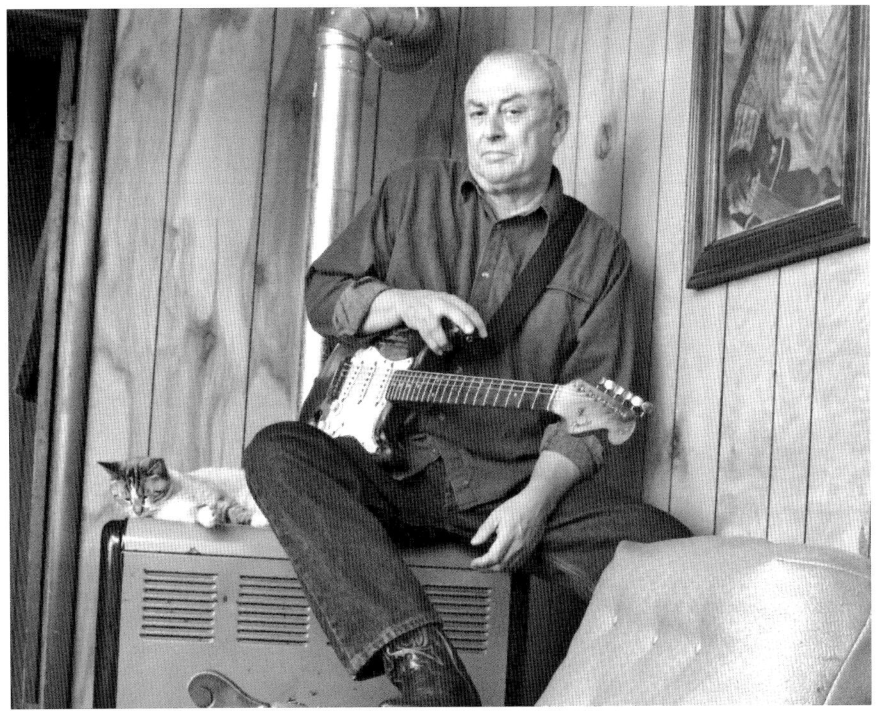

Russ Nasset, originally from up on the highline in Montana, is known for his unpretentious, honest delivery of original Montana roots music. *Photo by Sarah Daisy Lindmark, courtesy of Sarah Daisy Lindmark/the* Missoula Independent.

books, having written hit songs for Nashville stars. Stephanie Davis and Kostas top that list, while John Lowell in Bozeman has made a name for himself on the more modest bluegrass charts.

Lowell spent some time in Billings as a child, but his family moved around a lot. He graduated from high school in Arizona and immediately headed back to Montana, arriving in Bozeman in 1980. In high school, he had picked up a guitar, learning his first licks from his mentor and friend Peter McLoughlin, a virtuoso picker from Arizona. "But for the most part, I taught myself," Lowell said. "In this kind of music you're always picking things up from other people, but in kind of an informal way."

Lowell made his mark on some of Montana's best bluegrass bands in the 1980s and 1990s, including Wheel Hoss, where he first began writing songs. "I still play in one bluegrass band," he acknowledged, "but the bulk of what I do now is solo, and when I play my own songs, alone, it definitely falls into the Americana category." As Lowell conceived of it, Americana is that odd category of American music that gets filtered into its own box by process of elimination: it isn't quite bluegrass, maybe not quite country and not rock-and-roll, so it gets called Americana. "I think of it as mainly acoustic music, but not exclusively so," he said, and pointed to Tim O'Brien as a performer who epitomizes what Americana means to him. "He can play stellar bluegrass, classic old-time, but when he does his own stuff on his original records, I would call that the essence of Americana."

Lowell began writing songs in the early 1990s. It wasn't long before several nationally known bluegrass acts were recording his songs. The Colorado band Front Range was first, recording "Fergus County Jail" on their 1997 Sugar Hill release *Rambling on My Mind*. His song "Sarah Hogan" has been recorded by more than a dozen artists, including Bryan Bowers and Joe Hermann. Bluegrass legend Cliff Waldron recorded his "You're Not the Same Girl" in 2002 for his Rebel release *A Little Ways Down the Road*.

One of the most successful songwriters to hail from Montana is a soft-spoken, humble guy whom everyone knows as Kostas. Born in Greece in 1949, Kostas (full name Kostas Lazarides) came to Montana in 1957 and has been here ever since. He played in rock-and-roll bands in Billings growing up but always had an interest in country. In fact, as he sees it, Americana strikes him as little more than a new name put on an old phenomenon: "Joni Mitchell, Cat Stevens, Bob Dylan—all that stuff today would be called 'Americana,'" he said. "I avoid categories like that. When I look at music, I see a universe of currents that flow through one another and connect, blending, moving in a kind of circle. Some points of that jump out at you, others don't."

In the 1990s, Kostas spent a few years in Nashville, and he continues to write hit songs for the likes of Dwight Yoakum, Patti Loveless and Travis Tritt, but his home is Montana. "I guess if I could live anywhere else, it would be Kauai," he admitted. But more than any other place, Montana has a way of connecting individuals to its geography. "Maybe the sparseness of the people here allows you room to breathe a little easier," he said. "When you can breathe easy, you're more observant of the world around you. A lot in this state captures you and feeds your soul."

That same relative sparsity of population tends to drive people toward creative outlets. "I think every town in every county in this state has musicians in one stage of development or another. There are great musicians out there and songwriters in every town."

One of Montana's most loved bands happens to be the band who must also hold the record for longevity: the Big Sky Mudflaps have been at

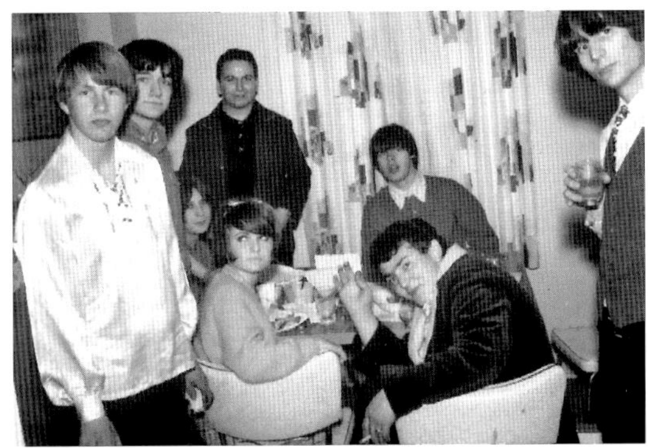

Left: The Wanderers, "with Chan Romero and Kostas right after the recording session for 'Don't Pity Me.'" *Courtesy of David Day.*

Below: The Big Sky Mudflaps have been entertaining audiences all over the United States for more than forty years. *From left to right*: Maureen Powell, Bob Packwood, Chuck Florence, David Horgan, Beth Lo, Rich Brinkman. Chuck Florence, photographer. *Courtesy of David Horgan.*

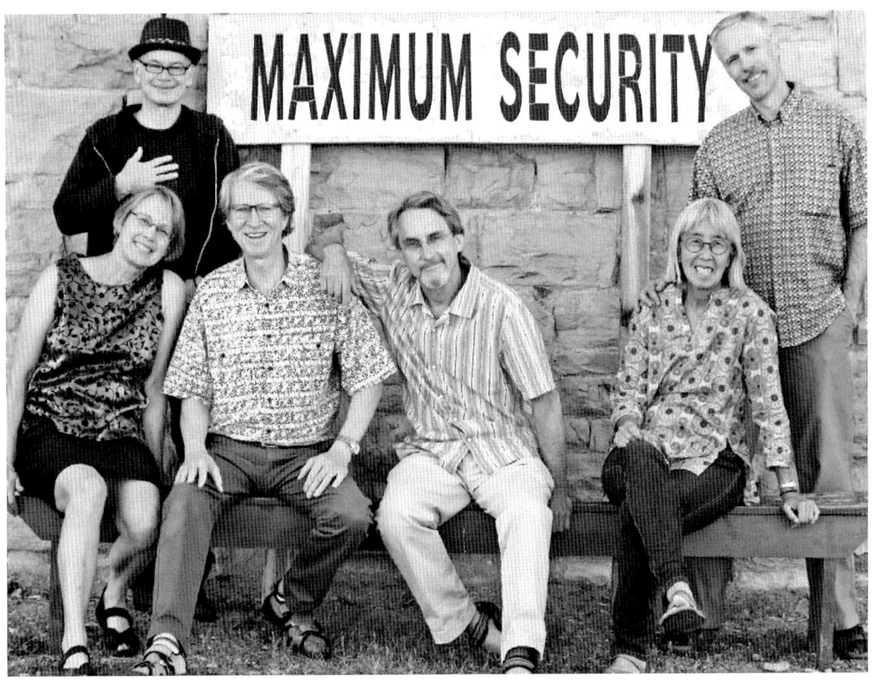

the forefront of Montana's music scene since 1975, and forty years later, they're still going strong. Although they have long been associated with Missoula, the various members actually came together in Hamilton, which in 1975 was still a sleepy logging and ranch town at the southern end of the Bitterroot Valley. David Horgan, guitarist for the band, explained how Montana offered an attractive environment for artists and musicians back in the '70s. "A lot of people from that era will tell you that western Montana had something, something about the region that made it really easy to try something different. There was a very laid-back, welcoming atmosphere that was a real contrast to what was going on in the Bay area, for example, where I came from."

Horgan recalled how, following the turbulent and epochal years of the '60s, the music scene in the Bay Area had become stagnant for bands interested in something other than "big hair" and "proto-disco." The post–Grateful Dead scene had become a fallow field in contrast to the earlier fertile era that had also produced the Jefferson Airplane, Big Brother and the Holding Company, as well as dozens of other memorable Bay Area bands.

Montana, especially Missoula and environs, by 1975 had gained a reputation as a haven for creative people fleeing places or scenes elsewhere that they felt were becoming somewhat stultified or predictable. The Mission Mountain Wood Band offered a good indication of how simple and relaxed things were in Montana: there was the customary long hair and the odor of marijuana smoke, but the folks in these crowds drove pick-up trucks with gun racks and they were likely to have cow dung on their boot heels. "In general, there was just a pervading sense of freedom about everything," Horgan explained. "Not just musically, but in terms of art and literature, too. People felt free to try anything, and there was community support for it."

The core of the original band consisted of a pair of couples—David Horgan and his partner, Beth Lo (who plays bass), and Maureen Powell (who shared bass duties) and her husband, Steve Powell (on piano). Michael Lea played drums, and Dexter Payne manned the saxophone. Eclectic in their tastes, the band played whatever struck their fancy, but the central aim in their arrangements was to produce a sound that was danceable. Listening to the early albums, one hears the definitive influence of classic American jazz, especially the swing jazz paragons such as Charlie Parker and Count Basie. The band played several shows without a name, but it was clear from the exuberant response they got that the band had staying power. Paul Stanton (of Duckboy postcard fame) took the band aside after a Missoula show and told them that he had the perfect name for them: the Big Sky Mudflaps. "Half the pick-up trucks in the state will do your advertising for you," he wisely promised. Surely their moniker is among the most fitting band names ever, especially for a jazzy Americana band from the Treasure State.

The band soon expanded their stage presence from rural western Montana and Missoula to bigger venues to the west in Spokane and Seattle. They meanwhile honed their signature sound, distilling their potent brand of swing from a carefully steeped mash of roots music: hot jazz, country and western, rhythm and blues. There were traces, too, of rockabilly and old-time southern

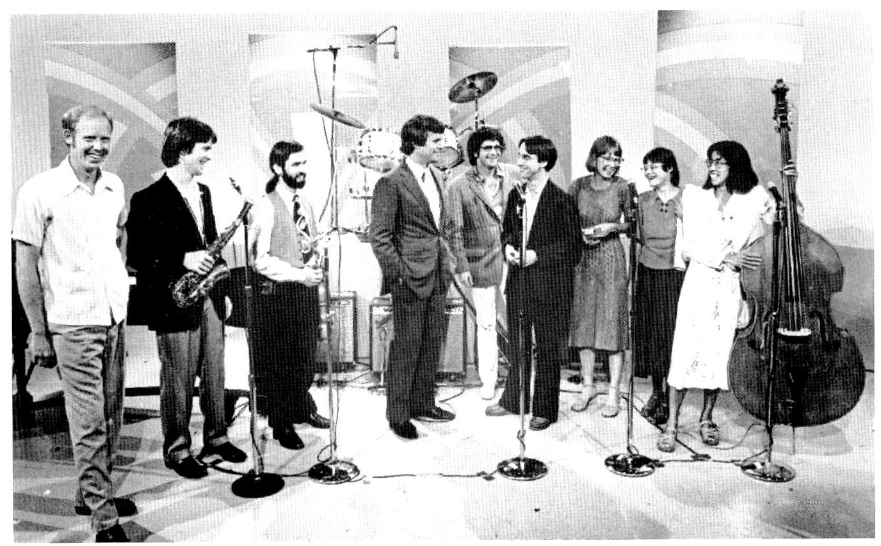

In the 1980s, the Big Sky Mudflaps played all over the country, including a few stints on NBC's *The Today Show*. *Photo by Jim Roderick, courtesy of David Horgan.*

country—the band routinely covers Hank Williams, for example.

The release of their debut album, *Armchair Cabaret* (1979), gave the band well-deserved national exposure, leading to a few live appearances on NBC's *Today Show* in the early 1980s. They also became favorites on National Public Radio's *Prairie Home Companion*, led by host Garrison Keillor, which has become a veritable showcase of Americana and roots music. A second album followed in 1983—*Sensible Shoes*—released on the seminal American label Flying Fish Records and singled out by *Billboard* magazine as one of that year's most "notable records." By 1984, the band was frequently touring the country, playing both coasts and gathering enthusiastic reviews in newspapers and magazines, including *Esquire*, the *Village Voice* and the *Los Angeles Times*. That year, however, saxophonist Dexter Payne left the band. His replacement was Chuck Florence, who, with only thirty-two years of playing with the Mudflaps under his belt, still calls himself "the new guy in the band."

All the members of the Mudflaps are accomplished and proficient musicians positively oozing with serious, professional talent. Adding to their aura, they have achieved impressive success alongside having accomplished careers as professors and teachers and artists in other media entirely. Beth Lo, for example, is a nationally known ceramicist and longtime art professor at the University of Montana. Most of the band members devote time to other musical projects on top of their commitment to the Big Sky Mudflaps. Horgan and Lo, for instance, front a straight-ahead western swing outfit called Western Union, as well as a salsa band called Salsa Loca. As with the Mudflaps, Horgan and Lo bring an enviable level of authenticity and high-caliber musicianship to Salsa Loca—so much so, in fact, that not long ago a disc jockey from a radio station in Colombia called Horgan up for an interview—their CD had been at number one on the playlist in the Central American country for weeks! "This fellow had no idea we were a bunch of gringos from up in Montana," Horgan said, laughing. "But that's an example of the feeling about this place I am trying to express: you can play any kind of music in Montana and get an audience." Of course, it helps tremendously to possess the sort of talent that allows them to play a variety of styles convincingly and authentically. To see the Big Sky Mudflaps perform makes it obvious that they feel quite at home in a number of Americana forms, and seasoned musicians all over the state envy their easy versatility on stage.

Another Montanan versed in western swing, Wylie Gustafson (born in Conrad, Montana, in 1961), achieved renown as the voice behind the famous "Yahoo!" yodel. He has toured all over the country with his band the Wild West, including performances on the *Grand Ole Opry*, the National Folk Festival and the *Conan O'Brien Show*. Although he now calls eastern Washington home, he has long been a legendary part of Montana western music, having released more than twenty albums of yodeling and western music. Baxter Black, probably the most famous cowboy poet since Curley Fletcher, offered high praise in *True West* magazine when, after witnessing a performance of Wylie and the Wild West at the 2010 Monterey Cowboy Poetry and Music Festival, remarked that the band had "changed the water level in the 'cowboy entertainment aquarium.'" Gustafson has also recorded an album with Great Falls poet Paul Zarzyski, including the song "Hang-n-Rattle," which earned them a Spur Award in 2010 from Western Writers of America.

The cowboy life attracts many songwriters and musicians to Montana, including Martha Scanlan. Scanlan might be alone among living American songwriters who can say that one of the country's greatest living writers has named a novel after one of her songs: Joyce Carol Oates named her 2009 novel *Little Bird of Heaven* after Martha Scanlan's song of the same name.

In the early 1990s, Martha was a shy young woman up from Wyoming who started playing folk and bluegrass guitar with local musicians in Missoula at house parties and jam circles around town. Occasionally, she'd

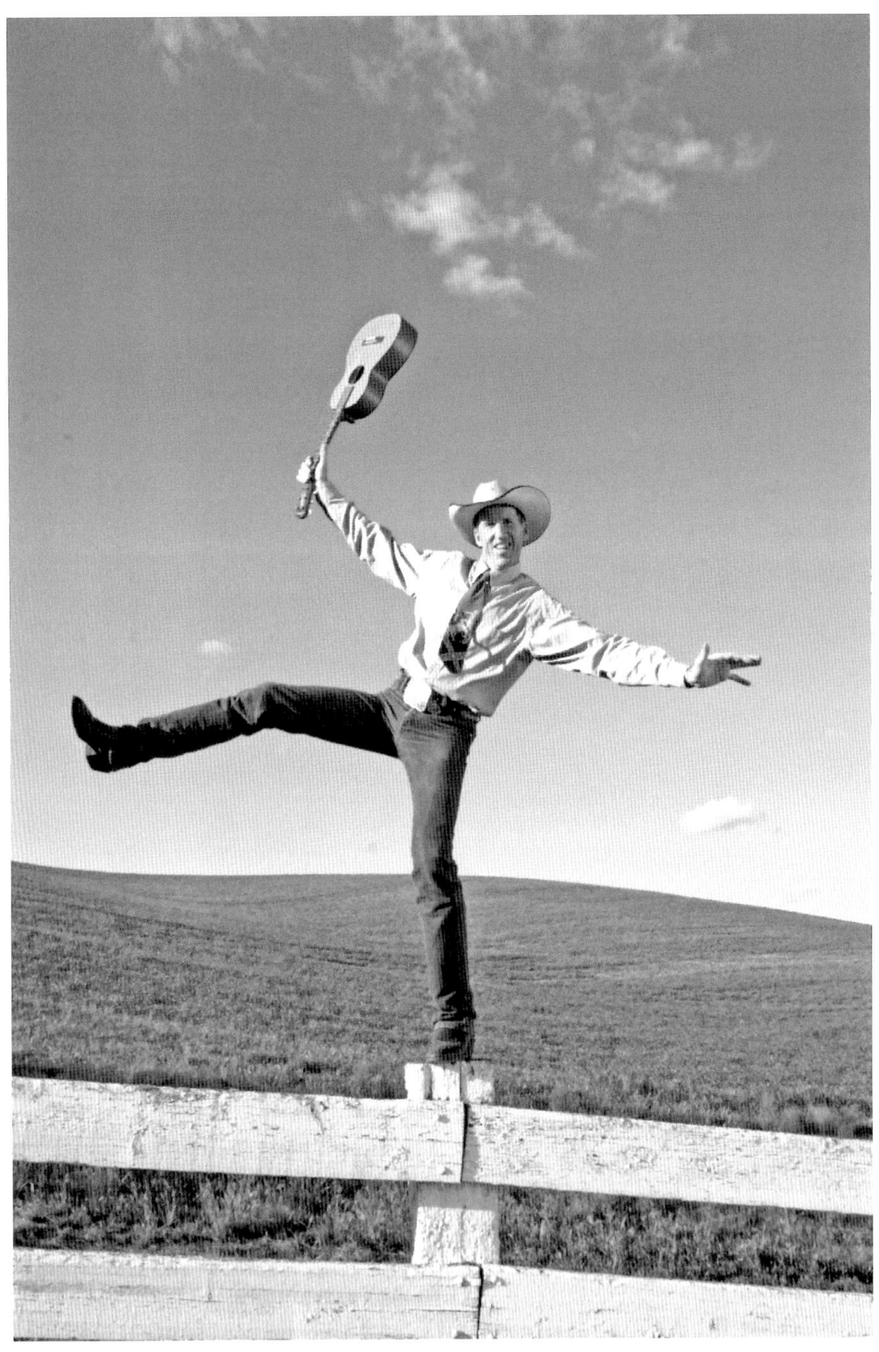

Wylie Gustafson of Wylie and the Wild West. *Photo by Bill Watts (CC BY-SA 3.0).*

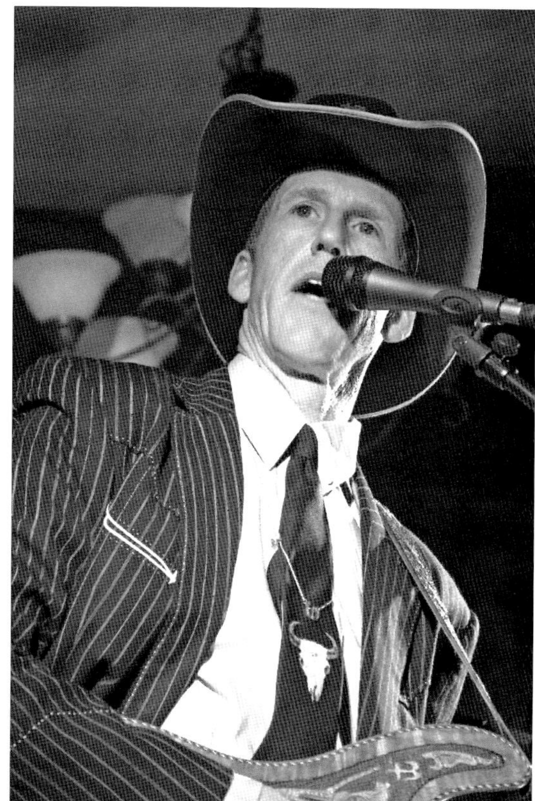

Right: Wylie Gustafson of "Yahoo!" yodel fame. *Photo by Jeri L. Dobrowski (CC BY-SA 3.0).*

Below: When she is not recording or performing, Martha Scanlan spends her time on a cattle ranch on the Tongue River in eastern Montana. *Photo by Yogesh Simpson, courtesy of Martha Scanlan.*

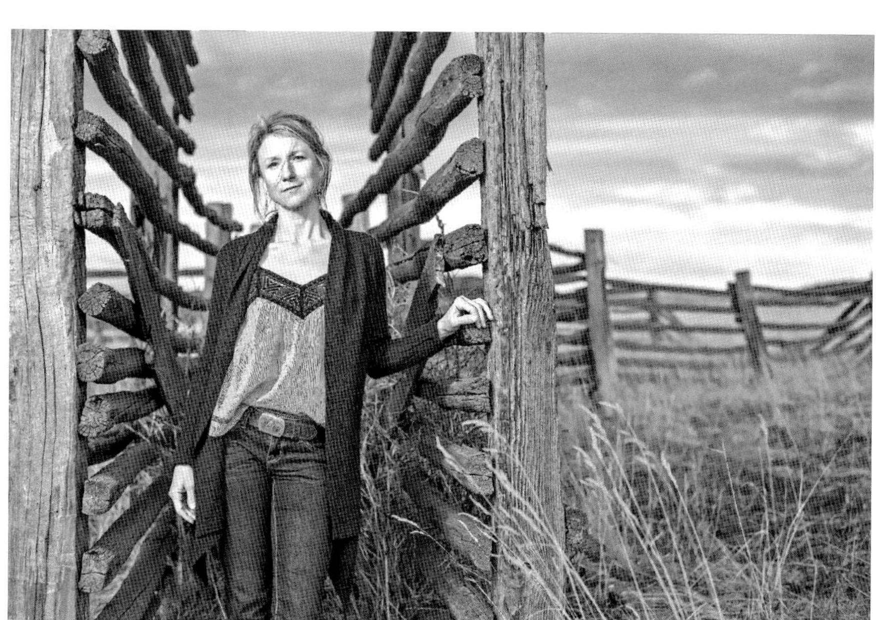

belt out a song in a plaintive, high voice reminiscent of Ola Belle Reed or Hazel Dickens. Originally from Minnesota, Scanlan had come west in 1990 to attend the University of Montana. Her family had ties to the state and would visit often when she was a child, and so after high school, UM was a natural choice.

Not long after arriving, she crossed paths with another bluegrass and old-time music fan named Thomas Sneed. He, too, was a neophyte among the seasoned musicians of Missoula, but he had engaging enthusiasm, a big, charismatic smile and a certain fearlessness when it came to learning tunes.

Before long, Thomas and Martha were playing music together every chance they got. Eventually, they decided to move to the South in 1997—to Johnson City, Tennessee—to search out the sounds they loved at the source. Johnson City happens to be just down the road from a town called Bristol, which figures prominently in the history of Americana music because many seminal Americana recordings had been made there in the 1920s, when Ralph Peer set up shop in the little Appalachian town. It sat right on the border of Tennessee and Virginia, with one of its main streets doubling as the state line. Peer temporarily recorded in Bristol on a two-month recording trip through the south for the Victor Talking Machine Company in 1927. It was in Bristol that he immortalized both the Carter Family and Jimmie Rodgers, initiating what many critics consider "the Big Bang" of country music, the original spark that gave birth to vast galaxy of Americana music so popular today in myriad forms.

The two of them got jobs—Thomas, in fact, found a position at the Archive of Appalachia—and began playing music in earnest with locals, frequenting the ubiquitous festivals and picking parties that compose the old-time music scene in southern Appalachia. Before long, the couple had connected with another pair of musicians who loved the music, a fiddler named Heidi Andrade and her husband, Roy Andrade, who played the banjo. They were joined later by bass player Brandon Story, from Bristol, Tennessee.

In short order, the four of them formed one of the most popular old-time bands on the eastern bluegrass festival circuit, the Reeltime Travelers. Their first record offered some genuine, heartfelt renditions of some classic gems in the old-time repertoire—"Twin Sisters," for example, and "Lonesome John." Their second album, *Living Reeltime, Thinkin' Oldtime* (2004), produced by Bob Carlin, also had respectable renditions of classic old-time tunes like "Elzic's Farewell" but, more importantly, featured a few originals that Martha had written and that had taken top honors in the songwriting contest that year at Merlefest in Wilkesboro, North Carolina. The Reeltime Travelers were soon on par with the Freight Hoppers and the Heartbeats, two other enormously popular old-time bands on the bluegrass circuit. Being one of the featured bands on the T-Bone Burnett–produced soundtrack to the film *Cold Mountain* (2005) really put them on the musical map.

Sneed's basic but rhythmic chops on mandolin worked especially well alongside Martha's driving country guitar, providing the perfect rhythm section for the core of any old-time band's sound: the fiddle and banjo, played by Roy and Heidi Andrade. None of them was an especially hotshot musician, but then old-time music doesn't deal in "hot licks" and bank on virtuoso picking performances the way bluegrass bands do. What counts most is an authentic delivery, and these kids had it. More importantly, they had a kind of relaxed, unaffected casualness to their sound, as if they really were having a great time picking in the backyard. And Martha Scanlan's sweet, melodious voice did hook your ear, and she was a fine songwriter.

The band performed all over the country on the festival circuit for several years. When the band eventually dissolved after the success of their contribution to *Cold Mountain* and the players all went their separate ways in 2005, Scanlan struck off on her own, dividing her time, when she was not touring, between a cabin on the border of Tennessee and North Carolina and a small cabin in the Tongue River Valley of eastern Montana. Being on the *Cold Mountain* tour in the company of Dirk Powell and Amy Helm and Olabelle exposed her to all kinds of music—old gospel, Irish ballads and strains of old-time and Americana that cross-pollinated with the old country and Dylan and Van Morrison she had grown up with. She began to focus more honing her songs and developing a distinct, Americana voice out of her experience in old-time music and her love for old-school country.

Her musical journey after the Reeltime Travelers culminated in an album of original songs called *Tongue River Stories* (2011). Her debut effort, *The West Was Burning* (2006), had also been a critical success, featuring the collaborative efforts of Levon Helm of the Band (as well as his daughter, Amy Helm) and others. But with *Tongue River Stories*, Scanlan wove together several threads of distinctly regional influence into a rich tapestry of distinctly Montana Americana. It's especially interesting that in composing the material, she spent her time working and writing in one of the most out-of-the-way regions of the state, far from the predictable allure of Missoula or Bozeman. Instead, Scanlan immersed herself in the desolate beauty of the eastern part of the state, with a population density, like its winter temperatures, hovering not far above zero.

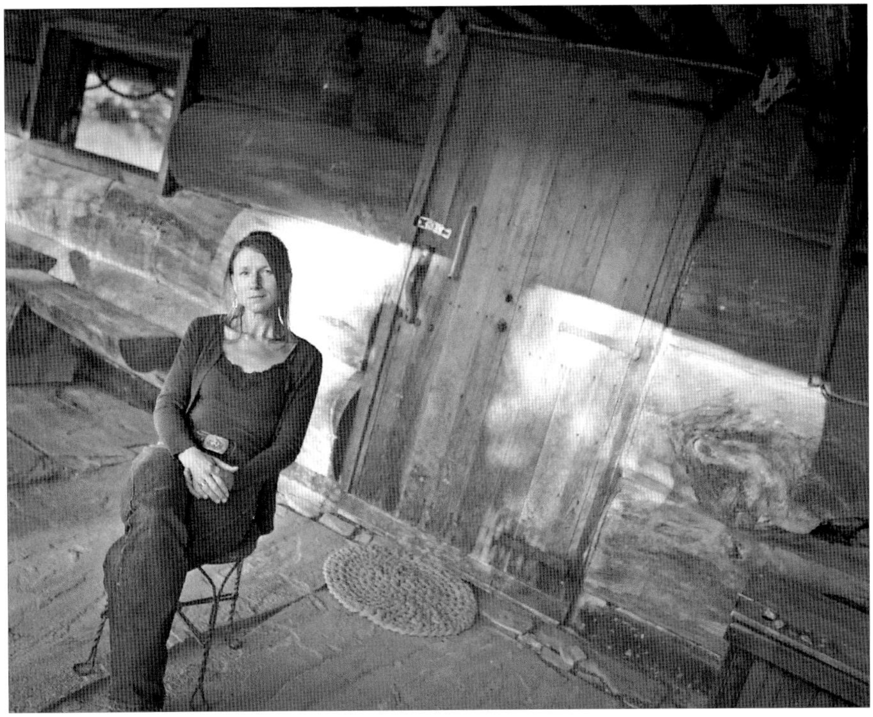

Martha Scanlan started her career in the seminal band the Reeltime Travelers. After winning the prestigious Chris Austin Songwriting Contest at Merlefest in Wilkesboro, North Carolina, in 2004, she began to devote her attention to songwriting full time. *Photo by Dawson Dunning, courtesy of Martha Scanlan.*

"All the songs on *Tongue River Stories* were written in Montana," Scanlan said. "In fact, the very first song I ever wrote—"Up on the Divide" [featured on *The West Was Burning*]—I wrote on that very ranch in the Tongue River Valley." Scanlan chooses her words carefully in trying to articulate the connection in her mind between what she writes and the overly broad category of "Americana." In the end, it comes down to an intimate association between the music and place. "In my mind, it seems that what makes the sort of Americana I am drawn to—starting with the old Appalachian tradition—is a connection between the people who play the music and the landscape they inhabit. Montana does that for me like no other place."

In fact, she sees the development of old-time and country music in Montana as in part a function of the history of people migrating into the Northwest from the southern region of the country—many of them to become cowboys and ranchers. "All over Montana there persists this sort of

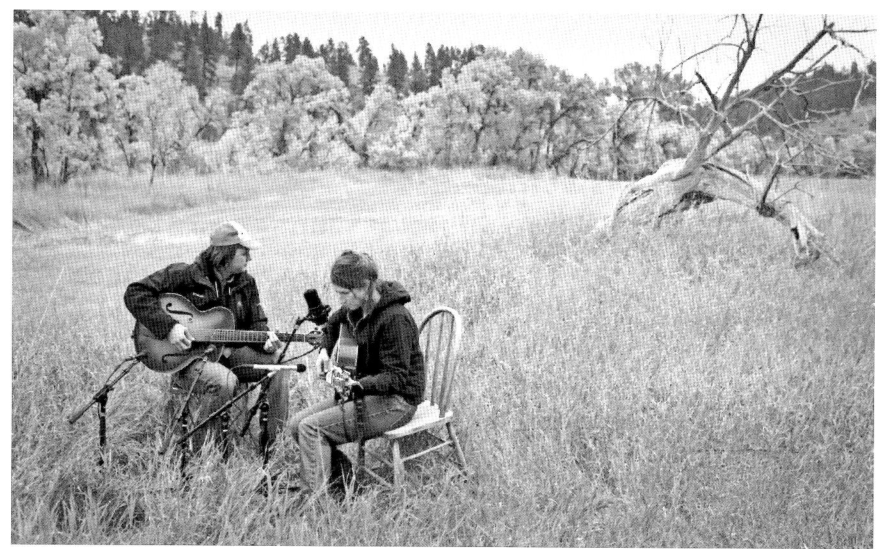

Martha Scanlan with Portland musician Jon Neufeld recording her song "The Meadow" in a meadow near the Tongue River, featured on *Tongue River Stories*. *Photo by Yogesh Simpson, courtesy of Martha Scanlan.*

'Cowboy Way,'" she said, "and with it, these subtle southernisms, for the lack of a better word." One example she gives is the way older ranch people in her community speak of their grandparents as "Mr. So-and-so" and "Mrs. So-and-so" rather than by the more informal "Grandma" or "Grandpa." Part of that social style does seem to echo the ingrained politeness that is still a part of southern culture and, though it is fading, remains more vibrant there than in many other parts of the country.

Martha Scanlan's sense of music inhabiting the landscape in which it was conceived is not, at least for her, an idle exercise in imagination. She actually recorded the songs she wrote in the very environment in which she wrote them. The songs from *Tongue River Stories*, including the haunting song "Guardian Angel," were literally recorded in the Tongue River country. "The Meadow" was recorded in a meadow ten miles up a creek from the ranch she works on, a meadow where she helps wean calves in the fall. "The films are the recordings," she explained. "What you hear on the video is the song as it was being recorded live." The results are astounding in their quality and clarity but even more so in the palpable connection to place that Scanlan stresses is so integral to the music she makes.

As with *Tongue River Stories*, her most recent album, *The Shape of Things Gone Missing, the Shape of Things to Come* (2015), arose out of time spent on an 120-year-old cattle ranch along a stretch of that same Tongue River. As Scanlan explained, "There's a beautiful congruence in music and working with cattle and horses—it's all about the flow, finding the current in things. I was curious about how that would translate in the studio, how the landscape would come through."

Quite often, Scanlan's lyrics rise to the level of poetry, so vivid are the scenes she evokes, especially on *Tongue River Stories*. Consider the opening lines of "The Meadow," for example:

Golden days up in the meadow
Autumn bright and border trees
Morning days, do you remember?
Horse's breath and horses feet…
(© 2011 Martha Scanlan, ASCAP)

Similarly, in "Guardian Angel," Scanlan condensed a wide range of images and emotions into a few lines, evoking a mood that at once captures homesickness and heartbreak and the immensity of the vast Missouri watershed carving its way through Montana:

Forty miles down this red dirt road
Forty flying geese
A ragged V crying "broken" and "broken"
Cross the broken breaks of the old Missouri
Forty-one days and your letter still burns…
Take my fear and transgressions
Take my love and grace
Take my two-faced guardian angel and go
Set her back up in her place.
(© 2011 Martha Scanlan, ASCAP)

Martha spends part of the year touring and showcasing new material created for her latest record, but when she's not doing that, she's working cattle and riding fence in one of the most remote regions of the West. Her intimate connection to the unparalleled beauty and lonesomeness of valley in the southeastern part of Montana, far removed from the rest of the country—and, for that matter, from the rest of Montana—furnishes the inspiration for and the substance of her art.

One of the most prolific and poetic songwriters in Montana right now is a fellow you almost certainly have never heard of, unless you haunt the more obscure alleyways of Soundcloud and Bandcamp on the Internet. His name is Cameron Boster—born in 1990 in Helena, Montana—and he has written and recorded more than 250 songs, almost every one of them a brilliant snapshot of life and the complex emotions it triggers as a matter of course. Each one of his songs also happens to epitomize an Americana sound that many would say reflects an approach inarguably influenced by having spent his formative years in Montana. For one thing, he makes his own recordings, relying almost entirely on unsophisticated equipment and simple, low-fi techniques.

The results are catchy and often haunting tunes tastefully embellished with harmony lines he sings himself. The lyrics are evocative and unforgettable aural paintings—vignettes of American life, mostly rural panoramas that cast a bemused eye on love and culture in the West.

Curiously, Boster almost never plays out live, which is unusual for any committed musician but especially for one in the Americana vein, where performance is an integral part of the connection to the audience. It's not

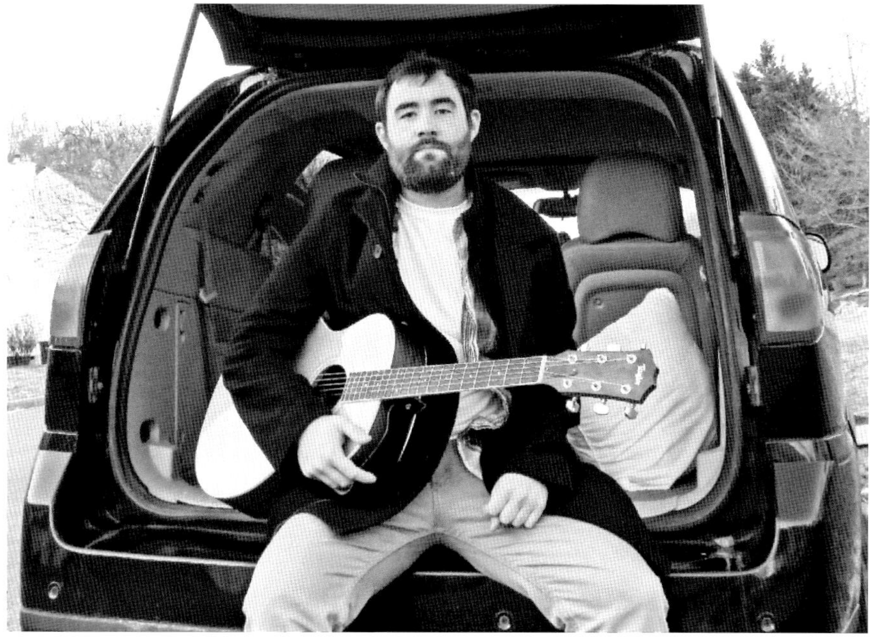

Songwriter Cameron Boster has recorded hundreds of masterfully crafted original songs ranging from haunting and heartbreaking to humorous and quirky. He epitomizes the do-it-yourself approach that has revolutionized the way original music is being produced and presented to the public. Photographer unknown. *Courtesy of Cameron Boster.*

that he actively avoids the stage; it's mainly the result of his focus on other things—finishing up a degree in law at the College of William and Mary, for example. But there's also a philosophical element involved in his approach to producing music. He also seems to be following in the footsteps of other great Americana musicians—J.J. Cale leaps immediately to mind—who approach songwriting as a craft akin to sculpture, and what matters most is the artifact that results: the song itself. "I don't put out the majority of stuff I've done," Boster said. "A lot of tracks are sitting in folders on laptops I don't even use any more. My approach is not quantity of quality. It's more like quality through quantity."

Boster takes the view that, over the long run, making a lot of songs will yield higher quality music than, say, spending months perfecting a single track. But that formula only works if you have some talent to begin with, and we all know that even professional production with its bag of cosmetic tricks cannot save the worst artists. By contrast, Boster balances undeniable raw talent with a sort of understated humility and respect for crafting soulful, writerly music.

When asked about his influences, Boster is voluminous in his praise for an impressive panoply of artists ranging from the Beatles to Glen Campbell, but the central core of what he loves is rootsy, singer-songwriter kind of material—John Prine, for example, who tops his list of great writers.

Boster started cultivating his musical tastes and talents at an early age. "I was a radio junky," he explained. "My favorite station in Helena was an AM oldies station. I tried to have it on in the car, in my room, everywhere. I even had a transistor radio that I took to Spring Meadow Lake, and I listened to it while I read or napped. That station had Beatles' Wednesdays, which I lived for—I waited all day to hear "Magical Mystery Tour," which was my favorite song then. There is a lot of melodic juice in that tune, and it still makes my ears happy."

As a result, the cumulative influence of all he's absorbed is actually a point of passion. "Essentially what I do is play only the music I've learned, and I learned it from listening to 'roots.' But I'm not consciously trying to derive or develop anything. It's like I put all the 'roots' into the hopper of a modern life and couldn't help what shook out the other end. I think that qualifies as Americana."

Boster reflects that probably the definitive Americana record is Tom Waits's epic *Nighthawks at the Diner* (1975). "It might draw on jazz for its 'roots,' as opposed to 'country,' but that whole album is an hour of brilliant musicality expanding on simple American symbols: coffee, diners, waitresses, weather, narcotics, family. I don't think he missed anything symbolically American in that album." *Nighthawks at the Diner* does seem to capture sonically and lyrically the same lonely, sordid side of the American landscape that Edward Hopper had captured in his oil painting of the same title in 1942. It's a wistful, almost forlorn view of American life that Boster himself is adept at swiping glimpses of. Consider for example the lyrical still-life he presents in his song "House on the River":

Cold winter is gone, and the house is empty.
Nobody to bring a comfort to.
But I've got my guitar and an empty parlor—
I'll sit on the cold wooden boards.
In your house on the river, you leave when the summer ends.
You say goodbye on the ice.
You're my oldest friend. [...]

Don't know when I'll go back to Virginia.
It's colder riding on the rails.
For now I'm fine walking through the backyard,
Finding wood to gather for a fire.

In your house on the river, you leave when the summer ends.
You say goodbye on the ice.
You're my oldest friend.
(© 2014 Cameron Boster)

Similarly, in "Old St. Paul," he spins a yarn of love lost that is both bitter and sorry and funny at the same time, achieving a pathos that is hard to find outside the masters—Tom Waits, Bob Dylan, Paul Siebel:

Sittin' in the corner with a gallon of tears,
I had a gal on my arm for a couple of years.
She smelled like smoke and she spoke so clean—
But sometimes I like it when they're dirty and mean.
She slept on the bed and I slept on the floor
and she gave me the eye and I showed her the door.
I don't know her name I didn't like her at all,
but that's the way it goes in Old St. Paul.

One day I'm gonna live on a boat on the river
Doin' chores on the boat and puttin' sores on my liver
Screaming at the women and the children on the shore
Where the water rings and the fire roars,
Going through the valley looking up at the stars,
By the bridge and the snow and the road and the cars,
If you want a ride just give me a call—
We'll both head right on through Old St. Paul.
(© 2014 Cameron Boster)

Throughout his often deep and philosophical musical analyses, however, Boster never loses sight of the intensely personal experience that music provides. "I think, to put it more poetically, Americana is a kind of music that affects a certain sort of person. I think we all have an image of that person in our minds—the simple appreciator, the rustic, the person in which the rivers of feeling run deep." Boster contrasts that ideal listener with a perhaps even more ubiquitous type of listener, one with whom performing musicians are constantly having to contend, a sort Boster identifies as having music "bounce off their big, insensitive Greek-life foreheads."

He pointed out that, in a way, we all use musical taste as a litmus test for romance and that we tend to have superficial friendships with people with whom we have little musical common ground. "In many of my ill-fated romances, not caring about this sound—'Americana' if you want to call it that—was a bad sign. And my best friendships, and the trysts I do remember fondly, were with people who react to this music the same way I do: a kind of dazed paralysis, inner seizing, mental relaxation, a desire to think over your entire life, sometimes with sadness."

The sheer volume of Boster's musical output reflects an immersive approach he traces to earliest childhood. "I was a compulsive listener. A real addict. I think my parents would confirm this. Nothing else interested me more than the act of listening. Pure listening, too: focusing on the changes and relationships, words and so on." And then a family friend made him a tape of favorite Dylan songs. That marked a seminal moment in his development. As he put it, "I remember some music critic once described 'Like a Rolling Stone' as a sound that 'kicked a door open in their mind.' Well, I still remember exactly what I told a friend when I listened to Dylan for the first time. I said, 'Holy shit! This is what I've been looking for all along.' It's pretty surprising how easy it is to avoid Bob Dylan, especially if listening to the radio is your main source for music."

Later discoveries included the band Iron and Wine and Sufjan Stevens. "I went home and tried to copy some basic stuff from Sufjan on the banjo. But as you know, the banjo has a remarkable propensity to sound like shit. So I stopped doing that." Instead, he turned to a cheap, old guitar he found hiding in his mother's upstairs closet.

> *The first day, I listened to "Naked as We Came" by Iron and Wine. I got the fingering down and the picking in about three hours and could do a decent imitation. People have doubted this story because the music sounds so complex, but if you have musical intuition and you know how simple the chords and fingering actually are, it's not that impressive or surprising. But I was impressed and surprised at how simple it was, and I realized at that moment that every damned song was now within my reach—Dylan, every old country song, anything—I could now be that, I could do that.*

By this time, the family had relocated from Helena, Montana, to the country in North Dakota. Boster became obsessed with learning songs. "I took that guitar and practiced playing and singing outside, on someone's property in North Dakota. I played under this big tree on the edge of a field and at the edge of a small cut bank by a creek that ran outside of town and at the ruins of some burned down brick house by that creek."

Boster started writing songs of his own when he went off to college (where he took a degree in philosophy) but feels that only recently has his writing reached maturity. He admitted that an early motivation for playing (and writing) was to "show off to women," but growing up has revealed more meaningful reasons for his art: "Lately, as I've bumbled over quarter-life with drinking too much and compensating for uncertainty, I've found that singing and writing is a fundamentally pure act. So I've steered away from music as a means to an uncomfortable end and tried to focus on the craft." For a man who is all of twenty-four, that's a remarkable insight to at which to have so casually arrived, especially when a visit to nearly any live music venue often reveals how many older and (one would think) wiser musicians continue to perform music primarily as a way to impress the opposite sex.

Boster feels an intimate connection to his formative years in Montana and the way it shaped his approach to songwriting. "John Steinbeck said that Montana was his favorite state, and I know why: It's got spiritual magic, man. That magic lives in the best landscape in the world and fills its natives with unusual vigor."

Boster even gets a little wistful and glossy-eyed in describing his sense of being a part of that singular landscape: "Once, after we had moved to North Dakota, my family returned to Montana for a funeral. On the road between Helena and Townsend, on a bright dewy morning that made the mountains really shine, my dad said without prompting, 'This is where I'm from. This is where we're from.'" While he acknowledged that probably everyone feels pride in being from wherever it is they happen to be from, he argued that "Montanans are especially stricken by this emotion."

Boster admitted that he's similarly affected by the same subtle chauvinism about where he's from. "When I think about who I am, I think in terms of my identity as a mountain person. Who else can say they've grown up with those mountains in the distance, around an unusual concentration of sincerely passionate, insane Montanans?" It's inevitable that where you live and the culture you grow up with will have an impact on what you end up doing with your life, but it isn't always easy to analyze who exactly all that factors out. "My music is going to be filled with an unavoidable Montana quality, because I am a Montanan," he agreed. "But I can't judge what it is. Maybe a willingness to say things directly. Maybe a 'playful' rudeness, too. There's going to be a lot of definitional crossfire when you try to sort out the difference between the questions, 'What extent do people and their creative acts define a place?' and 'To what extent does a place define a person?'"

Unlike a lot of musicians or philosophers, Boster is adept at providing examples for what he tries to express. "This summer I was at the General Mercantile [in Helena] enjoying a damned good cup of coffee prepared by a woman behind that wooden bar," he said. "I don't remember how we started on the subject of art, but we got there, and she pulled out her phone to show me the things she made. Her mode of creation was to go into nature, the deep backwoods, and construct little things out of sticks, leaves, ice, ferns and berries; take a picture of it; and then walk away." He smiled in re-creating the image. "Obviously, it's ironic," he said, "because what she's doing is perhaps the most basic, natural, land-oriented form of creation possible, but the only way to preserve it is through the most modern, soul-threatening object in our lives: the cellphone camera." He immediately saw the similarity between what she was doing creating art in the woods out of actual bits of nature and his own method of songwriting: his songs are simple, rustic and basic and preserved only by hyper-modern, instant distribution platforms like Soundcloud and Bandcamp.

By putting his music out in the world on these platforms almost exclusively, Boster represents and embodies what will strike older generations as a completely new type of musical artist—a type that the mainstream listening public and the industry itself has not fully come to comprehend. The people making it happen refer to it as DIY, as in "do it yourself." As Boster put it, "These platforms actually represent a fundamental shift in music culture," the upshot of which is that "anybody can be heard by anyone, anywhere, instantly." And what's more, the sonic quality of these uploads is often indistinguishable from what twenty or thirty years ago would have taken an army of studio engineers to accomplish. And it helps that low-fi is the new hi-fi—Neil Young, in fact, recorded a recent album on a Dictaphone!

The DIY approach accords perfectly with Boster's sense of what Montana, defined by its remoteness and rural sensibility, amounts to in practice: "I thought the similarity between her mode of artistic expression and my own was more than coincidental. Perhaps, being Montanan and feeling like we have a unique right to the emptiness, seclusion and beauty of the land we live on, we try to keep our music and art basic."

Keeping it "basic" refers not to the technical elements of composition in either case but rather to the usually complex features of connecting art or music to a venue or network of distribution. Boster theorized that perhaps being from and living in Montana has a profound effect in this regard as well. "If you think about it, there's a lot of self-diminution in both our approaches—she creating where nobody else can see, with no effort to commercialize or distribute the results…I creating in the privacy of my room, with no effort or desire to commercialize and distribute the results."

He also speculated that perhaps living in Montana itself minimizes the impulse to broadcast or show off. "If you live in Montana, you know what real expansive, explosive, vast beauty looks like," he observed. "Knowing that might cause you to abandon any hope of being as significant or important. When I was in Montana this summer, I was always thinking that I could do anything for a living and be happy as long as I could do it there. Sort of surrender my own goals and identity, just to be in a place."

In fact, he connected his almost surreptitious mode of delivering his music to a public hungry for a "new sound" to the effect Montana has on the psyche: "Knowing a place like [Montana] exists, and planning to go back there, has got to be responsible for my lack of motivation for pushing my creativity on the public. The Montanans I imagine don't need to have a damned thing pushed on them—they'll find it on their own, at community concerts or on their own time. I feel that if I meet them on those terms—if I just play for the sake of playing—those people, whose attitudes I respect, will respect me in return."

In the past, Montana has hardly ever been perceived by the rest of the country as having a particularly attractive music "scene," outside the bluegrass or old-time fiddle world. Its sparse population is a tough sell, in spite of two vibrant college towns, and the more ambitious musicians in search of stardom invariably end up in Seattle or Los Angeles. The Internet may change all of that, and the sheer number of promising songwriters who call Montana home bodes well for a vibrant musical future. To take one example, Christy Hays, an Austin musician who also makes her home in Butte part of the year, put out an album in 2014 called *O' Montana*, which contains several songs that reference in an indirect way the tension between yearning for a place with wide open spaces and the reality of having a job in another part of the country:

> *O' Montana, with your blues eyes so wild.*
> *The sage along the fences, the eyes of a child.*
> *O'Montana where my dreams go to rest.*
> *The sun is a gift, so even and deft.*
> *(© Christy Hays 2014)*

The title track thus captures an intimate view of the state from an outsider's perspective and reveals the powerful resonance between the idea of Montana as a place and some of the perennial themes of Americana music, including the notion that the West has always represented the promise of unspoiled land and new opportunity.

Chapter 4

"Music Is a Reverberation of Sunlight"

Native Americana in Montana

The first people to ever play music in Montana were Indians because the first people to inhabit the region now called "Montana" were Indians.* Although today Montana is more than 90 percent white, Indians account for the largest minority group (at 7 percent), and the state is home to seven reservations and a dozen tribes. In fact, evidence of the presence of aboriginal people in Montana dates back at least twelve thousand years, and the oldest human remains in North America are found in Montana. It so happens that some of the most important scholarship on Indian ethnomusicology has been done in Montana, including Alan P. Merriam's *Ethnomusicology of the Flathead Indians* (1967) and Bruno Nettl's *Blackfoot Musical Thought* (1989).

The two main traditional instruments of indigenous people were the drum and flute, although many other percussion instruments figured in Indian music as well. While most non-Indian audiences in Montana have heard the sound of powwow drumming, few are aware of its complex "system of sound and structure worthy of comparison with the classical European tradition," as Nettl put it, or know that such musical forms often have a religious or sacred dimension of meaning that does not have an obvious Western counterpart. It also makes little sense to talk of "Indian" music or

* While there are many terms in popular use today, including "First Peoples," "Native American" and so forth, literature put out by the Office of Public Instruction in Montana as part of the constitutionally mandated Indian Education for All makes clear that in Montana at least, the term that indigenous people prefer is simply "Indian."

culture monolithically, as what makes sense for one tribe may not apply to another, in the same way that to speak broadly of "European" music would unhelpfully obscure the obvious difference between Italian opera and, say, Klezmer music.

Indian music and culture have exerted important influence on the development of Americana music, although this influence is not always obvious or apparent. In fact, Nettl has noted "an absence of a repertory that makes substantial use of the stylistic elements of both Western and Indian music." At the same time, some of this country's most famous and influential Americana musicians claimed Indian ancestry. The universally acknowledged patron saint of country and western music, Hank Williams, for example, claimed Cree and Cherokee ancestry. Other famous Native American musicians who play in genres that fall under the umbrella of "Americana" include Buffy Sainte-Marie (Cree), Buddy Red Bow (Lakota), Floyd Red Crow Westerman (Dakota) and Gary Small (Northern Cheyenne).

In the 2009 work *American Indian Music: More than Just Flutes and Drums (A Guide to American Indian Music)*, author Scott Prinzing acknowledged that "without a doubt, the most widely disseminated genre of American Indian music is the powwow drum group. Growing from traditional tribal dances and feasts, the powwow has become a pan-Indian mainstay all across Indian country that finds dancers and drum groups from tribes all over North America coming together." He noted that at least two Montana powwow drum groups have been nominated for Grammy awards (as well as "Nammys," the prizes awarded at the Native American Music Awards): Black Lodge (Blackfeet) and the Northern Cree Singers (Cree).

But as Prinzing's title suggests, modern Indian music contains dimensions far beyond what the uninitiated listener might chance to hear at a powwow. Jack Gladstone provides an excellent example.

Jack Gladstone has been called "Montana's Troubadour" and "Montana's Native Ambassador" and has earned accolades from impressive critics all across the country; he can produce a résumé that would make academics as well as musicians jealous. On top of all that, he's an engaging conversationalist who feels at home among a lot of topics—philosophy, anthropology, history, music and literature, to name a few. For an intellectual, he's a pretty down-to-earth fellow who talks about what he calls "Native Americana" with both humility and contagious enthusiasm.

Gladstone has produced more than fourteen CDs of music in the last twenty years and played in hundreds of venues in forty-six states. "I think I've played over a thousand college campuses," he estimated. "I take seriously

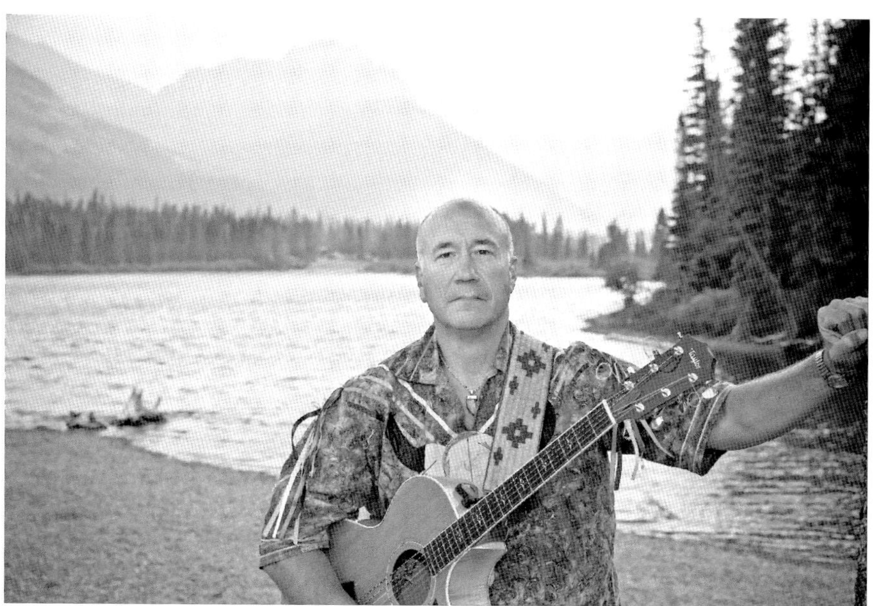

Jack Gladstone has been called "Montana's Troubadour." Billing his music as "Native Americana," Gladstone is an ambassador of storytelling, bridging cultural gaps and bringing people together in an appreciation of the healing power of music. *Photo by Rebecca Drobis, courtesy of Jack Gladstone.*

my responsibility of sharing my story, our Blackfeet story, and of getting it as correct as I can get it." Gladstone is not just a player—he's a scholar who meticulously researches the stories behind his songs and narratives. "I want to be able to defend my rhetorical strategies and words," he said. "I want to get it right."

Gladstone claims a mixed ancestry: his mother is of German descent, and his father is Blackfeet. In the mid-nineteenth century, the Blackfeet were the most powerful tribe to call Montana home, although their range extended far into Alberta and into Saskatchewan as well. With a foot in both cultures, Gladstone is especially well positioned to be the leading emissary of Native Americana. He's a natural musical ambassador—he is eloquent and genuinely excited about what he does. And it doesn't take listeners long to realize that his philosophical vision of both the human connection to music and its power to transform us spiritually transcends genres, categories and cultural or ethnic identity. Above all, Gladstone is an advocate for human connection through music, although he starts from a much broader conception of what music is than probably most musicians.

The common thread that runs through the various practices Gladstone is engaged in—scholarship, teaching, musical performance, poetry—is storytelling. "We are story-based beings," he said. "It's embedded in our DNA." He pointed, for example, to the *Iliad* and the *Odyssey*—the literary cornerstones of western culture—which were originally stories sung as songs. All over the world, the stories we tell compose the bedrock of the communities we inhabit, and this is particularly true for oral cultures. As he explained it, oral culture provided a critical method for keeping Indian identity alive and ensuring that native culture would endure the European invasion. As an example, he cited the 1880s in Montana history: "By the late 1880s, the buffalo were all gone and, with them, the Indian connection to the land. The buffalo provided food and shelter and tools for an entire culture, and when it was gone, what was left were stories."

Anthropologists and literary critics both agree that storytelling—often in song form—is a human cultural universal. "Stories are a form of sacred communion," Gladstone noted, and then he added with a chuckle, "and there's no 'app' for that." In his mind, at the root of all this is language itself, since without language, there can't be stories. And virtually the world over, from the *logos* of Christianity to the Egyptian god Thoth, language is connected with the divine. "To be fully present in the sacred," Gladstone said, "is a union created with language."

But what's especially interesting about his take on language is that it isn't all spoken or written. Many musicians would agree that music is often capable of expressing something ineffable. Gladstone goes further and suggests that "literacy can impoverish our experience." When he speaks on behalf of these points and insights, he isn't philosophizing from an armchair. His voice rings with a sincere sense of urgency. The philosophical side of things is important to him because philosophy seeks the fundamental nature of our experiences on earth and what it means to be human, and many people—musicians or not—would agree with him that we've lost a profound sense of our connection to nature and to one another. Gladstone believes that connection can only be recovered or healed through communication and empathy, which means that understanding the precise power of language itself is important. Gladstone offered an off-the-cuff definition of empathy that actually quite nicely summarizes the core of his approach to music: "Empathy is the surrender of your own perspective to assume through your imagination another's perspective."

As a result, the upshot of what Gladstone strives for in his music is something beyond cultural identity, beyond "white" or "Indian," and so he casts the term "Americana" in a somewhat metaphysical hue. "We are all children of a common mystery," he said, for example. The specifically Blackfeet view of that mystery resonates especially well for him, since that culture understands the world as a function of *Natos*, he said, or "sun power." He paused and then threw out a casual observation carrying all the power of a Nietzschean aphorism: "Music is a reverberation of sunlight." In a further flourish of culture-bridging, Gladstone went on to connect Joni Mitchell's "We are starlight, we are golden," to St. Francis of Assisi's "Canticle to Brother Sun," deftly illustrating how what might strike some ears as new-age mysticism is actually an old idea, expressed through the ages in various musical forms.

For Gladstone, Americana must refer on some level to a storied experience that all human beings share, such that the particular expressions of Americana music, especially in Montana, contain elements that must extend far back beyond the few hundred years that Europeans have been here. "Native Americana is like an iceberg," he suggested. "What you see is a very small part of the whole, and the rest extends much deeper than you might be aware." His own songs reflect this sense of deep history, both in the sense of showing how as human beings we are all connected to the earth we call home and to a common human culture, but also in the sense of reminding the dominant culture that what the history books and legends have said about the West frequently ignores or blatantly misrepresents the Indian point of view.

His song "Colter's Run," for example, attempts to set the record straight about the man who purported to outrun "half the Blackfeet Nation":

North of the Country of the Plains Cheyenne
Out west of the Bands of the Sioux
We Blackfeet were set to defend our range
What else could Napi's people do?
Our barefoot scheme to advertise
Backfired into HIS STORY
And to tell the honest truth
We never should have turned him loose!
(© 2016 Jack Gladstone)

By contrast, a passage from his well-known song "Tappin' the Earth's Backbone" provides an example of his desire to take a comprehensive view of the universal nature of human cultures everywhere—in this case our storied connections to the earth's mountain ranges:

Cold flows, snow blows up the Andes,
Alps, Ayers Rock, Himalayas and Rockies.
Uh-oh, Kilimanjaro is Tappin' the Earth's Backbone.

Well, you can spend your time in an uphill climb
Paying interest on the loans you find.
You can simplify and re-humanify
Celebrate relation with creation.
(© 2016 Jack Gladstone)

Cary Morin represents a different style of Americana and offers a more soft-spoken, almost shy, approach in talking about Native American influence. Morin plays country-blues guitar with a natural flair and finesse that would make most Delta musicians jealous. He has twice won the Colorado Blues Challenge and has made the semifinals at the International Blues Competition in Memphis. He has been hailed as the "Native American Taj Mahal" and as the "Dylan of Durango," monikers that invoke two of Americana music's hallowed godfathers. That's especially impressive for a guy who grew up in Montana, a region not ordinarily associated with blues music.

Born in Billings, Morin belongs to the Crow tribe, but he grew up in Great Falls, Montana, where his father was in the U.S. Air Force and where Morin first picked up a guitar. "My father played some guitar and had a lot of old country song lyrics printed out on sheets," Morin explained. "But I never had any real concept of different genres until much later. I just thought of songs I liked as songs, not 'country' or 'metal,' or this or that." Although he grew up surrounded by music, he didn't approach the guitar on his own until he was in the sixth grade. "My older brother played briefly, and he left a guitar around. I think I started on that." A respected musician by the time he graduated from CMR High School in 1981, Morin spent the next twenty-five years playing in various bands, including a moderately successful and highly acclaimed reggae band called the Atoll. He also played with Pura Fé, a musician in North Carolina best known for her Ulali project, which produced music that relies heavily on American Indian roots music.

Morin's eclectic musical education and tastes translate well to his unique style. His forceful fingerstyle has echoes of Mississippi John Hurt as well as Merle Travis, but you catch an occasional lick more reminiscent of AC/DC or the Rolling Stones. Morin's cover of Steely Dan's "Black Friday" (available on YouTube) offers a great example of how engaging a performer he can be: as one man with a guitar and a powerful voice, Morin gets across

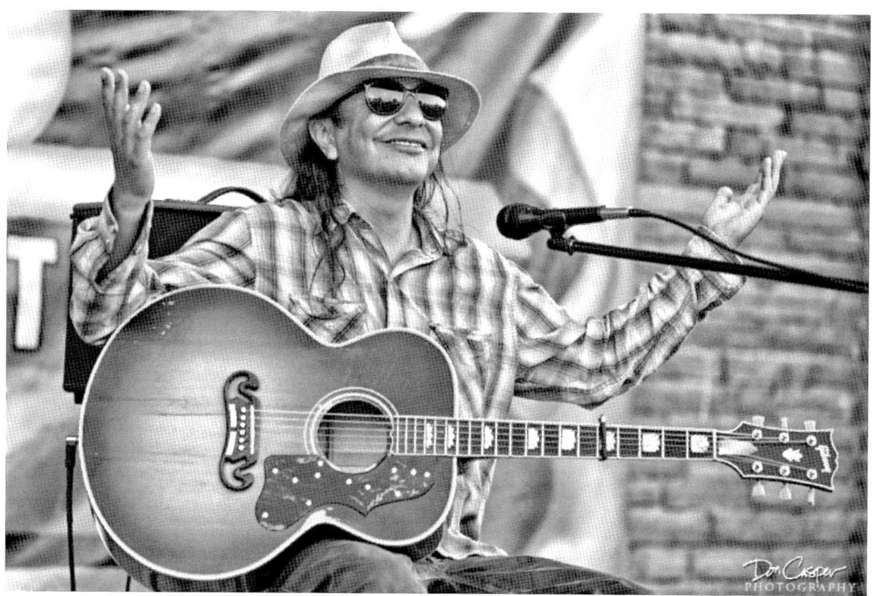

Born in Montana, Crow Indian Cary Morin has been called the "Dylan of Durango" and the "Native American Taj Mahal." *Photo by Don Casper, Courtesy of Cary Morin.*

as much energy and soul as the original band while stamping the song with something entirely his own.

Having started in music with a background in rock and country, Morin began learning the blues in about 2005, immersing himself in the sounds of the great blues fingerpickers. He learned by ear, all the while writing songs and performing a lot of solo shows, although he also regularly plays with other musicians in at least two working bands.

"I play with a couple guys in Fort Collins in a band called the Young Ancients," he mentioned casually, downplaying the fact that his bandmates hail from one of the most influential and important roots bands going: the Subdudes from New Orleans. The Young Ancients features Morin alongside John Magnie and Steve Amedée. In that band, Morin also occasionally plays pedal steel guitar, another instrument on which he is unusually adept. On top of that, Morin also plays in a duo with his wife, Celeste. "We play a lot of the country standards," he said. They bill themselves as Cowgirl and NDN.

In their own language, the Crow call themselves Apsáalooke, or "children of the large-beaked bird," a designation that was mistranslated by French trappers as "*gens du corbeaux*," which English speakers abbreviated to "crow." A more familiar variant of the name Apsáalooke is *Absaroka*, which is also

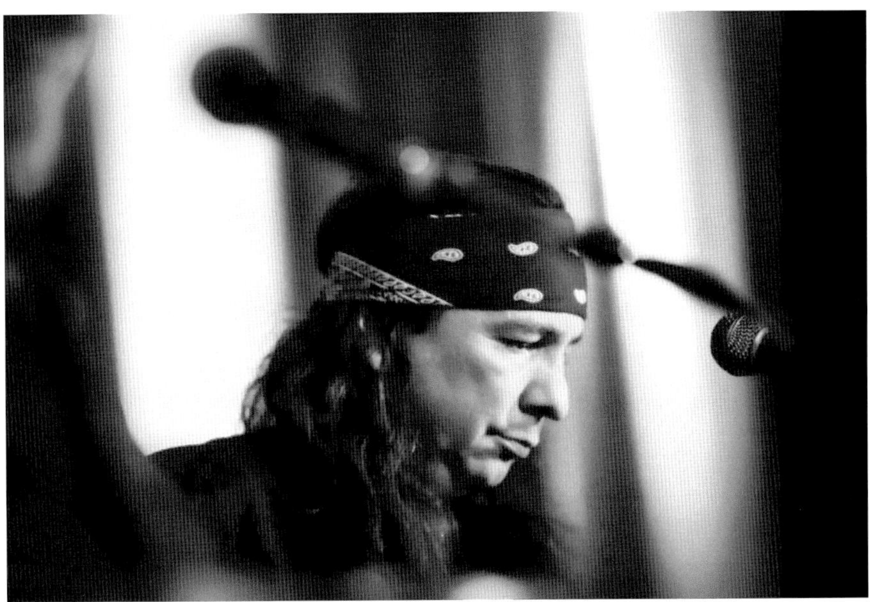

Cary Morin in a pensive moment on stage. *Courtesy of Cary Morin.*

the name for one of Montana's majestic mountain ranges within what was the traditional range of the Apsáalooke when the European fur trappers began to infiltrate what is Montana in the late eighteenth century. In fact, the Crow lands stretched from Yellowstone Park down the entire length of the Yellowstone Valley to what is now North Dakota.

Morin maintains a deep connection to his heritage, but as far as his music is concerned, it provides just one of many influences. "I have an understanding of native heritage and memories of my grandparents and relatives back home," he recently said. "I write songs from that perspective, although it's not real obvious in most of my songs. I'm not really influenced by traditional [Indian] music, but lyrically, it's there."

Morin has put out three solo records now featuring his signature driving guitar style that sets the backdrop for his powerful, soulful singing. The overall effect is some of the best Americana music on the airwaves today. Although his home base is Colorado, Morin spends a good part of the year touring the country, playing shows at festivals and bars all over the South and the West.

At twenty-six years old, and representing a completely new generation of Americana musicians, Joseph Running Crane is already a seasoned veteran of the Missoula music scene, having played in some of the state's most respected hardcore bands. There is an odd but well-traveled trajectory from hard-edged rock-and-roll to country Americana, but lots of big names having made the transition, from Dave Alvin to Robert Plant and John Paul Jones. Running Crane made a name for himself playing guitar and bass in what might be the best-named band ever to come out of Montana: Goddammitboyhowdy (although the Big Sky Mudflaps must also be a contender for that honor). Lately, however, he has softened his delivery into a distinctive Americana country sound.

Joey was weaned on punk rock and hardcore, a huge fan of the Minutemen and the Dead Kennedys since practically grade school. He grew up in Browning, Montana, on the Blackfeet Reservation, and his early influences were loud, heavy and hard rock. "As far as the Indian music influences go, my dad sang some spiritual Blackfeet songs, but any heritage comes out mainly in the lyrics." Although he admitted a fascination with the idea of integrating Indian drum circle and singing into the framework of more country Americana, he himself has not attempted to do so. Still, his recent songs have taken on a more wistful tone and use an acoustic sound far removed from the angsty and frenetic electric punk sound. "The album I am working on now is a bit of a departure from my previous stuff," he agreed. "The early punk stuff I did, especially lyrically, was an angry young Indian man sort of shouting—the themes were all a reflection of issues on the reservation. I would call it 'Indian music' in the sense that the locale—the reservation—and the culture influenced the lyrics and the attitude, but the form was just hardcore, or punk rock."

Like a lot of songwriters, Running Crane emphasized the fact that "writers write what they know," but he was careful to make clear that he doesn't see his own story as somehow more important than any other writer's, even if having grown up and started his musical career on the reservation informs much of his writing. "It's just 'my story,'" he said, "and I'm not conveying any kind of grudge." What does matter, he added, is that an Indian songwriter should have the same chance at being seen or heard, and if opportunities in a rural state like Montana are relatively slim compared to a city like San Francisco or Seattle, it isn't difficult to envision the greater challenge involved with being in a band from Montana—especially a band from one of Montana's reservations, all of which are geographically remote.

"I go back and forth on the 'Indian Songwriter' concept," he explained. "Goddammitboyhowdy, for example, was essentially a rez punk band. We edged into more countrified, cow punk stuff, but it was kind of a caricature of country. Lyrically, the music referenced local tribal issues, so in a sense,

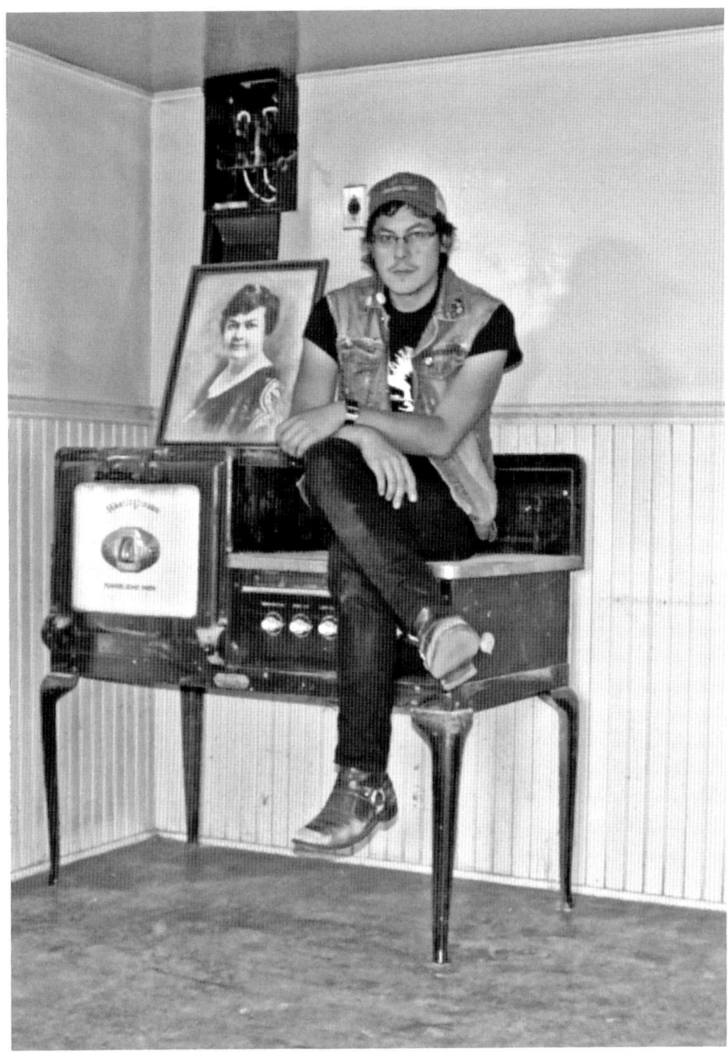

Joey Running Cane was a founding member of one of Montana's best punk bands, Goddammitboyhowdy, the title of whose seminal album was *Goddammitboyhowdy Is Rez Punk. Photo by Dark Sevier, courtesy of Joey Running Cane.*

there's the Indian part, but at the same time, I'm really sensitive to the risk of being 'tokenized.' I have for sure strayed away from the 'angry young Indian guy,' but I think there is a little bit of a crisis of identity. I'm not sure where the line is."

In spite of his youth, Running Crane has a lot of bands and tours under his belt, and he's experienced with media. He even made an appearance in the film *Winter in the Blood* (2013), directed by Montana brothers Alex and Andrew Smith and produced by Sherman Alexie, based on the novel of the same title by Blackfeet author James Welch. As a consequence of all he's done and seen, Running Crane is sensitive to how Indians, especially Indians from reservations, get presented in the media. On the one hand, he supports what he sees as a positive interest in modern life on the reservation, and in an interview with *Missoulian* writer Cory Walsh, for example, Running Crane said, "In a lot of ways, people are tired of seeing the quote-unquote poverty-porn depiction of contemporary North American indigenous people." Millennials especially are looking for documentary verisimilitude, as opposed to "the early 21st century person of Iron Cody crying by the side of all this garbage," he said. On the other hand, while a sincere interest in exposing problems, such as the actuality of widespread poverty, may be a noble and necessary undertaking, "it's important not to fixate on it and make it a defining characteristic because that is another form of dehumanization," he said.

From the moment he started bringing his music to the public, it seems clear that Running Crane was not just seeking out his own musical voice but rather was experimenting with an entirely new genre for the sort of music he was creating—a fact reflected in the title of the Goddammitboyhowdy debut EP: *Goddammitboyhowdy Is Rez Punk*. Even someone unaccustomed to the idioms of punk or hardcore listening to that album today will recognize the raw talent of this group of young kids from the Blackfeet Reservation showcased in their frenzied delivery and strident vocals. Goddammitboyhowdy caught the interest of documentary filmmaker Matt Cascella, who produced a documentary about the group in 2013 called *Howdy Montana*. The film provides a cinéma vérité glimpse into the realities facing a young band from the Blackfeet Indian Reservation, and there are some revealing scenes where the band talks frankly about what it means to try to forge a punk metal band in a small town in Montana.

As Running Crane described it, Goddammitboyhowdy "morphed" into another band, King Elephant, which strove for a little more "pop" sound and sought to distance itself from the "rez punk" marker. Although the earlier band took great pride in what they had created, they had begun to second-guess the nature of their appeal. In an interview with journalist Tim Goessman, Running Crane expressed the sort of doubt that was affecting the band: "Are we really getting interest for what we're saying? Are we really getting interest for whether or not our songs are good, or is it just that we're impressive because we're three rez kids?"

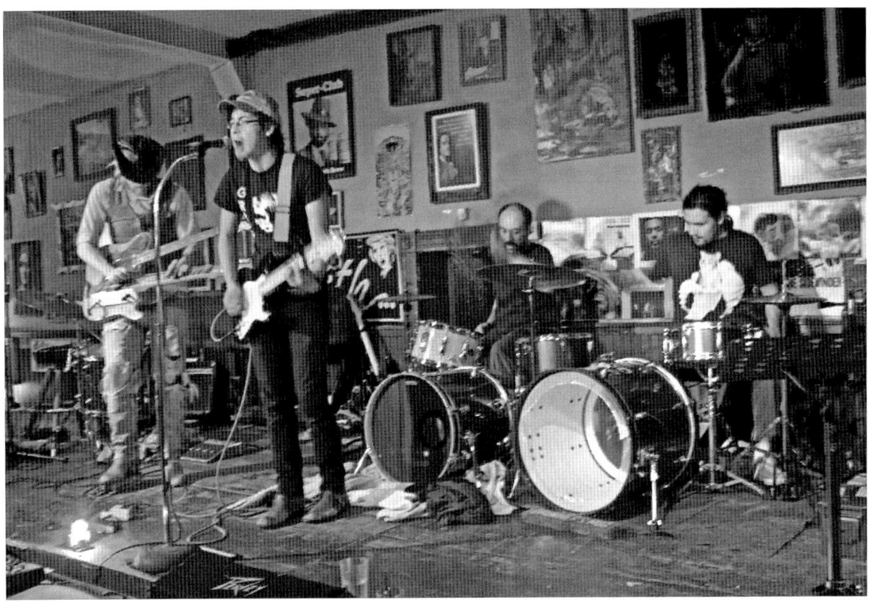

Joey Running Cane and the Dirty Birds. *Photo by Dark Sevier, courtesy of Joey Running Cane.*

King Elephant inspired Goessman to make his own documentary after traveling along with King Elephant on a tour of the United States in the summer of 2012. The result was a film called *We're Going Home*, which ended up being an emotional and ill-fated ramble across the country that climaxed with an ugly incident in Illinois in which the band endured racial slurs. Shortly after that, a window was smashed out of their van, and with money running out, the frustrated band agreed with Running Crane, "We're going home."

"My interpretation of 'Americana' is pretty loose," Running Crane said. "I think of it as pretty much anything from Appalachia, as well as black spirituals." He contrasted Americana country with mainstream, Toby Keith–type material, in that Americana "adapts to changing times." He also noted the relevance of Native American musical traditions and how, to a large extent, that influence on Americana music has been overlooked. He recommends the three-album compendium of Indian music from the United States and Canada put out in 2013 by Light in the Attic Records called *Native North America (Vol. 1): Aboriginal Folk, Rock, and Country 1966–1985*. He cited listening to that collection, along with the experience of playing in King Elephant, as bringing about a turning point in his songwriting. While some of the slower and more melodious material performed by King Elephant would qualify as Americana, most of it was "fast and loud" and closer in feel to the rez punk sound of Goddammitboyhowdy.

A 2014 profile in the *Missoulian* documented his more recent stage presence: "Accompanying himself on an acoustic guitar strummed with punk energy, he sang in a preternaturally scratchy voice for a 24-year-old, gruffly relaying lyrics that compare sacrifices for loved ones to venturing out into the harsh winds in Browning, where he grew up." Other recent performances available on YouTube also reveal a sound more in line with Bruce Springsteen than Jello Biafra. For example, in the short film *Montana Songwriter #9: Joey Running Crane*, Marshall Granger documented Running Crane alone with a Taylor guitar performing a soulful rendition of Running Crane's song "Always Out of Town." In the interview prefacing the song, the singer contrasted his tenure in Goddammitboyhowdy with the more melancholy, country sound he's currently creating. A lot of the rez punk stuff he describes as him "shouting and two other guys playing really loud," with lyrics about typical reservation topics such as "enrollment reform" and "blood quantum issues," but also more mundane subjects like "the price of orange juice." The more country Americana songs he's working on now are about love and heartbreak and the ordinary pain of being alive. Take, for example, the powerful lyrics of a verse from "Faith and Thunder": "God has left and the night is growing dark and I don't know where you are," which lead into a chorus that turns what might have been a clichéd love ballad into a more ominous, almost religious invocation:

> *Throw out your hand*
> *There will be faith*
> *There will be thunder*
> *Throw out my hands*
> *It'll just be me and you and there will be no others.*
> *(© 2015 Joey Running Crane)*

Montana, especially the remote and rural parts of the state, can evoke a profound sense of separation from the rest of the world. That feeling—what Bill Monroe meant by the word "lonesome" in the "high, lonesome sound"—emerges in many genres of music, but for folk and country, it's a basic requirement. Many Montana Americana musicians refer in some way to that quality as having had an influence on their sound, and Running Crane is no exception. When asked about how being from Montana influences his writing, he doesn't hesitate: "*Isolation* is the first word that comes to mind.

Absolutely. When you're not in a 'music town,' like Seattle or Austin or San Francisco, you pull influence from everything and everywhere, but you filter it through your own guts. There are tons of talented musicians in Missoula, but no way can that scene measure up to the effect of southern music in the South or hippie music in south California. In Montana, that isolation compels you to draw from all over, but it comes out with that distinct stamp of being so far away." It's a viewpoint articulated by other Montana musicians of the same generation like Cameron Boster (see chapter 3).

Both Boster and Running Crane also exemplify the DIY ethos that marks so much of the art and music scene unfolding in the second decade of the twenty-first century. The tech revolution of the 1990s and the proliferation of the Internet allowed artists and musicians to short-circuit the standard industry model that lavishly rewards agents and labels and an army of executives for marketing a product at the expense of the person who actually produced the artifact. Each middleman in the chain carves away a slice of the pie until artists are left a handful of crumbs, if they are lucky. Many musicians who sign record deals wind up bankrupt or in debt or somehow other legally beholden to an office suite of managers and producers. The DIY approach, made possible by open-source recording software like Audacity and dozens of host platforms such as Bandcamp, ReverbNation and SoundCloud has prompted a renaissance of homegrown music production. The economics of the thing often work out in the favor of even an aspiring band with a respectable following: what is lost in not having the juggernaut of marketing behind you that comes from a major label is balanced by being able to control virtually the entire process—from making the recording to collecting the money from the sales of digital downloads. For the typical garage band or unknown group making an initial foray into the music scene, it's a no-brainer: DIY involves very little overhead or up-front expense and provides an indispensable crash-course in what is actually involved in producing music for public consumption.

The concept of crowdsourcing has taken that revolution a step further: using launch platforms like Kickstarter or GoFundMe, artists and musicians can present an ambitious concept to the public and raise money for it by taking advance orders. Once their funding target is reached, they can then pay for the recording or artwork or CD manufacturing and shipping and deliver the CDs to fans who have already paid for them. It's essentially the same concept as the ubiquitous book subscription services that operated with great success throughout the nineteenth and early twentieth centuries, an approach Mark Twain, for example, used to publish and sell *Tom Sawyer*.

In 1976, in the height of the Aber Day Kegger years and when the Mission Mountain Wood Band was at the top of their game, up in the north-central part of the state on the Rocky Boy Reservation an obscure band called Jerry Denny and Buddy Russette and the Cree-ations put out what is now a rare but interesting 45 rpm record. The label bears the imprint of Kessler Music down in Billings. The B-side contains a love song called "Love You," an enjoyable but unremarkable ditty. The A-side, however, features a tune called "Indian Country," written by P.F. Russette, which invites repeated listening. It opens with the sound of a rattle or shaker into which blends a stately powwow drum, followed by a mellow, almost skiffle-sounding guitar. The lyrics begin thus: "Montana, it's the land of the free / it's the home of all Indians / it's the land of the Chippewa-Cree," sung by Jerry in a pleasant melodic voice. Both the opening lyric and the last stanza strike a subtle and powerful message that sort of cuts to the heart of Indian Americana, at least as it has developed in Montana. In the first place, the opening lines assert that Montana is the home of "all Indians," which may be read a variety of ways but in any case provides a nice contrast to the subtle and probably innocuous chauvinism expressed by so many Montanans of European descent—whereas white culture in the state tends to emphasize the ways in which Montanans are unique from the rest of the country, the Cree-ations song takes the opposite point of view: Montana is the home of all Indians because before the arbitrary placement of borders on maps, Montana was merely one particular region in a continuous landscape home to all the original inhabitants. At the same time, the last line runs counter to what the dominant culture, in its tendency to romanticize the tragedy of cultural invasion and replace it with the myth of the noble savage, might lyrically predict. That line, instead of something like, "We're proud people, no matter what was done to us," states rather, "We're all a proud people, no matter what we do," a phrasing that avoids the passive voice and emphasizes autonomy.

While the songs may not be otherwise particularly memorable, they do represent the indomitable spirit of musicians everywhere, as well as of Indians in Montana specifically. Because western Montana tends to gather the headlines and see itself referenced in Hollywood film credits, people forget that two-thirds of the state lie on the Great Plains and that the state is home to a relatively large Indian population—almost seventy thousand, in fact. The Cree-ations record stands as a reminder that the plains of Montana inspire as much musical rhapsody as do the mountains. As a musical artifact, that 45 record also drives home a truth already known to astute collectors: there is no place in this great state where someone is not making music. Drive far enough down any overlooked coulee or up any washboard gulch or any rural county road in Montana and you will inevitably find a musician unable to resist the muse putting words to paper and tracks on tape. And even if those efforts go unrewarded in the here and now, rest assured that some fellow traveler will come along to track them down and offer them another chance to change the world.

Chapter 5

A Brief History of Old-Time Fiddling in Montana

The old-time fiddle tradition represents the oldest example of Americana music, especially in Montana, since its earliest incarnation involved the intersection of the indigenous Indian music with a Scotch-Irish tradition inherited from Europe. When members of the Lewis and Clark Expedition periodically paused to "jam" with Indian drummers along their route through Montana, they initiated a long tradition of Americana in Montana.

The earliest references in the historical record to fiddling in the region now known as Montana appear in the journal entries for Sunday, June 9, 1805, made by Sergeant John Ordway and Captain Meriwether Lewis of the Corps of Discovery. Ordway wrote that "in the evening the Capts. Revived the party with a dram. They had a frolick fiddled & danced & Sang untill late in the evening," and Lewis noted that "Cruzatte gave us some music on the violin and the men passed the evening dancing singing &c and were extremely cheerfull." On that day, the men of the Lewis and Clark Expedition were camped in the vicinity of the Marias River, with a view of some mountains (probably the Highwoods) to the south.

A little more than a month earlier, they had camped on a point at the juncture of the Yellowstone and the Missouri and enjoyed a similar celebration, as noted by Lewis on April 26: "[W]e ordered a dram to be issued to each person; this soon produced the fiddle, and they spent the evening with much hilarity, singing & dancing, and seemed perfectly to forget their past toils, as they appeared regardless of those to come." Later, in the midst of their preparations for the great portage around the Great Falls, Ordway remarked on July 4, 1805, that "the fiddle put in order and the party amused themselves dancing all the evening untill about 10 oClock in a Sivel & jovil manner." Musicologists have identified some twenty-seven references in the journals to occasions on which the fiddle was played, the majority of them in Montana.

Although they may have been preceded by some long-forgotten French trader or trapper who happened to be musically inclined, Pierre Cruzatte and George Gibson—privates in the Corps of Discovery in 1805—initiated the history of old-time fiddling in Montana. The one-eyed navigator and translator Pierre Cruzatte is the better known of the two men, perhaps most remembered for his shooting Lewis in the rear on the return journey, myopically mistaking him for an elk. But the journals remind us that the corps enjoyed the performances of two fiddlers, and we should remember that George Gibson also played, although he is mentioned in this capacity only once in the journals.

For those unfamiliar with the instruments, the fiddle is identical to the violin—any difference between them has to do with the style and tradition in which they are played rather than the construction of the instrument itself. The journals refer to the instrument with both terms, as do many more contemporaneous writers. But the violin—primarily associated with symphonic music—belongs to history more as an artifact of "high" culture than the fiddle, which is often relegated to a mere curiosity for anthropologists or musicologists interested in "folk" culture. Accordingly, the fiddle is, in many ways, a signature instrument in Americana music, appearing in "country" genres as diverse as zydeco and Delta Blues to bluegrass and old-time. The violin, we might say, has the aristocratic appeal of city life, while its country cousin the fiddle wanders the hills outside town. Or, as old-time fiddler and luthier Dave Anderson of Great Falls even more bluntly put it, "a fiddle is a violin with an attitude."

The term "old-time fiddling" has been employed for well over a century, indicating that even one hundred years ago, fiddlers understood themselves as belonging to a tradition that reached far enough back in time to warrant the nostalgic epithet. Unfortunately, old-time fiddling is, as cultural geographer John M. Crowley noted, generally "unknown and nearly invisible" except to those inside the "fiddlers' circle."

Old-time fiddling may be identified according to several features, all of which are elastic enough to include dozens of regional styles under the general heading. First, musicologists note that old-time fiddling is a traditional style of playing that is passed from person to person and from generation to generation, much like a language. Fiddler and musicologist Stuart Williams, for example, makes the important point that "the blending of styles is not an arbitrary or contrived mix based on whims or current fad" but rather is a phenomenon that mirrors in many ways the shifting of language from one generation to the next. Williams has also compared the different fiddling styles as particular inflections, similar to "the brogue of a Scotsman or the Texan's drawl." In the same way that linguists can plot the migrations according to speech accents, Williams suggested that different fiddle styles "reflect the movement of peoples' migration and integration."

This explains why in spite of stylistic variations, the repertoire of old-time fiddlers in 2015 is, in general, not much different from the repertoire of old-time fiddlers in 1870—in fact, it may not be too different from that of Cruzatte and Gibson. Once a tune has become appreciated enough to be passed on from one generation to the next, it is unlikely to slip out of the canon of common tunes. Second, old-time fiddling is closely associated with stylized dances—as one old-time Montana musician pointed out, "If you can't dance to it, it's not old-time fiddle." This is perhaps the most important distinction, since it distinguishes old-time fiddling from one of its cousins known as "Texas" fiddling or "contest fiddling." Contest fiddling valorizes melodic finesse and has all but divorced itself from the older dance-oriented fiddling tradition. It therefore lacks the last definitive characteristic of what all the different old-time styles have in common, which is a definitive "drive," or rhythmic pulse provided by the fiddle. Whether traditional Appalachian, Métis, Norwegian Hardanger or Irish (to name only a handful of styles that continue to be played in Montana), old-time fiddling may be identified by its obvious pulse or rhythm, which is essential for dancing.

Many of the books devoted to the journey of Lewis and Clark and their contingent of hardened woodsmen make clear the point that the men were drawn from the periphery of the United States—both socially and geographically. As frontiersmen, they were by definition more rural than urban, although Lewis and Clark themselves would have enjoyed at least a familiarity with the more genteel setting of Washington and the other population centers of the East, including Philadelphia, New York and Pittsburgh. But by and large, the men who made up the corps were backwoods folk, and the music they would have entreated Cruzatte and Gibson to play would have been primarily "folk" music. A large percentage of the Corps of Discovery was made up of men who were Métis, including Cruzatte, who was half French and half Omaha Indian,

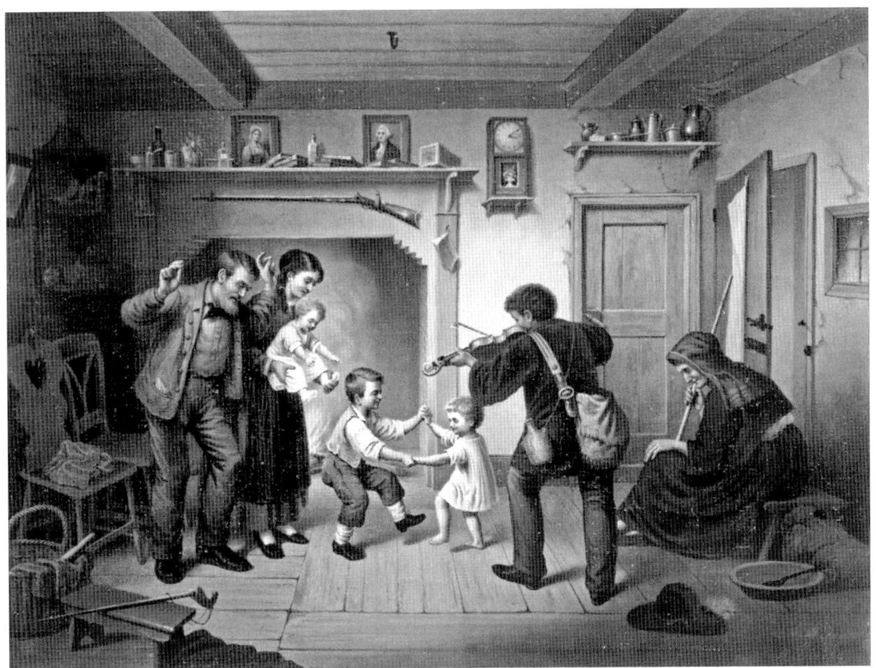

Power of music chromolithograph of *Duval & Hunter.* Philadelphia, Jas. F. Queen after A. Dircks, 1820/1821–86, New York, published by A. and C. Kaufmann, circa 1872. *Library of Congress.*

and they would certainly have been encouraged to play tunes drawn from that tradition. Taken together, those two traditions epitomize Americana, illustrating its "soul" as distinctly connected to the country, to rural life in general and to ethnic origins.

Cruzatte and Gibson's fiddling kept the men of the Corps of Discovery in good spirits as they struggled upriver through terra incognita, but their music served an additional, and perhaps more important, ambassadorial purpose: as a tool of what Métis scholar Nicholas Vrooman called "fiddle dance diplomacy." The journals indicate that many of the occasions on which the fiddle was played were encounters with Native Americans, who considered music a form of "medicine" or spiritual power, and they were eager to exchange their forms with those of the white travelers at dances that lasted late into the night. University of Montana music professor emeritus (and onetime mentor to the fledgling Mission Mountain Wood Band) Joseph Mussulman has written an article that specifically focuses on this function of the music that takes its title from one of the journal entries: "The Greatest Harmoney: 'Meddicine Songs' on the Lewis and Clark Trail."

Unfortunately, none of the journals mentions any of the tunes they played by name, but as Hunt noted, because of Cruzatte's French heritage, musicologists "assume that many French Canadian folk tunes of the era made up a considerable part of his repertoire." Their repertoire might have therefore included such tunes as "Jolie Blonde" and "The Old French Hornpipe," tunes that are still popular today. Hunt also reconstructed a likely repertoire based on the type of dancing the men were most likely to have engaged in. Given that most of the recruits hailed from Kentucky and other frontier regions, scholars have surmised that when the journals mention dancing, they most likely refer to what was known as "buck dancing," or "hoedowning," both ancestors to what is now known as "clogging." Excellent illustrations of such dances as practiced by subsequent Missouri River boatmen can be seen in the paintings of Caleb Bingham (1811–1879), particularly *The Jolly Flatboatmen* (1846). Quite likely the men would have also performed more formal dances now known as "country dancing" or "contradancing," a more complicated forerunner of modern

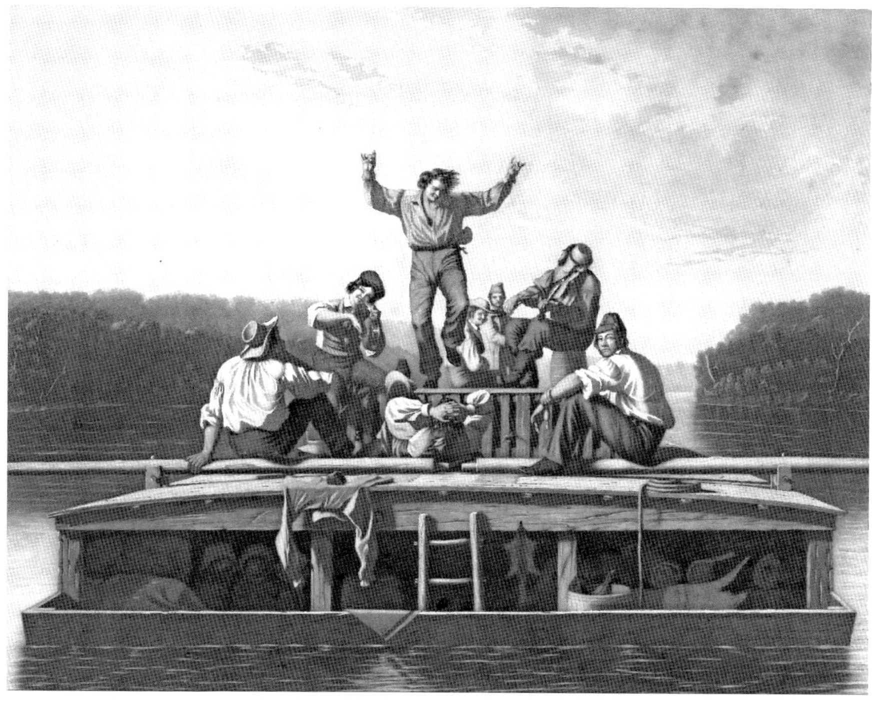

The Jolly Flatboatmen, painted by G.C. Bingham and engraved by T. Doney, printed by Powell & Company, circa 1847. *Library of Congress.*

square dancing, especially when called on to share their medicine songs and demonstrate their dance forms to the Indians.

Howard Marshall, a professor of archeology and art history at the University of Missouri who happens to be an extraordinary old-time fiddler, has also investigated the question of what tunes would have been likely in the repertoire of Cruzatte and Gibson. As a result of his research, he has recorded a CD called *Fiddle Tunes of the Lewis and Clark Era*. Many of the tunes Marshall identified are also tunes that remain active in the repertoires of old-time fiddlers today, such as "The Fisher's Hornpipe," "Soldier's Joy," "Leather Britches" and "Yankee Doodle." The persistence of such tunes in the old-time repertoire over the course of almost two centuries is evidence of the enduring power of folk tradition.

Joseph Mussulman remarked that we can never know for sure what tunes might have issued from the fiddles of Gibson and Cruzatte, although "some of the popular songs of that era are still within earshot today, and it may be that their very durability is sufficient grounds for some informed guesswork." At the same time, we can rule out some contenders as having arrived on the musical scene too late: such still-popular tunes as "Turkey in the Straw" and "Arkansas Traveler," for example, do not appear until the 1820s or 1830s.

One of the most popular songs of the day Mussulman noted would have been "Yankee Doodle," a "short-breathed, neatly shaped, crisp little tune that was a natural for doggerel of all descriptions." In other words, it was a tune that lent itself well to improvised verses and parody. Popular "airs" would have included "The President's March" and "The Federal Overture," tunes that the corps musicians might have played to impress the Indians. As well, they might have played an immensely popular tune called "The Anacreontic Song," first published in England in 1778 and better known today (and with lyrics added in 1814 by Francis Scott Key) as "The Star-Spangled Banner."

Since Cruzatte and Gibson were the most likely candidates to have inaugurated old-time fiddling in what is now recognized as Montana at the relatively late date of 1805, it is safe to say that the development of a specific regional style in Montana has lagged some decades—perhaps as much as a century—behind the development of styles in those eastern regions from which they first brought the music. It is perhaps too soon yet to speak of a distinctly "Montana" style of fiddling, but we can identify many of the strains that will inevitably make up whatever that style eventually becomes. Since the art of fiddling is transmitted from individual to individual and from generation to generation like a language, taking a diachronic glance at the form as it appears in the historical record can assist us in analyzing what might constitute a style of fiddling that may eventually be recognized by old-time musicians as "the Montana sound."

Current practitioners of the art such as Mike Williams in Helena and Bill Sevores in Missoula describe present-day old-time fiddling in Montana as a mish-mash of various styles—a fabric of different strands contributed by different ethnic groups. Williams argued that, unlike certain areas of the East such as North Carolina or New England, Montana has no distinctive fiddling style as yet because the tunes and styles that are played here are diverse and relatively recent imports from those older areas. Sevores also speculated that the lack of a significant population base in Montana has inhibited the critical cultural mass necessary for the development of a distinct, shared style.

Williams's assessment is corroborated by the memoirs of late nineteenth- and early twentieth-century fiddlers. Bill Carlson, for example, noted in *Eighty Years of Rosin and Floor Wax* that he learned to play from his father, who first learned Swedish tunes from his mother, but then was influenced by the Texas cowboys with whom he came into contact in the 1890s. "Father learned his dance fiddling from them," Carlson wrote, but expanded his repertoire from playing with "Scotch, Irish and English settlers in the area." He noted that, eventually, "people from nearly every state in the Union" settled in his native McCone County, each group bringing with it a particular fiddling style. Carlson said that the hallmark of good dance fiddlers in the days before radio was that they could play to suit whatever crowd they happened to be performing for: Germans and Scandinavians wanted their waltzes "fast and lively," eastern Europeans wanted polkas and Scandinavians were fond of schottisches. Canadians preferred their tunes played at a faster tempo than usual, and the Irish and Scottish crowds expected jigs and reels.

As the groups immigrating to Montana originated from different areas, so, too, did their music. What Stuart Williams has remarked of Washington State fiddling applies equally to Montana: "The Northern Europeans especially loved waltzes and schottisches; the Canadians brought a rich assortment of jigs and reels, and the Midwestern settlers brought hoedowns (distinguished from reels and hornpipes by the Southeastern, African-American influenced phrasing)." As a consequence, a number of distinct styles may be found alongside one another, and a considerable degree of blending may be discerned.

Unfortunately, the record of fiddling in Montana between 1806, when the Lewis and Clark Expedition left the region on their return trip home,

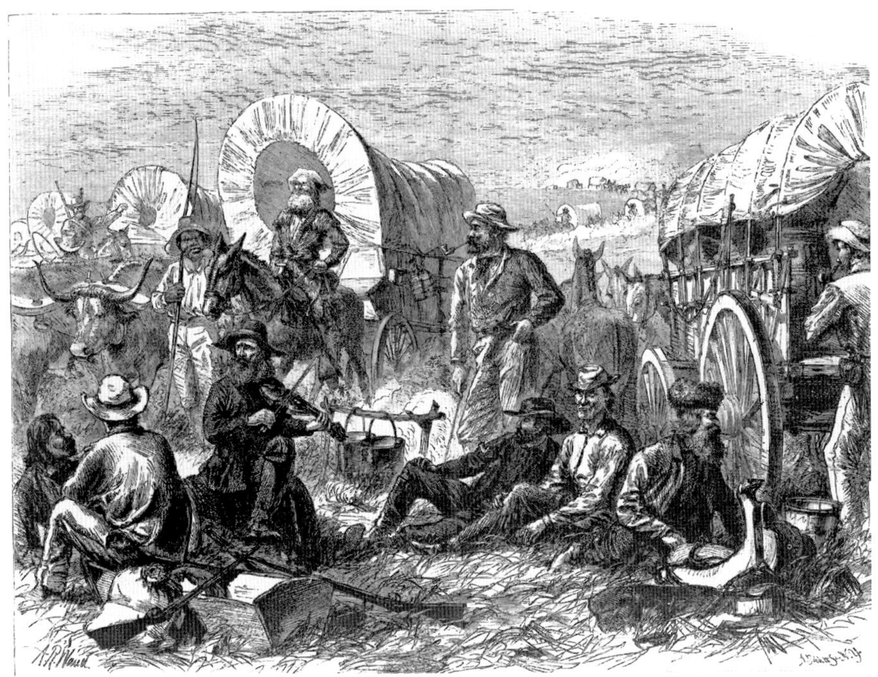

"Pilgrims of the Plains" by Alfred Rudolph Waud, from *Harper's Weekly* 15, no. 782 (December 23, 1871). *Library of Congress.*

and the arrival of the first gold seekers in the late 1850s and early 1860s is, like the history of the region in general, lamentably scant. Nevertheless, we may assume that the fur traders heading upriver that the Lewis and Clark Expedition encountered on the return journey had men like Cruzatte and Gibson in their ranks who passed their idle hours by breaking out the eminently portable fiddle.

As the fur trade gave way to the gold rushes, what passed for civilization gained a foothold in the form of the small villages in the gulches whose dominant features were the taverns and dance halls that immediately sprang up. Those who wrote about Virginia City and Bannack, or later Butte and Helena, repeatedly described wild, unruly frontier towns in which the incessant song of the fiddle competed with whizzing bullets. Every street was lined with saloons, and every saloon had a dance band. Unfortunately, the names of the men who provided the music at such venues and the precise tunes they played were facts the writers seldom considered worthy of note. We can see in the historical record that the early "dance bands" were entirely ad hoc affairs—two fiddlers might be accompanied by only a flute or a drum, for example. And while we seldom find in the historical record any mention of the specific tunes the early settlers danced to, we do encounter descriptions of the sorts of dances they conducted, which does yield some indication of the kinds of tunes that would likely have been played. Similarly, although the records seldom provide the names of the fiddlers who graced the stages at Bannack, Virginia City, Butte or Helena, we can get a clear sense of the kinds of environments such musicians performed in and the personalities of those with whom they consorted.

Two of the early fortune hunters in the mining camps of Montana were the Stuart brothers—Granville and James—who kept a journal during their early years in Montana. Both men were closely acquainted with two of the first fiddlers to be mentioned by name after Cruzatte and Gibson. The entry James wrote for January 1, 1862, notes that even though a blizzard was raging outside, they held a dance in John Grant's cabin at Grantsville (near modern-day Deer Lodge) and that "the music for these dances was two violins; and the dance most popular was the old-fashioned quadrille." Humble log cabins would have made for cozy if not crowded dance quarters. A similar account described one of the earliest events to take place a few years later in Butte: on Christmas Day 1866, "The first dance was held in the cabin of Dr. Olman. Fifty men, women and children attended and two fiddlers furnished the music."

Stuart indicates in his entry for February 1, 1862, that the miners exhausted themselves in dancing again: "Danced last night. Oh! Joy. It is not often that we have a fiddler, and when we do have one, we try to keep him in practice by having a dance every evening." On July 23, 1862, an apparently new fiddler appeared, "a fine violin player accompanied by his handsome, seventeen year old wife. His name is J.B. Caven." Stuart offered some hint that Caven may have had some classical training, since he wrote that "we have the Cavens over often and enjoy the society of an intellectual white woman and good music." These entries are made by James, but a few months later, Granville took up the pen again and echoed his brother on November 23: "There were two good fiddlers in camp, 'Buz' Caven and Lou P. Smith."

Before long, the isolated enclaves of log cabins the Stuarts described gave way to rough-and-tumble gold rush villages such as Virginia City and Bannack. A contemporary of the Stuarts, Professor Thomas Dimsdale, famous for his "correct and impartial narrative of the chase, trial, capture and execution of Henry Plummer's notorious road agent band," *The Vigilantes of Montana* (which, having been published in Virginia City in 1866, may claim the distinction of being the first book published in Montana), provided a picture of the sorts of dances held in the taverns of Bannack and Virginia City a year or so after the Stuarts were in the Deer Lodge Valley. "In every frequented street," Dimsdale wrote, "public gambling houses with open doors and loud music are resorted to." As quickly as the hopeful miners could erect a few crude shacks, "dance-houses sprung up as if by enchantment," echoed Nathaniel Pitt Langford, "and the crack of the revolver was often heard above the merry notes of the violin." By all accounts, the mining camps were raucous places lined with houses of ill repute—taverns, dance halls and gambling parlors—and the fiddle usually provided the soundtrack. Few writers can match the fustian hyperbole of Langford, however:

> *The number of drinking and gambling saloons was greatly in excess of stores and private dwellings, and to nearly all of these was attached that most important attraction of a mining town, the hurdy-gurdy. The sound of the violin which struck the ear upon entering the street, was never lost while passing through it, and at many of the saloons the evidence of the bacchanal orgies which were in progress inside was often apparent in the eagerness exhibited by the crowd which surrounded the building without.*

Dimsdale described these frontier taverns as all-purpose entertainment havens: a miner could drink, gamble or choose a dancing girl, or "hurdy-gurdy," with whom to step through a dance called by a "prompter" shouting, "promenade, eight," or "all hands round." Dimsdale did not identify the instruments in the "orchestra," but since he was describing a square or contra dance, we can assume that the key instrument was a fiddle. Moreover, he wrote, "an Irish tune or a horn-pipe generally finishes the set."

Albert D. Richardson's lively account of traveling across the West, published a year later in 1867, also gives a vivid description of the musical environment of the "hurdy-gurdy" houses in Virginia City, complete with an oft-reproduced lithograph depicting a dance band composed of two horns and a fiddler. The festivities Richardson described commenced at nine o'clock in the evening and continued until daylight, "interrupted only by two fights." The scene depicted in the accompanying lithograph matches precisely Richardson's literary snapshot of the interior of the bar: "At one end of the long hall, a well-stocked bar, and a monte bank in full blast; at the other, a platform occupied by three musicians; between, many lookers-on, with cigars and meerschaums."

Another writer of the same era who had been a miner and resident of Bannack corroborated in his memoirs the scenes Richardson had encountered in 1865. Robert Kirkpatrick recalled in his *Reminiscences* "hurdy gurdy houses runing [*sic*] in full blast until nearly daylight Monday morning with their wide doors on the ground floor wide open all a day and night, with string band and clarionet [*sic*] that could be heard the whole length of town." Kirkpatrick also alluded to the typically inebriated state in which the fiddlers performed: "a string band of first and second violins and bass Viol cost from forty to $60.00 a night, and the musicians often got so drunk they could hardly keep their seats."

A "dance" could therefore refer to a rural affair held at a miner's cabin, a party held in one of the town taverns with hurdy-gurdy girls or a presumably more formal affair held in one of the other town buildings. Such dances were a much-needed diversion from the rigors of mining camp life, but they also served a practical purpose as well. Jean Davis reported that the early communities such as Bannack established schools and funded their teachers' salaries with "benefit dances held in a home or in a saloon." As evidence, Davis cited a letter in the *Helena Weekly Herald* from December 18, 1874, that details the fundraising method, in this case, for the community of Clancy:

> [L]*ast but not least, on the list of improvements of the burg is the "School House on the Hill" which is a credit to the builders and an honor to the town. For the furnishing of the same everybody and his wife, the bachelor and the sweetheart, and his or her friends, are going to have a grand ball on the 22nd as you have already had due notice. One of our fellow townsmen, S.S. Harvey, proposes to contribute his share toward the ball by tendering the use of his stable and sheds, to any of you Helenaites, or any other man who comes to the party with a team.*

Soon after miners began striking their picks in the rugged gulches of the Rocky Mountains, cowboys and ranchers began to move their stock through the plains. Cowboys became so much associated with the music they brought with them that the enduring image of this western figure in the popular imagination is a man who worked in the saddle by day but settled down at dusk with a guitar or fiddle to serenade the cattle. The stereotype was vividly reinforced with the advent of motion pictures, which celebrated crooners like Tom Mix and Gene Autry. Although the real-life cowboys no doubt lacked the fancy duds and sparkling spurs of their celluloid counterparts, many of them were, in fact, musicians. The reminiscences of the late nineteenth-century cowboys refer often to the calming effect music had on the herds. As cowboy Lake Porter recalled, "Often have I taken my old fiddle at night when on the trail, and while some of my companions would lead my horse around I agitated the cat guts" (quoted by Douglas Branch in *The Cowboy and His Interpreters*).

As the open range gave way to rural ranch towns and railroad hubs in eastern Montana, those places, like the mining towns before them, relied on fiddle music and dancing as their main source of entertainment. Jean Davis described one such event held at Maiden in the Little Rockies in the 1880s that involved the infamous western bad man "Kid" Curry. It seems that the "Kid" had a brother named Loney Curry who, in addition to being a fiddler, had fallen in love with the foster daughter of Pike Landusky, who had forbidden the young woman from seeing a man of "such unsavory reputation." The feud came to a head at a Christmas celebration in 1884, a community dance that the *Kalispell Times* later described as "a real old frontier jamboree." Another of the Curry brothers, Johnny, held the dance at his new barn, with the music provided by Loney Curry, "a fiddler of no mean ability." The dancing went on for two days and nights, at the climax of which Kid Curry and Pike Landusky had their famous showdown that left Landusky dead and Curry's name inscribed in the pantheon of ignominious western outlaws.

This was not the first time a fiddler had been observed in the vicinity of typical Old West violence: a year earlier in 1883, Davis related the tale of a fiddler named Professor Glab in the town of Junction "who was employed in a saloon as an orchestra leader." The bully of the town entered the saloon with a rifle and a pistol and pressed everyone in the room to share a drink with him. Exhibiting somewhat atypical behavior for a fiddler, Professor Glab declined, and "the town terror shot a hole in his hat." The fiddler took his drink but then secreted himself in a closet near the exit with a borrowed shotgun. When the miscreant came past, "[the fiddler] let him have both barrels at once," and a doctor later spent the evening removing birdshot from the bully's back.

Although early writers in the mining camps such as Stuart and Langford offered some description of the kinds of steps that were danced at the dances they attended—the quadrille, the Virginia reel, waltzes and so on—it is not until we encounter the narrative histories of Teddy "Blue" Abbott in *We Pointed Them North* (1939) and Con Price in his 1945 memoir, *Memories of Old Montana*, that we get any indication of the specific tunes that were played by fiddlers in nineteenth-century Montana.

Edward Charles Abbott was born in England in 1860 and came to Montana in 1883. His memoir contains a chapter called "Cowboy Songs," in which he provides a desultory overview of specific songs he recalls having heard on the trail as early as 1876, including tunes popular with fiddlers even today such as "The Cowboy's Lament" and "Bury Me Not on the Lone Prairie." In reference to the latter, Abbott observed wryly that "like a lot of songs on the radio today, they sung it to death. I first heard it along about '81 or '82, and by '85 it was prohibited."

Price was born in 1869 in Iowa and had come to Montana as a cowboy in the 1880s. The camp cook for one of the cowboy outfits he worked with in 1887 played the banjo and harmonica, Price reported, "and had a kind of frame fixed around his head so he could play both at once." Price revealed that the cook only knew "two or three tunes," but that was enough to furnish the music at the dances. According to Price, the cook played "Turkey in the Straw, Hell Among the Yearlings, and a waltz or two." Both of the tunes he names happen to continue to be popular tunes in the canon of modern old-time fiddlers more than 120 years later, attesting to the power of the traditional mode of tune preservation and transmission. We can similarly infer that they were popular tunes before 1887, since it is likely that the musicians then had had the tunes handed down to them in similar fashion.

Both the miner and the cowboy embraced their hours of recreation with a gusto directly proportional to their capacity for hard work. And the perennial choice of entertainment in both worlds was dancing to fiddle music, which as we have seen was often associated (though perhaps not by choice) with violence and characters of "unsavory" reputation. Then, as now, nightclubs, bars and roadhouses tend to attract the sketchier elements of society. Accordingly, fiddling and dancing has often encountered resistance from the moral sector. The "fiddle" has long represented for many "the devil's music," and as we have seen in the historical record, fiddling and dancing were never far from the vicinity of the whiskey jug or fisticuffs. Then, too, musicians tend to become obsessed with their art: the unnamed wife of one Montana fiddler remarked that "the fiddle is called the devil's box because those who play it are possessed by it."

The WPA anthology of Butte lore, *Copper Camp*, documents a raucous party that had occurred at one of the taverns on the flat that inspired someone to write the ballad "The Hopheads' Ball." The ballad describes how "Three fiddlers from the red light / and some junkie with a flute / Were hired to play such music / like ne'er before was played in Butte." The ballad does not identify any of the specific tunes played, nor the fiddlers, but it does

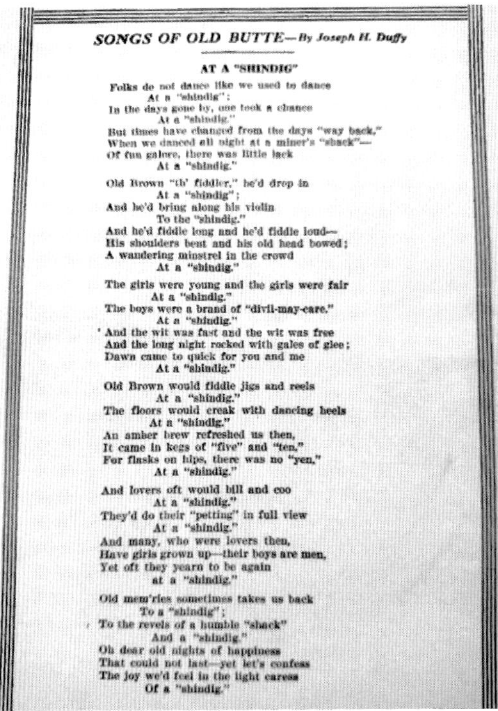

SONGS OF OLD BUTTE—*By Joseph H. Duffy*

AT A "SHINDIG"

Folks do not dance like we used to dance
At a "shindig";
In the days gone by, one took a chance
At a "shindig."
But times have changed from the days "way back,"
When we danced all night at a miner's "shack"—
Of fun galore, there was little lack
At a "shindig."

Old Brown "th' fiddler," he'd drop in
At a "shindig";
And he'd bring along his violin
To the "shindig."
And he'd fiddle long and he'd fiddle loud—
His shoulders bent and his old head bowed;
A wandering minstrel in the crowd
At a "shindig."

The girls were young and the girls were fair
At a "shindig."
The boys were a brand of "divil-may-care."
At a "shindig."
And the wit was fast and the wit was free
And the long night rocked with gales of glee;
Dawn came to quick for you and me
At a "shindig."

Old Brown would fiddle jigs and reels
At a "shindig."
The floors would creak with dancing heels
At a "shindig."
An amber brew refreshed us then,
It came in kegs of "five" and "ten."
For flasks on hips, there was no "yen."
At a "shindig."

And lovers oft would bill and coo
At a "shindig."
They'd do their "petting" in full view
At a "shindig."
And many, who were lovers then,
Have girls grown up—their boys are men,
Yet oft they yearn to be again
at a "shindig."

Old mem'ries sometimes takes us back
To a "shindig";
To the revels of a humble "shack"
And a "shindig."
Oh dear old nights of happiness
That could not last—yet let's confess
The joy we'd feel in the light caress
Of a "shindig."

Like the anonymous "Hophead's Ball," Butte poet Joe Duffy's poem "At a 'Shindig'" celebrates a raucous Butte party featuring old-time fiddling. *Courtesy of Aaron Parrett.*

mention that that they were fluent in all of the old-time idioms: "Waltzes, mazurkas, two-steps / They never passed one by; / There ne'er was dance invented / That the hopheads didn't try. / The fiddlers kept on fiddling / Like they didn't give a dang; / When one of them was tiring, / He just took another 'bang.'"

The ballad reinforces many of the negative stereotypes associated with fiddling and rural music forms in general—the violent chaos it engenders, the reliance of its practitioners on drugs and alcohol—but it also illustrates the hypnotic power of the genre. "The fiddlers kept on fiddling / like they didn't give a dang" represents rather accurately how absorbed old-time fiddlers become in their performances of tunes.

George A. Bruffey wrote in his memoir of life in the Sun River Valley at Fort Shaw in the 1870s that "we had a fine celebration on July Fourth, 1876. A general invitation was extended. All were there. A dance floor was laid. Some of the 'good' ones objected to this. Some held it would not do to allow any fiddling. There were others who were 'in for it.'…some danced who had never danced before or since."

John Barrows in his memoir *Ubet* also chronicled similar events in the Musselshell Valley in the 1880s and was one of the few witnesses to notice the toll such marathon sessions must have exacted on the musicians: "[T]he fiddler and his music grew very mellow as the hours advanced, but a 'pleasant time was enjoyed by all.'" In *Montana's Little Legends*, another writer recounted the burden imposed on the fiddler in humorous if somewhat hyperbolic terms: "These frolics began early and lasted until the wee hours, and the fiddler, growing weary, often fell asleep and whittled away on the same tune until someone woke him and started him off on a new one." The writer also made the point that frequently more men were in attendance at the dances than women and that "it was sometimes necessary to tie a white kerchief around a gentleman's arm, thus marking him as a 'lady' for that set." Bill Carlson described this expedient more colorfully in *Eighty Years of Rosin Dust and Floor Wax*. At one particular dance he recalled as having been held "in about 1905 or 1906," the men outnumbered the women eighty to three. Carlson wrote that "some of the men 'Heifered' themselves by tying handkerchiefs on their arms, and took the part of ladies."

A few common threads emerging from the general fabric of all these accounts perhaps reveal why fiddling is so often associated with individuals of questionable morals or reputation. In the first place, fiddling frequently occurs in the vicinity of alcohol—whether consumed by the musicians themselves or the crowd for whom they are performing. Musicologist Alan Jabbour suggested that the relationship between drinking and fiddling is "serious and complicated, reflecting the deep ambivalences in the larger culture about the fiddle." He pointed out that "everyone wants to give the fiddler a dram—and [then] to malign his character for drinking too much. They keep him up all night—then gossip about him for not managing his farm well."

And even if alcohol is not a factor, the revelry and rowdy behavior that tends to emerge at dances strikes many as boorish if not downright sinful. More importantly, fiddling tends to be the choice of entertainment for those pursuing occupations at the absolute frontier of the land: miners, cowboys, gamblers and so on. And because it is so lightweight and portable, the fiddle was the natural instrument of choice for the itinerant pioneer. In her memoir *Homestead on the Kootenai*, for example, Jacoba Boothman Brad described an early twentieth-century tramp who traveled through on his way to Kalispell whose "passport was a violin from which he drew the most lovely music… he played for us as he sat on the porch, his foot tapping time to the music."

In a similar vein, Con Price related a story told to him by Charlie Russell about the irresponsibility of fiddlers (and artists in general) when it came to legitimate work. Apparently, the captain of the Judith Basin Roundup appointed Charlie and another cowboy who happened to be a fiddler to attend the Moccasin Roundup to collect any cattle that had wandered from one range to the other. When the two returned empty-handed, the boss of the latter outfit laughed at the boss of the former outfit and said, "What the Hell could you expect? You sent a fiddler and a painter over there to act as cowboys."

The initial wave of immigrants to Montana from the East was composed largely of single men—many of them disgruntled soldiers or refugees from the failed Confederacy—and so the early mining camps were relatively free from moral reformers. But the wagon trains that moved westward on the Oregon Trail were family affairs, and as ranchers and cattlemen moved into the valleys of Montana, moralists were quick on their heels. As David Dary noted, "Strongly religious settlers disliked dancing because they believed the 'waist-swing' was indecent" and because "dances often attracted the worst characters in the neighborhood." Such moral revulsion did not spring merely from the religious suspicion that dancing was, as they say, the vertical expression of a horizontal desire, since "even if a girl danced alone to the music of a fiddle, the act was deemed sinful." Such aversion to popular folk music has a long heritage—rumor has it that even Martin Luther composed many of his famous hymns because he thought it "unfair that the devil should have all the good tunes."

Although the moralists might have been vocally critical, they seldom succeeded in stamping out the devil's music. Dances remained the most popular version of frontier and rural entertainment in Montana for more than half a century. The historical record between the 1860s and the 1920s is filled with the reminiscences of those who participated at fiddle-fueled dances across Montana, from Libby to Glendive. Wherever a fiddler could be found, all-night dancing and general revelry was the entertainment of choice.

It may also be the case that unremarkable old-fashioned racial prejudice played a part in the moralists' repugnance for such entertainment forms. As Joseph Kinsey Howard observed in *Montana: High, Wide and Handsome*, at dances in the nineteenth century, "musicians frequently were the half-breeds, famous fiddlers." The less offensive and historically more accurate term for "half-breed" is Métis, and no history of fiddling in Montana would be complete without an account of the Métis.

As noted earlier, one of the first two known fiddlers in Montana, Pierre Cruzatte, was Métis, and given the profound significance of fiddling in Métis culture, Howard is no doubt accurate in ascribing much of the music provided in the early days of Montana history to Métis fiddlers. John Grant, with whom the Stuart brothers wintered in the Deer Lodge Valley in 1862, was Métis, for example, and in addition to Caven and Smith, the Stuarts would likely have been acquainted with Métis fiddlers in the early days in the Montana territory.

The term "Métis" comes from French and literally means "mixed." The Métis emerged sometime in the eighteenth century as a distinct people in the

Red River area of Manitoba, Canada—the result of interbreeding between the French settlers moving westward across Canada and the indigenous tribes they encountered. After several doomed attempts at establishing an independent nation in the second half of the nineteenth century, the Métis have endured through the twentieth century as a landless people with a past of which history has remained largely ignorant. The Métis have long been noted for their aptitude for languages and music. In the nineteenth century, some of the Métis followed the dwindling bison herds from the Red River Settlement into the Milk River drainage and then later into the Judith Basin of central Montana.

Musicologists describe Métis fiddling as a "syncretic form" that draws from both Indian rhythmic and European melodic forms, a kind of synthesis of Scottish, Irish, French and Indian music that emphasizes a distinctive, single beat pulse throughout the tunes that, as in many other fiddle styles, is critical for the execution of dance figures. As with other fiddle traditions, such as the Appalachian, the melody is supported by the rhythmic pulse, and the fiddler must be responsible for both, especially if it is the only instrument available. Because of its unusual time signatures and departure from symmetrically numbered measures, Métis fiddling is difficult to learn and quickly discernible from other styles. In this respect, Métis tunes resemble a class of tunes that old-time Appalachian dance fiddlers refer to as "crooked," meaning their unusual bar lengths make them unsuitable for strictly choreographed contra dancing. Nicholas Vrooman explained that the unusual phrase length in Métis fiddling stems from its close alignment with an Indian drumming and vocal tradition in which the fiddle duplicates a melody that follows a vocal line and a rhythm that follows the beat of a hand drum. In many other traditions, the process works the other way round: the vocal line imitates the melody as set out by the fiddle.

In any case, the Métis style of fiddling, like its Appalachian counterparts, is closely connected to a dance tradition, and the informal Métis anthem "The Red River Jig" is both the name of a particular tune as well as a style of dancing that draws on "elements of Native dancing as well as the jigs and reels of the French and Scots." Métis fiddling also shares affinities with its Appalachian or midwestern old-time cousins with respect to unusual fiddle tunings—for example, ADAE, or AEAC#, instead of the standard GDAE. For fiddlers in the old-time tradition, "standard" pitch ("A" as 440Hz, for example) is an impractical if not meaningless concept. Julia Harrison remarked that traditionally Métis fiddlers "were said to tune their fiddles to the 'cry of the loon and the bellow of a rutting moose.'" As musicologist

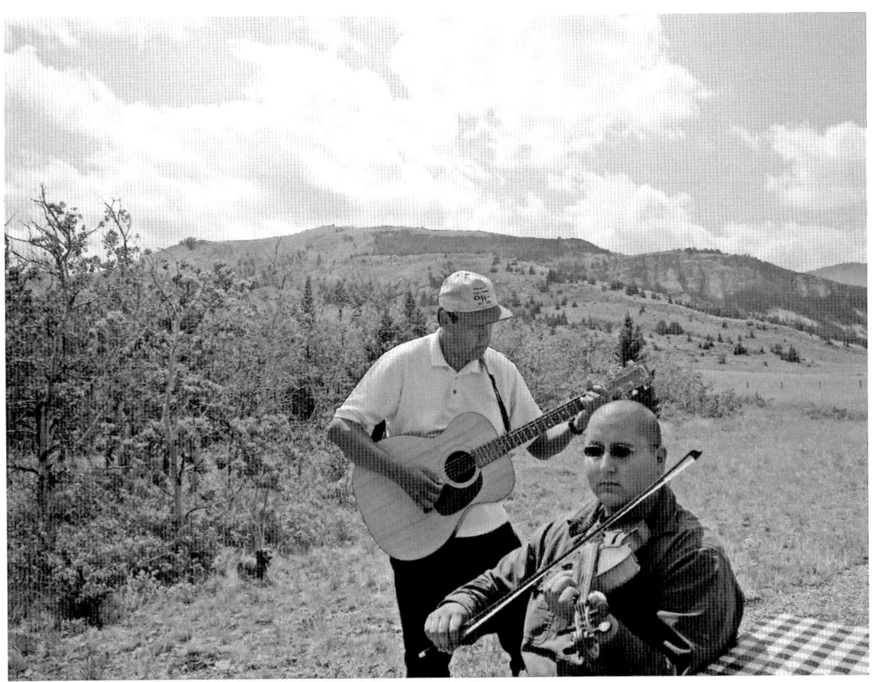

Jim Fox, on the guitar, and his fiddle-playing son, Vince, perform at a dedication of a display that honors the history of the Métis at Ear Mountain. The Métis style of fiddle is unique to the people, whose culture is a mixture of French Canadian and Native American. *Copyright* Great Falls Tribune. *Photo reprinted with permission.*

Lynn Whiddon has noted, Métis fiddlers also employ double-stops, slides and syncopated accents, "practices adopted from American fiddling." Like practitioners of other forms of old-time fiddling, Métis fiddlers also typically hail from rural and impoverished regions and often play their music on handmade instruments.

As with other versions of old-time fiddling, one of its most salient cultural features is the mode of transmission it depends on for survival: tunes are passed from one fiddler to next like messages that tend to take on in some small way the identity of each successive fiddler. Whiddon related how one of the best-known Métis fiddlers, "Teddy Boy" Houle learned by watching his stepfather and uncles play. Like many bearers of such a fiddling tradition, Houle maintains reverence for "the old-time Métis fiddling where every individual has his own version of a tune."

Although the Métis are primarily associated with the Red River region in Manitoba, Canada, the Métis fiddle tradition thrives in Saskatchewan and Alberta as well. Although Canada officially recognized the Métis in 1982, the estimated fifty thousand Métis in the United States, many of whom live in Montana and the Dakotas, have yet to be granted official government recognition. During the 1920s and 1930s, hundreds of Métis lived on Hill 57 outside Great Falls, as well as on the outskirts of other Montana towns. By the year 2000, there were more than four thousand Métis enrolled as Chippewa-Cree. As a result, the Métis fiddling tradition continues in Montana, although its most well-known practitioners (in the United States) are associated with the Turtle Mountain region of North Dakota.

Among the most famous Métis fiddlers in Montana history is Mary Trotchie (1911–1982), who in 1969 won first place in the women's division at the National Fiddle Contest at Weiser, Idaho. Like other fiddlers in the tradition, she learned from older family members who played—her father and uncles. She also cited Métis fiddlers Andy Dejarlis and Ned Landry as important influences. At present, members of the Fox family from the Fort Belknap reservation (parents James and Krystal, son Vince and daughter Jamie) are among the most active proponents of Métis fiddling in Montana.

Jamie Fox is Assiniboine and Gros Ventre, two tribes who share the Fort Belknap Reservation in north-central Montana. "For me, music—Métis music and powwow drumming both—are just part of natural life. I grew up just assuming that that music was just a part of everyday life for everyone." While she acknowledged that some fiddlers learn from CDs or sheet music, the tunes she has acquired for her repertoire are tunes she learned growing up. "The first time I went to the fiddle camp down at Monarch, it dawned on me that there are so many different styles of old-time fiddling," she said. That experience opened her eyes to the broad spectrum of American music in general and the various approaches to old-time music.

But she also noted a rhythmic kinship of those styles with certain elements of Métis fiddling: "I learned from Fatty Moran, his bowing technique especially, which involves a lot of 'jumping' with the bow. I'm not sure how to describe it, but it is very percussive—it emulates the beat of the drum—and to me, that's what defines Métis music." Fox is quick to point out that not all Métis fiddlers use that "pulse," but it is at least specific to her experience in learning at Fort Belknap.

Métis music is, in many ways, the epitome of Americana music, especially because the very name, meaning "mixed," is also a definitive part of America and Americana. As Fox put it, "It really is a reflection of rural, local life and what the identity of an American is—we are all mixed, really." In the last few years, Fox has been traveling the world with her husband, Kristian Bugge, who is from Denmark and is also a fiddler. He plays the old-world

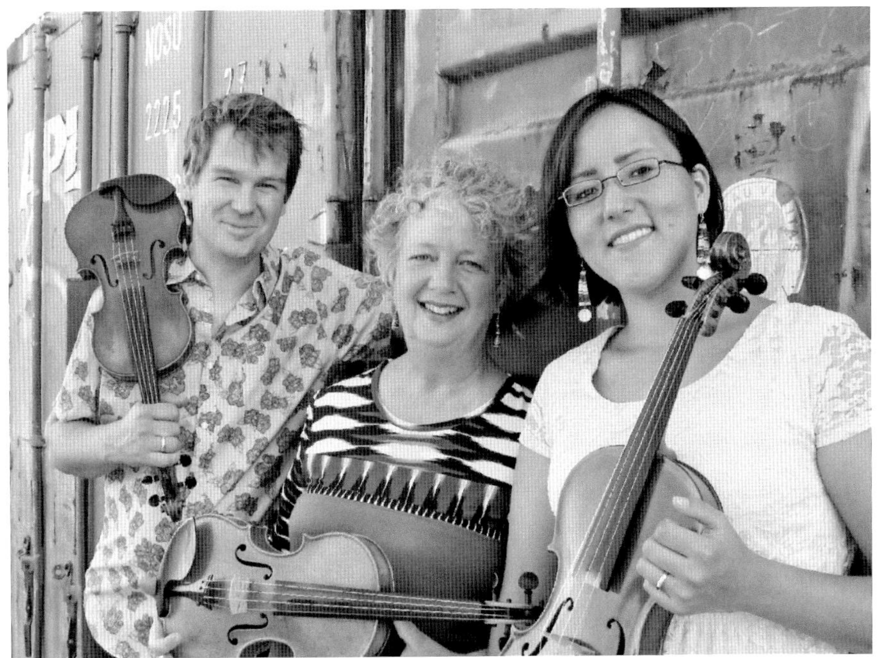

Fiddler Jamie Fox from Fort Belknap, Montana, presents Métis fiddling as part of Three Fiddles, Three Traditions, a band that tours all over the world. Jamie Fox, Kristian Bugge and Ruthie Dornfeld. *Courtesy of Jamie Fox.*

styles of Scandinavia, and with one other fiddler, the three of them bill their shows as Three Fiddlers, Three Traditions. Traveling the world as a musical ambassador has reinforced for Fox what makes Americana music what it is, especially in its old-time country and fiddling traditional aspect.

In the definitive historical work written on the Métis, *Strange Empire*, Joseph Kinsey Howard referred to the heritage of Métis fiddling as he described the wedding of the charismatic nineteenth-century leader of the Métis, Louis Riel:

> *After some of the feast had been consumed the dancing began, with a Métis fiddler supplying the music—the Red River jig, the "pair o' Fours," the "Reel o' Cats," and traditional French steps centuries old. Save for intervals for more eating and drinking the dancing continued all night and sometimes all of the following day...the youngest and most enthusiastic leaped high into the air and executed intricate figures; the Métis braves pounded their heels on the floor and shouted "Ho! Ho!," signal for the ride through the buffalo herd, or "Hiah! Hiah!," the universal alert of the Plains Indians.*

> *Through all the clamor the mad cry of the fiddle knifed, stepping up the tempo of the dance. The solemn-faced Métis babies, silent and unafraid, gazed at the huge shifting shadows on the walls which chased each other faster and faster as the maniac fiddle sobbed and shrieked.*

It is worth noting that the tunes that Howard mentioned are tunes that continue to be played today by contemporary Métis fiddlers, such as Jimmie LaRocque in the Turtle Mountain area of North Dakota, Johnny Arcand in Saskatchewan and Jamie Fox, who studied with LaRocque and Arcand.

Incidentally, Howard also related an anecdote about a Métis fiddler in the late nineteenth century accused of stealing horses by Granville Stuart and his band of vigilantes, known popularly as Stuart's Stranglers. Although Stuart in the 1860s had been involved in a somewhat more defensible episode of vigilantism during the gold rush days in Virginia City and Helena, his role in this second incident in the 1880s was ignominious, as the pretext of rooting out "horse thieves" was more likely an effort to discourage homesteading. Apparently, the young fiddler was "was forced to play all evening for the entertainment of the Stranglers and coolly hanged the next day." Later, one of the Stranglers defended their actions by pointing out that "his being a fiddler hadn't nothing to do with his being a horse thief."

The celebration of Métis fiddling culture thrives in Montana literature as well. The protagonist of Montana writer Peter Bowen's Gabriel Du Pré novels, for example, is a part Métis who plays the fiddle. One of the greatest of all Montana novels—and among the most neglected—is the Métis writer D'Arcy McNickle's *The Surrounded* (1936), which features main character Archilde Leon, who is also of mixed ancestry (Spanish and Salish) and who occasionally makes money playing fiddle in a traveling band.

Through the nineteenth century and up through the first part of the twentieth century, Métis fiddling, like other culturally distinct styles of old-time fiddling, could have been identified by its particular repertoire of tunes. But with the advent of radio and cheap portable phonographs in the 1920s and 1930s, fiddlers in various traditions suddenly gained access to other repertoires, which resulted in a great deal of crossover. Mary Trotchie, for example, claimed to have learned her trademark tune "Foggy Valley" from listening to KOBB radio (out of Great Falls) in the 1930s. In addition, fiddlers in various traditions adopted into their repertoires contemporary popular songs, from Tin Pan Alley or Broadway. Today, one is as likely to hear "I'm Always Chasing Rainbows" or "The Good Old Summertime" played by an elder fiddler at an old-time fiddler's jamboree as often as "Arkansas Traveler" or "Leather Britches."

Nevertheless, the programming of Montana's earliest radio stations reflected the popularity of old-time fiddling. According to Mary Murphy, for example, the conventional wisdom at KGIR in Butte was "Ditch Dvorak. They want 'Turkey in the Straw.'" Unfortunately, old-time fiddling enjoyed only a brief tenure on the airwaves before becoming drowned out by kilowatt after kilowatt of popular music and an emergent form that, thanks to the popularity of WSM's *Grand Ole Opry*, would eventually become known as "country and western." In the meantime, old-time fiddling receded from the horizon and began to disappear.

Although old-time fiddling lingered in the more rural areas of the state as a still viable source of entertainment for dances, it dwindled in general popularity so much that by the midpoint of the twentieth century it seemed in danger of dying out. Many old-time fiddlers in the '40s and '50s expressed concern for the vanishing style. With more accessible forms of entertainment competing for the attention of the younger generations—motion pictures, radio and especially television—fewer younger people were adopting the pastime.

By the 1960s, concern had reached a critical mass among the elder fiddlers, many of whom had been born in the late nineteenth century. In 1963, a group of concerned fiddling aficionados started the Montana Old Time Fiddlers organization. They were inspired by the foundation of a national organization in 1953 that began sponsoring the Grand National Old Time Fiddle Championships at Weiser, Idaho, that same year. To coincide with the 1964 Territorial Centennial celebrations in Montana, the Old Time Fiddlers published a catalogue of more than one hundred fiddlers and accompanists in the state called *Fiddlers Book*. With charmingly rustic diction, the ostensible editor, L.T. Johnson, lauded the dawn of the organization with the concomitant centennial:

> *Comes the Montana Old Time Fiddlers—representing the fiddler of by-gone days. These older boys that came with their parents in the covered wagons were the ones that brought the fiddle, banjo, guitar and accordion to this wide-open country. The "young sprouts" that have grown up and were never quite able to close their minds to the only entertainment they knew when they were young are the ones that are responsible for the fiddlers that are in existance* [sic] *today.*

The centennial provided a natural and appropriate occasion for the fiddlers to align themselves. As Johnson and many of the other fiddlers in the booklet giving testimonials attested, their direct ancestors had made the journey cross country in the several decades after Lewis and Clark, and like those first Europeans to travel through Montana, they carried their fiddles with them. "A hundred years later there are sons, grandsons and granddaughters who had a desire to continue along the same road of family enjoyments," Johnson wrote, "to gather together and relive the days of the dusty trails their forefathers had traveled, and enjoy the clean fun-making entertainment that even brings many friends and familys [*sic*] together today." Like many fiddlers who helped found the Old Time Fiddlers Organization in 1964, Johnson, born in 1893, was the child of immigrants from the Midwest—in his case, Lindberg, Kansas.

Other founding members of the Old Time Fiddlers included Jim Ring, Dave Baylor, Alfred Olson and Hazel Bradley. Ring recalled that "in the year before the centennial, or 1963, Mr. L.T. Johnson went to Weiser, Idaho to the National Fiddlers' Contest and came back with the idea of having a National Contest here, and starting an organization. The first meeting was held at his place." Ring, a fiddler himself, was born in Tecumseh, Nebraska, in 1895 and had picked up the fiddle at age ten. To coordinate their fledgling organization with the encroaching centennial celebrations, the Veterans of Foreign Wars sponsored Ring and Johnson "for a trip around the state to organize the 'layout.'"

By "layout," Ring referred to the division of the state into various regions, each one of which could sponsor local hoedowns and jamborees and then send representatives to the annual contest held by the state organization in Missoula and, later, Polson. For nearly two months, Ring and Johnson traveled around Montana, talking to local fiddlers and describing their vision of an organization that would sponsor a national contest in 1964 under the aegis of the Centennial Celebration. "So began the Montana Fiddlers," wrote Maxine Ness in her informal history of the organization, published in 1976 as part of the nation's bicentennial.

Although many locales around the state had held fiddling contests before 1964, none had been officially sanctioned by the national organization. The state contest that year was divided into two categories: Pat Colyer won the division for fiddlers under sixty-five years of age, and Mark Turnquist won in the over sixty-five category. The National Contest sponsored in conjunction with the Territorial Centennial was won by Byron Berline, a now-famous fiddler who was already beginning to make a name for himself in bluegrass

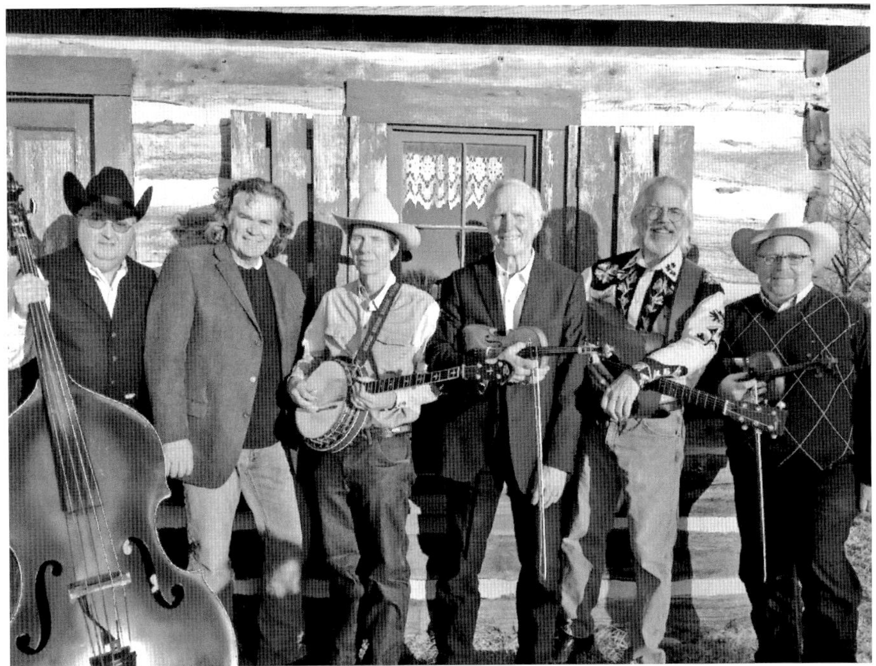

Virtuoso fiddler Byron Berline is nearly as famous for his cameo performances on various rock-and-roll records (including the Rolling Stones' *Beggars Banquet* and Rod Stewart's *Tonight's the Night*) as he is for his stellar bluegrass and swing performances, seen here with the Byron Berlin Band. *Promo material from http://doublestop.com.*

and swing circles and who was in high demand as a session musician. A few years after winning the national title in Montana, for example, Berline would be fiddling on the Rolling Stones' *Beggar's Banquet* album (1968), and their *Let It Bleed* (1969), the Flying Burrito Brothers' *Gilded Palace of Sin* (1969), Gram Parsons's *G.P.* (1972), Arlo Guthrie's *Hobo's Lullaby* (1972), Bob Dylan's *Pat Garrett and Billy the Kid* (1973) and Rod Stewart's *Tonight I'm Yours* (1981), to name a handful of highlights. The (Great Falls) *Tribune* in the Sunday supplement for June 1964 featured a photograph of Berline and Jimmy Widner of Snake River Outlaw fame (see chapter 2) fiddling together.

Widner was a great influence on many of the present-day generation of bluegrass and old-time fiddlers in the Missoula area and in the Bitterroot Valley, where he made his home for more than thirty-five years. He is cited in discographies as one of the definitive sources for such tunes as "East Tennessee Blues" and "The Bitterroot Valley Waltz."

The Montana Old Time Fiddlers Organization continued to grow in the 1970s, and a decade after its inauguration, representative fiddlers from the various regions of the state entertained the crowd at the World's Fair in Spokane, Washington (Expo '74), and were featured on the front page of the *Spokesman Review* on September 7, 1974. A year later, a registry of fiddlers called *Montana Fiddlers* listed many younger members alongside the ranks of the older founding members, which indicated that the organization was succeeding in its mission to ensure the preservation of the tradition. By 1989, the *Montana Fiddlers* registry (now called *Montana Fiddlers Hall of Fame*) had grown from a thirty-two-page booklet in 1975 to almost two hundred pages, divided into sections for each of the state's eight regions.

Today, the fiddlers' organization continues to thrive, although two of the eight regions happen to be currently inactive because of low membership. Those regions (five and seven) encompass the extreme eastern quarter of the state and suffer from limited population and extreme distances between fiddlers. The organization is otherwise vibrant and active in sponsoring various contests, and the annual Fiddle Camp in Monarch, Montana, each year features world-class instruction from such famous stylists as Stuart Williams, Brendan Bulger, Bobby Hicks, Brad Leftwich, Alice Gerrard and Geoff Seitz.

One of Montana's most energetic young fiddlers is Brigid Reedy. She's passionate about music and has been for longer than she can remember. She began yodeling at two years of age and picked the fiddle up a few years later. When she was twelve years old, the musically precocious Miss Reedy graced the stage at the annual National Cowboy Poetry Gathering in Elko, Nevada, holding her own alongside such luminaries as Tom Russell, Stephanie Davis, Wylie Gustafson and Ian Tyson, to name just a handful of those who have starred at the Gathering, now in its thirty-first year. Now fifteen, she has recently moved beyond just fiddling and yodeling to writing her own fiddle tunes and lyrics, including "When the Snow Flies," cowritten with her father and featured on her self-titled debut EP. In 2016, she will for the third year in a row attend the National Cowboy Poetry Gathering as a featured performer.

When asked about what genre she feels her music fits best into, Brigid is pretty adamant about avoiding pigeonholes. "I play all kinds of styles, all kinds of traditions—Irish, country, even Tin Pan Alley," she said, although undoubtedly one of the phrases even a casual listener would associate with the sound of her EP is "cowboy west," a term both she and her father, John Reedy, refer to often in discussions of their music.

Her father, John Reedy, is also a performing musician, and he and his daughter are frequent collaborators. John recorded an album of his own in 2007 called *Twisted Vignettes*, featuring a handful of his own compositions,

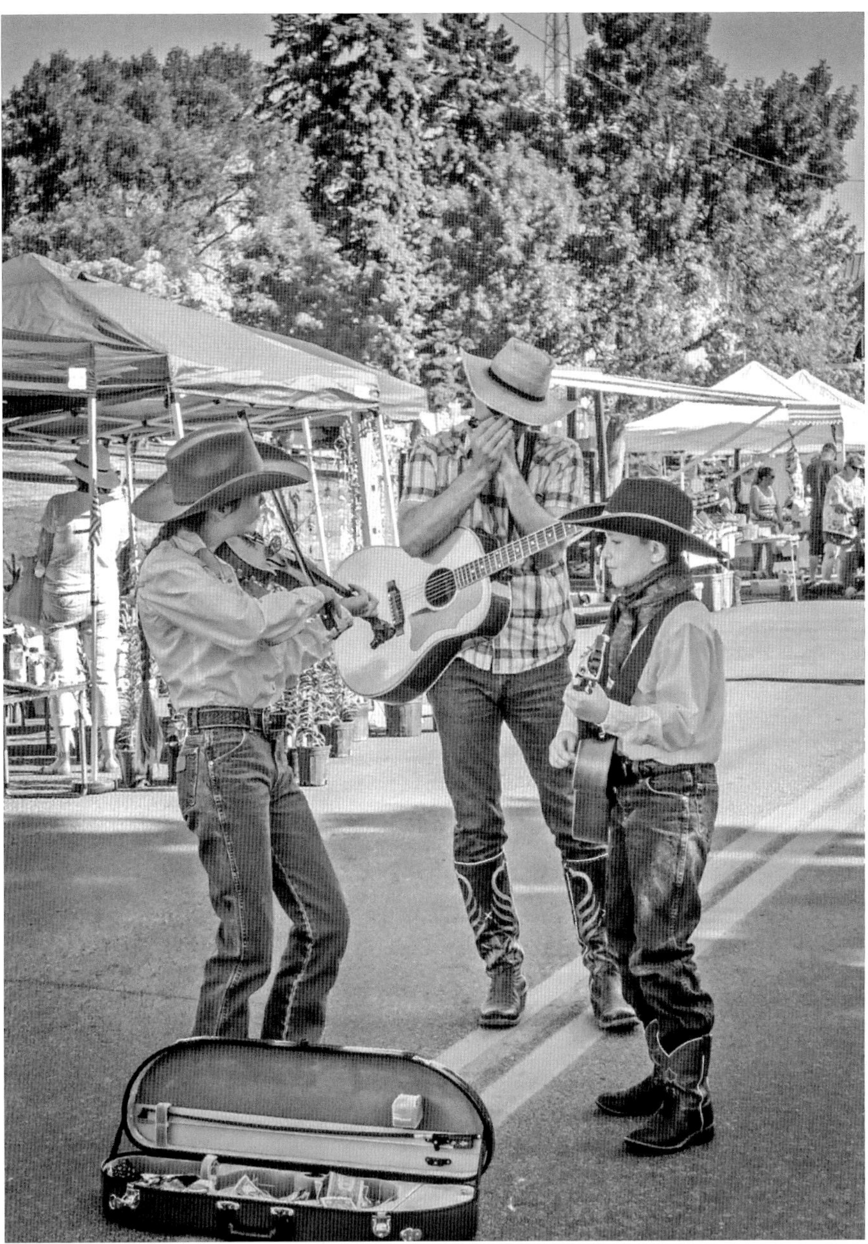

The Reedy family out of Boulder, Montana, embody the western strain of folk Americana. John Reedy is a songwriter and performer and father to young Brigid Reedy, who has been delighting the cowboy poetry crowd at the annual gathering in Elko, Nevada, since she was five years old. Pictured here are John Reedy, Brigid Reedy and Johnny Reedy performing at the farmers' market in Helena, Montana. Heather Reedy, photographer. *Courtesy of John Reedy.*

as well as a few rodeo songs and ballads by other writers. He happened to record the album in Belt at the Boone Productions studio of Dan Gliko (of Boone and the Buckskins notoriety; see chapter 1). Like his daughter, John Reedy is also wary of labels. "'Americana' is an OK way to describe our music," he admitted. "But if asked, we'd probably just say 'American music.'" While the Reedys' music references the blues and other traditions—one hears a touch of Celtic, for example—there's no denying that the dominant sonic strain coming through here is a hallmark of Montana tradition: the cowboy song.

Both Brigid and John also embrace an ethos of place that many people across the country associate with the West, by which they understand almost instinctively the rural life (the Reedys live outside Boulder, Montana) and the general aesthetic associated with ranching and the cowboy way. To see the photos on their albums, for example, one might think they've just come off a photo shoot for *Cowboys and Indians* magazine. But the truth is that they always look that way. Brigid, for example, is hardly ever seen without her signature vaquero hat (a gift from her mother). But alongside her profound and earnest sense of "place," and her own immersion in Montana specifically, Brigid understands music as a sort of universal passport to other people and cultures. Already she's done a lot of world traveling, and in 2015, she spent a month or so in Ireland. "I love to connect with people, and music cuts quickly through to the soul," she said. When her father suggested that music is a way of telling stories, Brigid elaborated with a poetic observation of her own: "It's an efficient way to spread beauty."

At the ripe old age of fifteen, Brigid Reedy probably represents a future for Montana Americana music that is just now beginning to coalesce and form, and what that future will sound like is perforce a matter of pure speculation. As for her own career, she's surprisingly philosophical and unwilling to look too far ahead. "I really don't know what I'm going to do with my life yet," she said with a smile and a glint in her eye. "I live in the moment, pretty much."

Even in the nineteenth and early twentieth centuries, when old-time fiddling was the main source of musical entertainment, it was nevertheless a peripheral phenomenon because Montana itself was at the periphery of the country. And although now old-time fiddling has been again relegated to the periphery of music styles—neglected by many in favor of bluegrass or the flashier "contest" style—it endures as the original "alternative country" music amid a plethora of derivative or competing forms. While most fiddlers in the old-time tradition would agree that even two hundred years of fiddling in Montana has not been long enough to result in a definitive "Montana" style, many of them—Mike Williams, the Fox family, Bill Sevores and Brigid Reedy—are among those who are presently contributing to what may eventually be known as the "Montana style" among old-time fiddlers nationwide.

Afterword

Oh Shenandoah, I long to hear you…Away, we're bound away,
Across the wide Missouri.
—old folk song of the Voyageurs

The cowboy aura of the West contains an inherently musical element, akin perhaps to the way the fiddle and banjo are among the first things people think of when they heard the word *Appalachia*. Historically, it is clear that boot heels cobbled in the South have made a deep impression on the Montana landscape, both by way of the cowboys during the years of the open range and by way of the gold prospectors who preceded them. For that matter, because Montana contains the headwaters of the vast Missouri drainage, it happened to be one of the earliest goals of the European explorers, many of whom carried with them accoutrements of a folk tradition stretching back to the seventeenth century, including instruments (especially the fiddle) that continue to define the Americana sound. The influence of native cultures on the development of country music in general and old-time "square" dance music is obscure only to those who lack a firsthand acquaintance with it, and it is likely that some graduate student in musicology is right now exploring the possibility that some definitive features of rock-and-roll can be traced to Indian drumming just as much as to African drumming.

Nearly every musician I talked to for this project mentioned the importance of the landscape itself as a factor in the production of whatever version of Montana Americana they happen to be playing or developing, and it hardly needs repeating that a preoccupation with "place" has overwhelmed Montana literary criticism for almost fifty years. Visitors to Montana routinely observe how passionate its residents tend to be about the state they inhabit. While it may be a benign kind of chauvinism, the pride Montanans take in their state seems to come largely from the emptiness of its wide-open spaces, although the character of the people also gets mentioned almost as often. It would be tempting to say that the latter derives from the former, but experience shows that in the broadest sense, people are pretty much the same everywhere—we're all *Homo sapiens*, after all.

The equation may work the other way around. After all, people tend to seek out those with whom they're spiritually similar, and we all like to congregate with other like-minded people. The last census showed that half of the state's residents were born outside the state, and the idea that over the last century Montana has developed a population especially appreciative of, if not geared toward, its peculiarities of geography and weather and lonely, unpeopled expanses makes a certain amount of sense. In other words, people self-select for the Big Sky Country.

How those factors might emerge in the music people make here in this state reflects the same problem. How definitive a "Montana sound" is there, really? The answer to that question, for the most part, lies outside the scope of this book, although an obvious first step would be a far more comprehensive survey of the music and the bands than I've offered here. In anticipation of the critics who will inevitably (and rightly) fault me for all that I've left out, I can only say that my approach here is tentative and without question a reflection of my own taste more than anything else. But anyone who loves music will recognize the perhaps obvious truth that, in the end, there's no other way to start. Collecting music is like collecting books: at some point, it dawns on you with the force of Gödel's Proof that a lifetime is hardly long enough to make an inventory both consistent and complete of what you've judged worth keeping. Naturally, it's hard to draw broad conclusions from such a brief sampling. Nevertheless, a few observations seem worthy of emphasis.

First, a small population spread over a large area creates practical problems that any musician in Montana has to contend with. Outside Billings and Missoula, and possibly Bozeman, it's almost impossible for a musician to make a living without having to travel—a lot. What counts as an urban center in Montana would amount to little more than a neighborhood in a city like Seattle or Minneapolis, and those "urban centers" in Montana tend to be few and far between.

Consequently, working musicians in Montana tend to be more eclectic and versatile perhaps than in other places—they have to be. Helena musician John Dendy provides a good example: he plays in a half-dozen bands, ranging from "hot club swing and jazz" (Cottonwood Club) to folky Americana (Tombigbee), but then he also does "country blues and ragtime" with Steve Laster and can even be cajoled into playing bass for the occasional contra dance. David Horgan and Beth Lo illustrate the same principle, although an interest in and inclination for a wide variety of styles is certainly a factor in all three cases. Meanwhile, Erik "Fingers" Ray—pound for pound probably the most capable performing musician around—has solved the problem in another way: he's made himself into a one-man band in high demand, as he incorporates everything from Cajun music to hard rock covers into his sets, all delivered within the framework of an award-winning fingerpicking blues style. (He also beats out rhythm on a bass drum and a high hat using his feet and blows harmonica solos the way Clarence Clemons might have if he'd chosen the harp instead of the saxophone.) I am eternally impressed by and harbor tremendous respect for Montana musicians such as Tom Catmull, Russ Nasset, Frank Ruffolo, Scot Wilburn, Martha Scanlan and many others who, against considerable odds, continue to make a living playing the music they love. Tom Catmull, in fact, has penned a song about, as he puts it, "trying to make a living out here." The song is called "Rome" (a cut off *Glamour Puss*); it's described as "mostly about me giving into Missoula (as home) after fifteen years of living here" and captures the problem poignantly:

They say that anything you do or don't do well,
turns out to be a can or cannot sell,
Missoula County never promised it would whisper where to go.
Might as well be Rome.
(© 2014 Tom Catmull)

It is equally evident that the small population of Montana makes for an unusually close-knit community of musicians of all stripes. Perhaps more than other states with bigger populations, musicians in Montana—whatever style they play—are seldom more than one degree of separation from one another, even if they live at opposite ends of the state. That propinquity might very well generate a higher rate of musical cross-fertilization in Montana than in more populous states, and most critics seem to agree in any case that Americana music is, to some extent, a reflection of the cultural melting pot we call home.

Accordingly, musicians in one part of Montana quite often feel they share an unspoken kinship with their counterparts in other regions of the state. People who lived here in the 1970s and were fortunate enough to be a part of the Aber Day Keggers or see their herald bearers, the Mission Mountain Wood Band, perform live, for example, often refer to a familial vibe running like a current through the music scene in those years.

Americana musicians in Montana continue to cultivate that sense of camaraderie and good times against the backdrop of the inimitable Big Sky Country and the sublime lonesomeness of the West, and as a result, they continue to contribute to an American stream of music as full of time and history as the wide Missouri itself.

Selected Bibliography

Abbott, E.C. *We Pointed Them North*. New York: Farrar & Rinehart, 1939.

Bloch, E. Maurice. "The Jolly Flatboatmen." *American West* (September 1968): 41–48.

Borchard, Jacquie. "Our Own Stradivarius?" *Great Falls Tribune*, April 9, 2000.

Brad, Jacoba Boothman. *Homestead on the Kootenai*. Caldwell, ID: Caxton Press, 1960.

Branch, Douglas. *The Cowboy and His Interpreters*. New York: Appleton, 1961.

Briggeman, Kim. "UM Student Collecting Archive of Mont. Bands." (Helena, MT) *Independent Record*, November 12, 2012.

Brown, Tom, with Jim Widner. *Fiddlin' Around the West*. Hamilton, MT: Sapphire Printing, 1984.

Bruffey, George A. *Eighty-One Years in the West*. Butte, MT, 1925.

Cannon, Hal. Liner notes for Snake River Outlaws, *Live Radio*, circa 1953, Missoula, Montana. Deep West Records/Western Folklife Center, 2008.

Carlson, Bill. *Eighty Years of Rosin and Floor Wax: A History of Old Time Fiddling*. Glasgow, MT, n.d.

Cohen, Betsy. "Fiddle Camp: A Bow to Tradition." *The Missoulian*, June 25, 2000.

Crain, Zac. "Charley Pride Turns 70." *D Magazine* (June 2008).

Crowley, John M. "Old-Time Fiddling in Big Sky Country." *Journal of Cultural Geography* (Fall–Winter 1984): 47–60.

Dary, David. *Seeking Pleasure in the Old West*. Lawrence: University Press of Kansas, 1995.

Dimsdale, Thomas J. *The Vigilantes of Montana*. Reprint, Norman: University of Oklahoma Press, 1953.

Foster, Martha Harroun. "The Spring Creek (Lewistown) Métis and Métis Identity in Montana." In *Métis Legacy: A Métis Historiography and Annotated Bibliography*. Edited by Lawrence J. Barkwell, Leah Dorion and Darren R. Préfontaine. Winnipeg, MB: Pemmican Pub., 2001.

Guntharp, Matthew G. *Learning the Fiddler's Ways*. University Park: Pennsylvania State University Press, 1980.

Harrison, Julia D. *Métis: People between Two Worlds*. Vancouver: Glenbow-Alberta Institute, 1985.

Havighurst, Craig. *Air Castle of the South: WSM and the Making of Music City*. Champaign: University of Illinois Press, 2007.

Howard, Joseph Kinsey. *Montana: High, Wide, and Handsome*. New Haven, CT: Yale University Press, 1943.

———. *Strange Empire*. New York: William Morrow, 1952.

Howdy Montana. Directed by Matt Cascella, 2013.

Hunt, Robert. "'Merry to the Fiddle': The Musical Amusement of the Lewis and Clark Party." *We Proceeded On* 14, no. 4 (1988): 11–15. Lewis & Clark Trail Heritage Foundation.

Kegger: The Story of the World's Largest Benefit Kegger. Directed by Bruce Barrett et al. MLAC, LLC, 2009.

Korn, Michael. *If You Can't Dance to It, It's Not Old Time Fiddle! Traditional and Old-Time Fiddle Music from Montana.* Booklet accompanying Montana Folklife Project LP MFP-002, 1986.

———. "A Violin's Just a Fiddle that Went to College...." *Rural Montana* (March 1980): 12–13.

Langford, Nathaniel Pitt. *Vigilante Days and Ways: The Pioneers of the Rockies, 1890.* Reprint, New York: Merrill, 1971.

McLatchy, Michael Gene. "From Wisconsin to Montana and Life in the West, 1863–1889: The Reminiscences of Robert Kirkpatrick." Master's thesis, Montana State University, 1961.

McMurtry, Larry. *In a Narrow Grave: Essays on Texas.* Albuquerque: University of New Mexico Press, 1968.

McNickle, D'Arcy. *The Surrounded.* New York, 1936.

Montana Territorial Centennial Fiddlers Book: Old Time Fiddlers. Helena, MN: Veterans of Foreign Wars Ole Beck Post 209 and the Ladies Auxiliary for Montana's Territorial Centennial Year, 1964.

Moulton, Gary E., ed. *Journals of the Lewis & Clark Expedition.* Lincoln: University of Nebraska Press, 1995.

Murphy, Mary. *Mining Cultures: Men, Women, and Leisure in Butte, 1914–41.* Champaign: University of Illinois Press, 1997.

Mussulman, Joseph A. "The Greatest Harmoney: 'Meddicine Songs' on the Lewis and Clark Trail." *We Proceeded On* (November 1997): 4.

Nettl, Bruno. *Blackfoot Musical Thought: Comparative Perspectives.* Kent, OH: Kent State University Press, 1989.

Never Long Gone: The Mission Mountain Wood Band Story. Directed by Michael Ballard et al. Montana PBS documentary, 2009.

Parrett, Aaron. "'Ditch Dvorak, They Want Turkey in the Straw': A Brief History of Old Time Fiddling in Montana." *Old-Time Herald* 13, no. 7 (Fall 2013).

Petrusich, Amanda. *Do Not Sell at Any Price*. New York: Scribner, 2015.

Price, Con. *Memories of Old Montana*. Pasadena, CA: Trail's End Pub., 1945.

Pride, Charley, with Jim Henderson. *Pride: The Charley Pride Story*. New York: William Morrow, 1995.

Richardson, Albert D. *Beyond the Mississippi: Life and Adventure on the Prairies, Mountains, and Pacific Coast*. Hartford, CT: American Publishing, 1867.

Stuart, Granville. *Forty Years on the Frontier*. Vol. 1, *Prospecting for Gold: From Dogtown to Virginia City, 1852–1864*. Reprint, Lincoln: University of Nebraska Press, 1977.

Time. "Pioneers" (February 28, 1927): 17.

Vrooman, Nicholas CP. "'Rielization' of the Greater Métis Traditional Historic Homeland." In *Métis Legacy: A Métis Historiography and Annotated Bibliography*. Edited by Lawrence J. Barkwell, Leah Dorion and Darren R. Préfontaine. Winnipeg, MB: Pemmican Pub., 2001.

Walsh, Cory. "Joey Running Crane Shows Versatility at VFW Monthly Residency." *The Missoulian*, March 16, 2014.

We're Going Home. Directed by Tim Goessman, 2012.

Whidden, Lynn. "Métis Music." In *Métis Legacy: A Métis Historiography and Annotated Bibliography*. Edited by Lawrence J. Barkwell, Leah Dorion and Darren R. Préfontaine. Winnipeg, MB: Pemmican Pub., 2001, 169–76.

Williams, Stuart. "Old Time Dance Fiddling in Washington State: 1830s–1994." *Fiddler Magazine* (Summer 1994): 12.

Interviews

Aaberg, Philip. Telephone, March 1, 2016.

Arnentaro, Louis. Telephone, July 29, 2015; February 3, 2016.

Barrett, Pete. Telephone, July 17, 2015; Helena, Montana, August 13, 2015.

Boster, Cameron. E-mail, December 3, 2015.

Cornette, Matt. Telephone, January 13, 2016.

Cowles, Monty. Telephone, November 7, 2015.

Darlington, Ron. Telephone, November 4, 2015.

Fochtman, Orval. Telephone, August 16, 2015.

Fox, Jamie. Telephone, 2006; January 16, 2016.

Gladstone, Jack. Telephone, August 28, 2015.

Gliko, Dan. Telephone, August 18, 2015; Belt, Montana, October 7, 2015.

Hartwell, Gibson. Telephone, September 9, 2015; e-mail, January 23, 2016.

Havighurst, Craig. Telephone, July 16, 2015.

Hawes-Davis, Doug. Telephone, June 8, 2015; Missoula, Montana, August 29, 2015.

Horgan, David. Telephone, December 17, 2015.

Horton, Jane. Helena, Montana, October 20, 2015.

Kostas. Telephone, February 3, 2016.

Lowell, John. Telephone, September 30, 2015.

Martens, Dave. Telephone, May 25, 2015; telephone, August 10, 2015; telephone, January 12, 2016; Havre, Montana, February 26, 2016.

Morin, Cary. Telephone, August 25, 2015.

Nasset, Russ. Telephone, January 19, 2016.

Newby, Rick. Helena, Montana, November 7, 2015.

Pavelich, Matt. Flathead Lake, Montana, July 11, 2015; telephone, August 16, 2015.

Purington, Michael. Telephone, October 23, 2015.

Quist, Rob. Telephone, June 11, 2015; e-mail, January 9, 2016.

Reinholdt, Richie. Telephone, August 22, 2015.

Rieke, Rex. Telephone, August 25, 2015.

Rimel, John. Telephone, August 24, 2015.

Rosenberg, Ivan. Telephone, October 2, 2015.

Ruffolo, Frank. Butte, Montana, August 14, 2015.

Running Crane, Joseph. Telephone, January 1, 2016; telephone, January 2, 2016.

Ryan, Rick. Telephone, July 13, 2015.

Scanlan, Martha. Telephone, September 8, 2015; e-mail, January 25, 2016.

Sevores, Bill. Missoula, Montana, July 23, 2005.

Stokes, Doug. Telephone, June 15, 2015.

Wilburn, Scot. Spokane, Washington, June 9, 2015.

Williams, Mike. Helena, Montana, July 20, 2005.

SELECTED DISCOGRAPHY

This discography is compiled from record collections all over Montana. Dave Martens and Doug Hawes-Davis were especially helpful and knowledgeable resources. Some of the recordings were digital files with scant information. I have included as much relevant info as possible (label, year of release, format and so on). I welcome corrections or added info for future editions.

Best Westerns. *High Country*. Black National Recording, 2014. LP.

Betty Jo Starr & Johnny Starr. "Copper Colored Klootch" / "Song of Great Falls." Montana Records (R-1281). 45 rpm.

———. "I'm Blue Again" / "Missoula Waltz." Alaska (OP-194). 45 rpm.

———. "Liberty Express" / "Montana Rainbow." 4-Star (X-74). 78 rpm.

———. "Missoula Waltz" / "When It's Peach Picking Time in Georgia." Alaska (OP-194). 78 rpm.

Big Sky Mudflaps. *Armchair Cabaret.* Helios Records (HR 440-2), 1979. LP. Rereleased on Spud Records (SD 21001), 2002. CD.

———. *Armchair Cabaret Live.* Spud Records (21000), 2000. CD.

———. *Cold Duck Time.* 1997. CD. Rereleased on Spud Records (SD 21097), 2002. CD.

———. *Sensible Shoes.* Flying Fish Records (FF-293), 1983. LP. Rereleased on Spud Records (SD 21002), 2002. CD.

———. *Shake, Rattle & Roll.* 1987. LP. Rereleased on Spud Records (SR 21087), 2002. CD.

Boone and the Buckskins. "Just Less than a Day"/ "Don't Let Our Love Fall Down" / "Somewhere with You" / "Bring on the Good Times." Valtron Records (R-2295), Helena, Montana. EP-45 rpm.

Boster, Cameron. https://cameronscottboster/bandcamp.com.

———. https://soundcloud.com/csb2.

Country Girl Kay. "Bluebird Yodel" / "First and Last Waltz" / Moonshine Party" / "That's Why I Couldn't Stay Up Late Last Night." Whitkay Records (502). EP-45 rpm.

———. "Blue Montana Skies" / "Don't Let the Moon Break Your Heart" / "Iowa Waltz" / Mockingbird Waltz." Whitkay Records (504). EP-45 rpm.

———. "Canadian Waltz" / Montana Stomp" / My Heart Says Forget You" / "No One Loves You Like I Do." Whitkay Records (501). EP-45 rpm.

———. "I'll Yodel My Blues Away" / "Apache Trail" / "Honky Tonk Boogie" / "Only One." Whitkay (509). EP-45 rpm.

———. "I Still Worry Over You" / Love Can't Stay Away" / "Moonshine Hill" / "Springtime in Montana." Whitkay Records (506). EP-45 rpm.

———. "Life Is Not a Bed of Roses," b/w "Arkansas Boogie." Whitkay Records (W-1001). 78 rpm. Only fifty copies were pressed.

———. "Montana Rockies" / "Heartache Millionaire" / "I'm a Fool" / "Leather Britches." Whitkay (507). EP-45 rpm.

———. "Raggedy Ann" / "Montana Special" / "Red Wing" / "Crackling Hen." Whitkay (510). EP-45 rpm.

———. "Utah Two Step" / "Life Is Not a Bed of Roses" / "Old Montana Trail" / "Canadian Waltz." Whitkay (505). EP-45 rpm.

Denny, Jerry, Buddy Russette and the Cree-ations. "Indian Country," b/w "Love You." Kessler Recording (USR-9317), 1976. 45 rpm.

Edwards, Jonathan. *Jonathan Edwards*. Capricorn Records (SD 862), 1971. LP.

Goddammitboyhowdy. *Goddammitboyhowdy Is Rez Punk*. Minor Bird Records (MBR-002), 2011. EP.

Hays, Christy. *O' Montana*. Self-released, 2014. CD.

If You Can't Dance to It, It's Not Old Time Fiddle! Traditional and Old-Time Fiddle Music from Montana. Montana Folklife Project (MFP-002), 1986. LP.

King Elephant. *Exhaust*. Minor Bird Records (MBR-008), 2013. LP.

Lil' Smokies. *Lil' Smokies*. Self-released, 2014. CD.

Lindy Ness & the City Dudes. "Beautiful Destiny Waltz" / "Ever Ever Time." Vega (453). 78 rpm, also 45 rpm.

———. "My Heart's in Montana" / "My Heart's in Montana (Instrumental)." Vega (4018). 78 rpm.

Live Wire Choir. *Live Wire Choir*. Helios Records (HR 440-1), 1978. LP.

Lowell, John. *I Am Going to the West*. Self-released, 2012. CD.

Lowell, John, with Kane's River. *Kane's River*. Doobie Shea (DSCD 4003), 2000. CD.

Mission Mountain Wood Band. *In Without Knocking*. M2WB Records (OU812), 1977. LP.

Morin, Cary. *Streamline*. Self-released, 2013. CD.

———. *Tiny Town*. Independent, 2015. CD.

Nasset, Russ. *Blue Highway*. Self-released, 2010. CD.

———. *Human Tongue*. Self-released, 2013. CD.

———. *Russ Nasset & The Revelators*. Self-released, 2003. CD.

Native North America (Vol. 1): Aboriginal Folk, Rock, and Country 1966–1985. Light in the Attic Records, 2013. 3-LP set.

The New Columbia Fiddlers. *Fiddle Tunes of the Lewis & Clark Era*. Voyager Records (VRCD 358), 2003. CD.

Reedy, Brigid. *Brigid Reedy*. Twisted Cowboy Music, 2014. CD.

Reedy, John. *Twisted Vignettes*. Twisted Cowboy Music, 2007. CD.

Rummel, Jay. "Lady from Missoula County" / "Montana Blue." Epson Records (no cat. #). 45 rpm.

Scanlan, Martha. *The Shape of Things Gone Missing, The Shape of Things to Come*. Self-released, 2015. CD.

———. *Tongue River Stories*. Self-released, 2011. CD.

———. *The West Was Burning*. Sugar Hill (1085), 2007. CD.

Snake River Outlaws. "I Won't Go Huntin' Jake" / "Orange Blossom Special." Snake River Records (101). 78 rpm.

———. *Live Radio c. 1953 Missoula, Montana*. Deep West Records/Western Folklife Center, 2008. CD.

Starr, Betty Jo. "The Beautiful Hills" / "You Sold Your Saddle." Keyboard (WES 501). 78rpm.

Starr, Betty Jo (The Starrettes with Waterhole Johnny Sten). "You Sold You're [*sic*] Saddle" / "The Beautiful Hills." Keyboard (WES-500). 78 rpm.

Starr, Betty Jo (Waterhole Johnny's Prairie Stars). "Boogie Woogie Yodel Man"/ "Montana Waltz." Keyboard (WES 502). 78 rpm.

Stokes, Tiny, with Betty Jo Starr & Johnny Starr's Rocky Mountain Trail Blazers. "Missoula Waltz" / "Sleeping with One Eye Open." (Vega 601). 78 rpm.

Tarkio. *Omnibus* (compilation). Kill Rock Stars (27213), 2006. CD.

3 Young Men from Montana. *Folk Song Favorites*. Cameo records (C-1025), 1962. LP.

Tiny Stokes & the Frontiersmen. "Blackfoot Boogie" / "Write My Name." Big T Records (OP-235). 78 rpm. Also (OP-235-45). 45 rpm. Rereleased as a cut on *Footloose and Fancy Free: Boppin' Hillbilly Series* (CLCD 2972), 2012. CD.

———. "Judy" / "Korea's Mountain Northland." Keyboard Label (WES 504). 78 rpm.

Tom Catmull and the Clerics. *Glamour Puss*. Cheap Strings, 2009. CD.

Young Ancients. *Fishstory*. Independent release, 2015. CD.

Index

K

L

M

N

O

P

Q

R

S

T

V

W

Y

About the Author

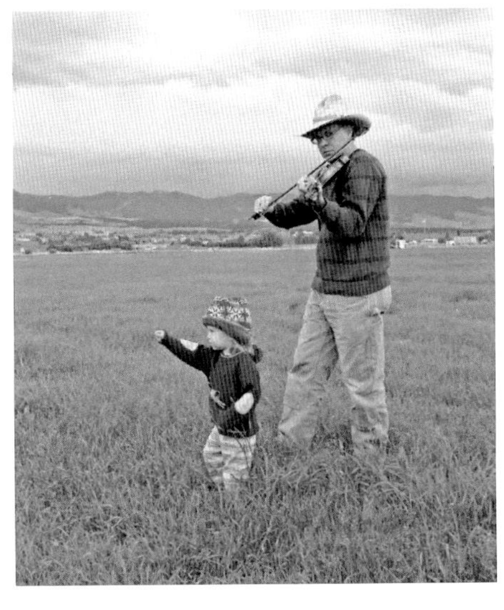

Aaron Parrett was born in Butte, Montana. He earned a degree in philosophy from the University of Montana and holds a master's and doctorate in comparative literature from the University of Georgia. He has published widely in many fields, including fiction. In 2004, he won the People's Choice Award from the Montana Historical Society for his article "Montana's Worst Natural Disaster: The 1964 Flood on the Blackfeet Reservation." He is the author of *Montana Then and Now* (Bangtail Press, 2014) and *Literary Butte: A History in Novels and Film* (The History Press, 2015). He has released several albums of acclaimed Americana music himself, including *The Sinners* (1996), *The Legend of Jim Collins* (with the Judge and the Jury, 2000), *Left of the Mason Dixon Line* (with the Judge and the Jury, 2001) and *Stumbo Lost Wages* (with Ivan Rosenberg, 2009). His music also appears in the Emmy-nominated film *Libby, Montana* (2007). He teaches literature and philosophy at the University of Great Falls.